Inspiring Women
of HAWAI'I

Inspiring Women
of HAWAI‘I

Dr. Loretta Chen

Mutual Publishing

Copyright © 2019 by Mutual Publishing

No part of this book may be reproduced in any form or by any electronic or mechanical means, including information storage and retrieval devices or systems, without prior written permission from the publisher, except that brief passages may be quoted for reviews. All rights reserved.

Front cover: Mazie Hirono © Frank Fey; Puanani Burgess © Paul Dunn; Maya Soetoro-Ng; Isabella Ellaheh Hughes © Don Gaboya; Raiatea Helm © Adam Jung; Lee Anne Wong © Hawaiian Airlines; Maxine Hong Kingston © Maryanne Teng Hogarth
Back cover: Kathryn Whang Inouye © Tracy Wright Corvo; Mary Philpotts McGrath © Tracy Wright Corvo; Marleen Akau © Harold Julian

ISBN: 978-1-949307-12-2
Library of Congress Control Number: 2019947592

Design by Jane Gillespie
First Printing, September 2019

Mutual Publishing, LLC
1215 Center Street, Suite 210
Honolulu, Hawaii 96816
Ph: (808) 732-1709
Fax: (808) 734-4094
e-mail: info@mutualpublishing.com
www.mutualpublishing.com

Printed in South Korea

DEDICATION

To my readers,
May we never lose the courage to do what is right.

Table of Contents

Foreword ix
Acknowledgments xi
Introduction xiii

The Alter-native Connector : **Puanani Burgess** 1
The Workhorse Fighter : **Mazie Hirono** 13
The Power Listener : **Connie Lau** 29
The Retail Doyenne : **Marleen Akau** 44
The Filmmaker : **Leanne Ferrer** 56
The Place Maker : **Mary Philpotts McGrath** 67
The People's Advocate : **Kymberly Marcos Pine** 77
The Controversial Storyteller : **Lois-Ann Yamanaka** 91
The Ad-Venture Capitalist : **Catherine Ngo** 100
The Peacemaker : **Maya Soetoro-Ng** 112
The Just Defender : **Crystal K. Rose** 126
The Renaissance Woman : **Ligaya Stice** 138
The Kismet Chef : **Lee Anne Wong** 145
The Game Changer : **Kim Coco Iwamoto** 156
The American Dreamer : **Christine Camp** 170
The Island Serenader : **Raiatea Helm** 182
The Dynamic Developer : **Kathryn Whang Inouye** 195
The Irrepressible Entrepreneur : **Isabella Ellaheh Hughes** 212
The Multi-Hyphenate : **Lauren Matsumoto** 227
The Woman Warrior : **Maxine Hong Kingston** 243
The Sharp Shooter : **Shirley Daniel** 257
The Community Innovator : **Karen Tan** 272
The Culinary Connoisseur : **Lynette Lo Tom** 284
The Chief Staffer : **Jennifer Sabas** 294

The Women of Waiʻanae Scholarship 309
About the Author 311

Foreword

The voices of women have taken many forms over the last century, and there have been much progress to have their voices heard in places such as the corporate board room and the educational arena. In today's world, where the cacophony of divisive stories fill conversations, these women's stories exemplify collaborative leadership. From the smallest act of kindness to the largest political and economic decisions, all make a difference in someone's life.

Here in Hawai'i where diversity is a common theme, the women in this book reflect the wide range of circumstances under which they persevered and found success. Their stories are of those who were born and raised in the Islands to those who came from afar and became part of the fabric of the Islands. In all cases, the women have common traits. They are forward-thinking, fearless but not reckless, and persistent. They all have grit.

It is important that the stories of these women are told, for they serve as role models for other women—women whose circumstances restrict their voices from being heard. In Hawai'i, there are still pockets of isolation, places where for a number of reasons—economic, societal, familial, educational, political—barriers still exist that suppress the voices of women. The women leaders in this book describe their journey in ways that are real, passionate, and most of all inspiring. Many of these stories will serve as the foundation for the next generation of women who must sustain the progress made and create more paths to women's success.

— Suzette Robinson

Acknowledgments

My deepest appreciation and respect to all the women who have generously given me their time, opened their hearts, bared their souls and allowed me access into their finely calibrated minds.

To Marleen, Auntie Pua, Christine, Shirley, Leanne, Raiatea, Senator Hirono, Bella, Kathy, Kim Coco, Maxine, Connie, Lauren, Mary, Catherine, Councilwoman Kym Pine, Crystal, Maya, Jennifer, Ligaya, Karen, Lynette, Lee Anne and Lois-Ann—you are all inspiring women in my book and eyes. I hope you continue to inspire the world with all that you do and touch.

But in particular, I wish to thank Kathy Inouye who helped connect me with many of her peers. Mahalo, Kathy, for believing in me, the project, and in the power of our collective voices. We are indeed stronger together.

My deepest appreciation to the previous interim chancellor of Leeward Community College, Suzette Robinson, for your support and willingness to take on the writing of the Foreword despite your hectic schedule. I can think of no better person to weave the intricacies of the changing face of women in leadership, the education climate, the Hawaiian landscape, and provide a nuanced view of the Women in Waiʻanae (WOW) for which proceeds of this book will go to.

To Mutual Publishing, Bennett and Jane, thank you for taking me on and trusting me with a gargantuan task of telling the stories of Hawaiʻi's most beloved women. I am indebted to you for allowing me to start, flow, and flourish on this journey. Thank you for the patience and I am already looking forward to the next collaboration!

To the Chen Clan and all my BFFs. Thank you for being my lifeline and pillars of support.

To my husband, Lee, for always loving me. Writing is a lonely activity. You have cared for me tirelessly throughout the process and taken on the tasks of cooking, cleaning, and caring for our fur babies even after a hard day's work.

Acknowledgments

And as always, my deepest gratitude to Daddy and Mummy for your selfless love and dedication. Thank you for the lessons on gratitude and compassion, virtue of striving, importance of giving back and leaving this world a better place than we found it. I love you both very much and hope to always make you proud.

Introduction

Writing the introduction always comes last for me as the journey and process of writing takes you places, and you are never the same person as you are when you first start writing; neither is the book. The ideas and words morph with each person you meet and story you hear.

When I first conceptualized the book, it really was my way of connecting with a new community I now call my home. I am from Singapore and moved to the Islands in 2015. I knew nobody when I first set foot on Oʻahu but was certain I wanted a way to continue with my life-long work in women's empowerment as well as engage in current, contemporary, critical conversations that matter. Having battled juvenile arthritis and now diagnosed with miserable malalignment syndrome, I knew from experience that some of our biggest trials and tribulations are our own best teachers, and that most illuminating conversations were not always the most comfortable. But I knew that it is in that space of discomfort that reflection and growth can occur and could not wait to hear what these inspiring women had to share.

In the course of research, I have met with countless individuals, all of whom have been nothing but supportive of this endeavor. In particular, I have had the privilege of meeting with and talking to some of Hawaiʻi's most illustrious and well-respected women across diverse backgrounds and demographics. They have shared with me their childhood struggles, countless challenges, personal tragedies, and little victories. In today's global climate, perhaps now more than ever, we need greater awareness and united support for diversity and solidarity amidst the rise of divisive rhetoric. And we can certainly do with more female role models right here in the Aloha State.

This book is a collection of honest, searing stories from many luminaries—leaders, activists, and specialists from various fields. In the sphere of politics, law, and diplomacy, there is Senator Mazie Hirono, Councilwoman Kymberly Pine, Representative Lauren Matsumoto, legal eagle Crystal K. Rose, ex-Board of Education member Kim Coco Iwamoto, and Jennifer Sabas, who used to be the chief of staff for the late Senator Daniel Inouye.

Many of them are entrepreneurs, expanding the job market in scores of industries. Chef Lee Anne Wong and Lynette Lo Tom are both passionate about food, one as a chef and the other as a critic and food writer, both leading teams of staff whether in the kitchen or publishing desk. Who can forget feisty Isabella Ellaleh Hughes who started Shaka Tea out of her disdain from not seeing authentic Hawaiian produce on the supermarket shelves and yet also found time to found the Honolulu Biennial? Today, she good-humoredly jests that she can finally afford dental insurance attesting to her start up success.

There are head honchos and CEOs Connie Lau of American Savings Bank and Hawaiian Electric Industries (HEI), Catherine Ngo of Central Pacific Bank, and Vice President cum General Manager Marleen Akau of the Royal Hawaiian Center, all of whom are all experts in their respective fields.

Then there are pioneers who break the proverbial glass ceiling and paved the way for women in the erstwhile male dominated industry of construction and real estate: Kathy Inouye of Kobayashi Group and Christine Camp of Avalon. While both women are established names in the field, many do not know that Christine considers Kathy her own personal mentor as she was one of the first to give Christine her early break. This is a fact Christine honors and the bond between the ladies is palpable even today.

From the realm of arts and activism, we are honored to have peace practitioner and Director of the Obama Foundation, Maya Soetoro-Ng; master connector Auntie Puanani Burgess; from the music circle, Grammy award-winner, Raiatea Helm; Mary Philpotts McGrath from print-making and design, from the world of film, Leanne Ferrer and Ligaya Stice who is a Renaissance woman traversing both the world of musicals and medicine. The two writers whose books I loved reading even before I set foot in the Islands—Maxine Hong Kingston and Lois Ann Yamanaka—round up our representatives from the arts and humanities.

In the human services sector, Karen Tan shows us the path towards infusing innovation, enterprise thinking, and creativity in the arena while Shirley Daniel, Professor of Accounting and my personal champ, reminds us why an education remains the best investment one can ever make.

Listing these luminaries in the way that I have above and in the header of their respective chapters belie the complexities of their identities as they are all so multifaceted. As you read their stories, you will discover other lesser-known descriptors, because amongst these women, we have playful professors, artistic businesswomen, entrepreneurial musicians, sensitive physicians, analytical writers, cancer survivors, poverty conquerors, nature champions, enthusiastic mothers, happy singletons, amiable divorcées, and so many more. All these women have courageously redefined what it means to be women of the twenty-first century and have bravely forged ahead with their dreams—fearing nothing and no one.

As work on the book took shape, I realized that any attempt at capturing the personalities of the ladies in prose would prove ultimately futile simply because they all had such distinct voices. Eventually, I decided that my format would include a one paragraph "op-ed" or a "first impression," followed by a short bio and an edited transcript that captures their speech patterns and stream of consciousness. I also figured that I would end the interview with a series of trivia questions so you, the reader, could get a sense of who they are through their spontaneous, spur of the moment answers that are uncensored and unfiltered.

The process of putting the book together was not quite as intricate as these women's lives but still required deft coordination. Planning the time to meet was itself a noteworthy feat because these women are busy. Interviews were scheduled in between a packed day of meetings; after work hours, over lunch meetings, and even across time zones. A couple opted to have their PR gurus and expert handlers on ground to assist. Some interviews were so intimate and heart-felt, we ended up trading personal stories that left me in tears. A couple of interviews were held in kitchens, one on the ruggedly, beautiful Wai'anae Coast, some in elegantly appointed offices while others in comfortable, well-worn and lived-in homes with books, paraphernalia, and toys strewn about. Some interviews blossomed into firm friendships with subsequent meet-ups and frequent chats, while a handful of the interviews allowed me a glimpse into my possible, desired future. Yet others allowed me the opportunity for close encounters with some of my personal heroines. Whatever the circumstances, all the interviews were unique, informative, and ultimately inspiring.

In the course of the next few chapters, you may read some familiar stories and some unfamiliar ones. Raiatea Helm, while no stranger to many in the Islands, is breaking new ground by sharing with us her new found activism following the death of her Auntie. In her interview, she reveals that she has traced her ancestry all the way back to King Kamehameha the Great. This revelation can have significant ramifications on published accounts of history and more importantly, on the allocation of asset and land ownership as it stands today.

In the past few years, gender equality has resurfaced as a major issue in the U.S. public sphere. The 2016 presidential election fueled a massive Women's March, leading to one of the largest protests in U.S. history held in January 2017 against the backdrop of Trump's inauguration. An anniversary Women's March took place across the country in January 2018 causing many to believe that this is not merely a moment but a movement.

The #MeToo movement that erupted in 2017 continues on today. The global airing of the Kavanaugh-Blasey Ford hearings brought issues of latent sexism, sexual predatory behavior, and toxic masculinity to the fore. When do we just let men be men or when is "enough" enough? And whatever happened to "no" means "no?" The #metoo stories in our book are not of explicit sexual assault but are encounters and experiences of gender inequities, discrimination, and harassment faced at work that range from belittlement and disparaging comments on the basis of sex; to a hand on the thigh, to even outright asks for sexual favors. But as Crystal K. Rose aptly summed up, "These issues of sexual and physical abuse all stem from an issue of power. It is not about sex. It's about men having power."

The Equal Employment Opportunity Commission (EEOC) reports receiving 25,000 allegations of sex-based harassment each year, with women accounting for about eighty-three percent of the complainants, and this figure is believed to be just the tip of the iceberg. In fact, according to the co-chairwomen of a commission task force, most women experiencing sexual harassment never tell anyone in authority about it but instead would "avoid the harasser, deny or downplay the gravity of the situation, or attempt to ignore, forget, or endure the behavior[1]."

---

1 For more, please read article by Beverly Engel on *Why Don't Victims of Sexual Harassment Come Forward Sooner* found on https://www.psychologytoday.com/us/blog/the-compassion-chronicles/201711/why-dont-victims-sexual-harassment-come-forward-sooner (accessed March 19, 2019)

In the interviews, some of the women like Marleen Akau, highlighted specific personnel in their work spheres that held them back simply because they were women, while Shirley Daniel shares with us details of a sex discrimination suit in the academic arena which is typically heralded as the arbiter of ideological change and social progress. The irony is not lost on this writer.

But, not all encounters with male counterparts are unpleasant. Several women took the opportunity to celebrate how the men in their lives have been champions and advocates. Many cited husbands as their pillars of strength and voiced their intentions to raise sons who will make a difference in the generation to come.

What is worthy of note, however, is that even today, some of these women leaders still refrain from wanting to discuss their own experiences and encounters of unwanted attention and unwarranted sexual intimations from men. This in itself underscores that we as a society need to do better and cultivate a climate where women can be better heard and less judged.

Discussions ranging from parental leave to the gender pay gap to sexual harassment in the workplace have made front-page headlines and sparked national debates—but the voices of adolescent girls and boys on these issues have not often been heard. As an educator and author, I hope this book will spark conversations and play a role in helping to raise woke youth leaders who will go on to become empowered change makers in society.

The other thing to note is that all the women in this book hold distinct views on the notion of feminism and the role of women in society. Their perspectives on marriage, motherhood, and career differ and many even challenge Sheryl Sandberg's notion of "having it all." In fact, many opted to re-define the notion of "having it all." Shirley Daniel even goes so far as to say that women "get it all." Some argue that we still have a long way to go, while some maintain that we have it good in Hawai'i. A few share that motherhood is tough business, while some Earth Mothers take it in gleefully and ask for more. A handful agree that the workspace today can still be hard on women with Representative Lauren Matsumoto reminding us that work life balance for women remains a big issue, most ironically in the legislature! It is where policies on breastfeeding and paid family leave for other businesses are set, but these don't yet apply to women who are elected officials! In fact, the U.S. Senate had to vote for the first time to allow Senator Tammy Duckworth to bring her baby onto the floor so she could cast her vote in 2018!

Indeed, for a first world country with one of the highest GDP in the world, we can certainly demand more progress and stage a concerted effort to increase the recognition of women in the work sphere. We should aim to offer better support and set up social structures to allow women to undertake and assert their multi-hyphenate roles.

To quote Brené Brown, "The real struggle for women… is that we are expected to be perfect and yet not look as if we are working for it. We want it to just materialize somehow. Everything should be effortless. The expectation is to be natural beauties, natural mothers, natural leaders, and naturally good parents, and we want to belong to naturally fabulous families. … And when it comes to work, we love to hear, 'She makes it look so easy,' or 'She's a natural.'"

While no two stories are alike, what is common in all these diverse accounts is the overwhelming sense of overcoming. These women unabashedly share what they had to undergo to get to where they are today. The climb can be arduous and unglamorous and certainly not always "natural." But what does make it beautiful is their unyielding passion, strength in spirit, and staunch belief that things will always get better. They have embraced challenges, pain, taken a stab in the back, a kick in the face. and a slam of the door, and they all somehow find the courage to say in their own way, "Okay, this is how the world rolls. So this is how I will *rock and roll*." They have never allowed their circumstances to define them, and instead saw it as a challenge to overcome. None of them used the victim card, "Boo hoo, poor me. It's all my parents', ex-husband's, soon-to-be baby and future lover's fault." None. Zilch. Nada. They instead had a similar rallying cry, "Whether I like it or not, this ball is in my court. So what can I do?"

Either consciously or unconsciously, these women have all marched on to the beat of their own drums. In so doing, they have crafted personal world views, distinct life philosophies, created their own style of authentic leadership, and are true beacons of light, worthy of being exalted as Inspiring Women all in their own right.

I truly believe that giving a platform to issues that matter is important. It is my sincere wish that the book will ignite conversations and raise awareness

Introduction

on issues that are prevalent and paramount and, above all, allow anyone to seek solace and inspiration in these diverse stories of overcoming and draw strength from one of your own Inspiring Women right here on the lush Hawaiian Islands.

THE ALTER-NATIVE CONNECTOR

Puanani Burgess

I use stories to move the people who aren't sure about what I do, as the stories allow them to be present in a way they haven't been before. I also allow for patience, and wait for people who are in a negative space and choose silence. In Hawaiian culture, we believe that silence is also the voice of God, so when people choose silence as their way, it means they are giving you a story that has no words or language.

P**uanani Burgess, or Auntie Pua as she is affectionately known, consults and does her work One-Peace-At-A-Time. Based in Hawai'i, her work takes her all over the U.S., the Pacific, and other parts of the world. She is also a poet, cultural translator, and has been a lecturer with the Department of Urban and Regional Planning at the University of Hawai'i, where she was the first community scholar in residence. She sat on the board of directors for the Positive Futures Network, the publisher of YES! magazine and was the Miles and Zilphia Horton chairholder for the Highlander Research and Education Center in New Market, Tennessee.

She is noted and much respected for her experience in community, family and values-based economic development, mediation, and storytelling processes as part of conflict transformation, as well as developing community-based organizations especially along the Wai'anae Coast. In 2000, she was ordained as a Zen Buddhist priest in the International Daihonzan Chozen-ji and among five people named as Hawai'i's Living Treasures in 2009.

Being in Auntie Pua's presence has an instant effect of calming you down, much like a panacea for all your daily stresses. Her talk story is entertaining, engaging, enlightening, and her words have a magical way of getting right to your soul.

You have an eclectic bio Auntie Pua! Share what you would like us to know about your long, meaningful path working with the community.

I was thinking about the people who put me on this path. One of them is my husband. We celebrated our fiftieth wedding anniversary in 2018. From the beginning, he told me, "Your job is not to be my wife. I intend to do the work I am meant to do while I'm here, which means you have to find your way and go do it." Initially, I was pissed off because I was raised in a very traditional family where women were raised to be supportive and to take care of family. Here was a very regular Hawaiian man who told me to go find my own purpose and destiny.

Since I was little, I wanted to be an attorney. My husband went to law school, which was outrageous for a Hawaiian man at that era. He was first admitted to the George Washington University Law School during the Vietnam War but he was drafted. So he returned to Hawai'i and joined the Air Force. When that was done, he went into Richardson School of Law. He was in the first batch of students at the law school and I met him in 1966 and basically went to law school with him as I was getting my bachelor's. My husband urged me to go back to school. I never thought it was possible to be a lawyer as no one in my family had graduated from college. But with his urging, I tried and was admitted as part of the seventh batch.

In my third year, I woke one morning two weeks before the semester finals. I asked myself, "Did I really want to take the bar and be a lawyer?" My answer was no, so I decided to come home. I called my husband and instead of admonishing me, he came with our daughter to pick me up and just like that, I started to work in this community.

Back then, I had no idea where I was going or what I was supposed to do. But, law school made me incredibly skilled at reading rules, understanding how institutions, or what I call "dragons" are, and how to "feed" them. I became a great "dragon feeder" and started to work with people in the community to build the infrastructure and nonprofits that worked on economic development, health, social development, and education. With my law school background, I helped develop about twelve different organizations and began to be the legal and cultural translator between the people and the systems that rule our lives.

You helped to lay the foundations for numerous community centers here in the Waiʻanae Coast. How did that happen and what was your inspiration?

I grew up here and lived here throughout the 1970s and 1980s. During this time, there was a group of religious leaders who came here including the Catholics and the Quakers, who ministered in a very different way, and they started to help us build our own infrastructure. So I began working with people who came from this place, who loved and respected where they came from and don't see negatives or impossibilities.

So back then, we had to go to town to get mental health services. But it was a time of community-based development, so I started to think about how we could make a change so that we could have processes and organizations which we could develop in our own frame of reference, with its own value system that would serve the people here. Hale Naʻau Pono or Waiʻanae Coast Community Mental Health Center was one of those places we successfully created. Later, I helped build the infrastructure for Kaʻala Farm, which is a taro and land-based cultural learning center in Waiʻanae up in the mountains, which is the caldera from which this island was born so that community is one of the oldest. A lot of things written about Waiʻanae are so negative, but if people only understood the kuleana it carries, it is incredibly dynamic and interesting.

You have a wonderful story to share about the Waiʻanae Coast Community Alternative Development Corporation (WCCADC). Please enlighten us.

During the 70s and 80s, the whole notion of community-based economic development was flourishing in the U.S. At that time, Koʻolina and West Beach was just starting to be built and the first hotels were about to be built. People were pushing back against that form of development as the argument was that these developments may provide jobs, but it is not providing work. In the Hawaiian principle, work is medicine and it is the second thing people ask you after they ask you for your name. If you are not proud of what you do, you have nothing to say even if you have a job.

We wanted to develop work for people in the community to allow them to earn, and yet not have to leave the community or their family to take one more job. Anyhow, one day, I was catching the bus back from town and an old Hawaiian man got on the bus. We chatted and he asked me, "What does the word alternative mean to you?" So I said, "Choices, different ways of looking at things" and he took my paper and wrote "Alter Native." The realization struck me and he said, "Yes, that's what they do to us. The natives were here before they came, and the trees, clouds, and oceans came long before even the natives did." That became the core of the organization, and so we renamed ourselves Waiʻanae Coast Comprehensive Alternative Development Corp., instead of the Waiʻanae Coast Comprehensive Economic Development Corp.

We decided to build alternatives for the community even as we focused on the economic aspects. If you trace the roots of the word "economics," you will see that its core meaning is "to take care of the hearth," which is the fireplace where people gather to eat. So when you take care of the hearth, you take care of family. We decided to focus on food to care for our community's well-being and how they share their food.

Our first project was to develop backyard aquaculture. Even though many people do not have enough land to build a farm, they have their backyard. At that time, I was traveling and was exposed to many small ideas and I wanted to translate that into our community. We decided to work on backyard aquaculture as Waiʻanae is a coastal town and people make a living from fishing. Rather than having individuals apply, we encouraged families instead. We implemented the concept in our own backyards first, as one of our major principles is to try and test out these ideas before we get others to follow.

What we understood, too, was that at least one in the family had to be literate, as we were getting funding and needed to churn out reports. It was a tricky question to ask, so what we did was to set up tables during the orientation meetings with the families and we would leave the application form and the pen in the middle of the table. The ones who would pick up the stationery were the literate ones and that was how we identified the team leads who would pass on the information to the family.

What if there was no literate person in the family?

We built cohorts between three to four families who lived close to each other, so they are also building their own neighborhood communities around economic development. The amount of fish that you could grow in six months was not enough to replace your income from a job, but it was enough to pay for car insurance so they can drive legally to get to work. There was a family who had four girls who made enough from the fish to buy new surfboards.

The other principle was teaching the children the relationship between "I work, I eat" and, by doing that, we share with them the idea of kuleana, neighborliness, and sustainability right from within the family.

I did this for about eighteen to twenty years and I lived many different lifetimes given that I am in my seventies now.

What was that aha moment two weeks before you were about to take the bar?

In my second year of law school, I interned for a woman named Cynthia Thielen[1] who is now a state representative. It was she who introduced me to the idea of Hawaiian activism, and I did the cultural research, writing, and negotiations for her. I had not grown up with this idea of resistance, so she was an inspiration. One of the most important lessons I learned came during my internship with Cynthia. It was about the hālau, as we had to negotiate with the navy to preserve the halau as a visual symbol of our presence and significance. The process also revived traditional skills and we had to learn all the chants and rituals that I learned from my kupuna, whom I see as a kahuna.

---

1 After graduating from law school, Cynthia was in federal court arguing on behalf of her client, the Protect Kahoʻolawe ʻOhana. She was successful in stopping the United States Navy from bombing Kahoʻolawe and gained access to the island for the ʻOhana and their kūpuna. During these years, Cynthia developed deep roots in the Hawaiian community. She continues to respect the sovereignty rights of Native Hawaiians, and shares their spiritual connection to the land. Cynthia built a strong reputation as a successful fighter to protect the environment.

Auntie Pilahi Paki[2], is also known as the "Keeper of the Secrets of Hawaiʻi" and her specialty was language and the sounds that were evoked that were spoken to the gods. She loved to talk story at night and I asked her for help with the prayer needed for the hālau. Instead of giving me the answer, she asked me, "Who are you?" She proceeded to say, "When you go outside, can you see the stars and the sky? Can you feel the wind? Can you feel and smell everything around you? When you put your bare foot on the ʻāina, can you feel the energy coming from your ancestors? And when you go into the water, can you taste the salt and see your ʻohana?" I said yes, and Auntie said that I have exactly what my ancestors had. They had to figure out what they needed and so would I. With that, I knew I had the answer. I learned that I need not only rely on what my ancestors did but that I, too, had to figure out new pathways for myself, in order for our culture to stay alive. And we did. We figured out all the hows.

I have been given the permission to invent and I learned that I could be both traditional and modern in the same space. I figured out how to do that and what has to be done to do it. I learned not to hold back just because I have not been told.

With that, I started to think about how we can help people have meaningful conversations with each other, especially if they're not sure about who you are or who they are. My aha moment came when I started to think how I could create processes that will work for at this moment—and that really was what made me turn away from law school and started me on a lifetime of service.

You also speak a lot on conflict resolution. How did this come about?

I learned by observing the conflict between the developers of West Beach, Koʻolina, and our community to see how we could bring people together to have honorable conversations to solve problems. We were met with a lot of criticism from people because we were mediating instead of protesting. We felt that it was important not to just say no, but to also articulate what we liked. That is why working on alternatives that come from core principles of how you relate to the world, earth, and each other is key. We need to design processes that allow people to see each other deeply and respectfully. That has been my work for the past thirty years.

---

2 Auntie Pilahi Paki tasked several of her students to be prepared for the future when the world would be in collapse. She spoke of the time when Hawaiʻi would have the remedy to save the world and the remedy was aloha. In 1970, at a governor's conference, she introduced modern Hawaiʻi to a deeper understanding of aloha. For more, look up http://www.tailsofaloha.com/wp/wp-content/uploads/2009/06/What-is-Aloha-Poster-Proof.pdf

I also had the opportunity to go to Highlander in New Market, Tennessee. It was where black and white people came to talk about race relations. It was a place that Martin Luther King Jr. went to meet white people interested in social justice, so it was a place that dealt with alternatives, a place of research and education where people from different backgrounds came to talk to each other.

In the 1970s, Miles Horton was one of the founders of Highlander, and I was invited to be the Horton Chair. This is where I began to look at issues of race relations, economic systems, and development systems that were destructive, and how people have to learn to walk away from the destruction, yet build systems to allow people to earn a living and be proud of what they do.

I went to the south many times to listen and meet people who are struggling. I wanted to figure out a way to take this work back to Hawai'i. With my exposure to Highlander, I learned how to design processes based on culture, food, music, poetry, and dance. Thereafter, I met lots of people in West Beach who became seminal to my work here.

Tommy Holmes[3] is one of those guys who started the Polynesian Voyaging Society and is a legend. He would surf those forty-five foot waves. One day, he showed up at the project site and told us that we had to stop talking between ourselves and go to the tables where decisions are being made and where power is held. He then opened the doors for us to talk to other people, like Kenny Brown, who introduced us to Bobby Pfeiffer, who, then, introduced us to the people in the Democratic Party.

I quickly learned that establishing relationships were important as it allowed us access into places that ordinary communities did not have access to. As I began to find my voice, I also began to find other like-minded people wanting to harmonize. A lot of my work now revolves around working with groups and communities, and teaching them the possibility of using processes and solutions to overcome obstacles.

Speaking of obstacles, what are some of the biggest challenges you face in doing the work you do?

Part of my work is trickster work, as most people have made up their mind when they ask you for help. The first story is called "The Poha and Popo Prin-

---

3 Tommy Holmes, one of the founders of the Polynesian Voyaging Society, died of a heart attack in 1993 while paddling an outrigger canoe off Waikīkī. One of his lasting legacies is *The Hawaiian Canoe,* the most comprehensive modern study of the subject, published in 1981 and reprinted in a second edition in September 1993. On August 28, his ashes were carried out to sea by the *Hōkūle'a* and scattered off Waikīkī. Hundreds attended the ceremony.

ciple," as Poha is my son's name and Popo is grandmother. When my son was a little baby, his Chinese grandmother, or Popo, would put him in the stroller and walk around the block to show him the pastures where the animals were. She thought my son would really enjoy the animals, but he had no response each time she went. Finally, Popo went down to Poha's eye level and realized that Poha never saw one horse or cow! So Popo understood that she had to see from where Poha was seeing, which is the first principle: We need to first show them what you are looking at and see if we are seeing the same things, and just because you don't agree, doesn't mean you disagree. All it takes could be more conversation. I share that from that sacred space of non-agreement, where we can establish a space of navigation. I always want to find the one thing we can see eye to eye on.

The second story is called "The Sylvester Stallone Principle One and Two." In the movie *Assassins*, Sylvester Stallone, who is the number one assassin in the world, is being challenged by the other assassin, played by Antonio Banderas. Anyway, the idea was Banderas wanted to kill Stallone so he could reign. He was taking aim at Stallone, who was in the bank, which only had one entrance and exit. The Julianne Moore character is watching out for Stallone across the street when the bank deal was happening. To calm him down, Stallone asks Moore to tell him a story and she tells the story of a bird in winter who flew toward the sun for warmth. In the flight, the bird's wings freeze and the bird falls to the middle of a pasture, where a cow comes and lands a pile of shit on it and its wings defrost so it comes alive again. But soon after, a cat comes around, digs the bird out of the poo and eats the bird.

The moral of the story is "not everybody who craps on you is your enemy and not everyone who digs you out of shit is your friend." You need to see the whole picture first before you make up your mind, so one should wait and not rush into judgment because you may make mistakes. And the other principle is, if you can learn something from a Sylvester Stallone movie, you can learn something from anybody if you are willing, so always keep your heart and mind open.

The third story is the one I learned the most from and it is called "The Gift." One of the activities I like to do is to get people to tell me the story of their names as your name carries meaning. When you tell the story of your name, you share your family's aspirations for you and your background. Then I ask people to tell me what their gift is. So I did this with a group of eleventh and twelfth graders at Waiʻanae High School and I had this boy who said he had no gift and he felt ashamed. I, in turn, felt ashamed, as I had made him feel that way. Anyway, days later, I ran into him in a store and he told me he found his gift. He said his gift was an ability to talk to the fishes and the sharks in the ocean, and that allows him to put food on the table.

When I go to the Department of Education and the schools, I ask the leaders how do we serve these youths whose gifts are not bound by the books and how do we teach to these gifts? They may not show up in our Western standards, but we need to nurture them.

You clearly have a gift with connecting and mediating, so how do you deal with people who are negative toward you?

I love them anyway. I also use stories to move the people who aren't sure about what I do, as the stories allow them to be present in a way they haven't been before.

I also allow for patience, and wait for people who are in a negative space and choose silence. In Hawaiian culture, we believe that silence is also the voice of God, so when people choose silence as their way, it means they are giving you a story that has no words or language. They are not ready, just like that boy who didn't want to speak in class, but, weeks later, the question worked on him and he was ready to speak when he was.

How would you deal if the opposition is not silence, but anger and violence?

I have never experienced that ever.

Has being a woman been a boon or bane in your career?

I am in such demand and can work every day of the week if I want to. *(laughter)*

I work with both men- and women-led organizations. I see that if the men are given permission to show up in a different way, they can and they are capable of emotions, tears, and great depth.

Do you think there are special needs or areas we need to look at for girls and women, or is gender irrelevant here in the Waiʻanae community?

My daughter runs a book mobile to support literacy along the coast, and she also provides snacks and school supplies to people. She started this for girls between the ages of twelve to sixteen, but many of these girls can only show up if they can bring along their younger sisters, as they have to take care of them. So the book mobile now supports girls from six to seventeen years old. My daughter also gave them a survey to fill out, and the questions asked them where they saw themselves in fifteen years and what are some deterrents to their dreams.

Many of the girls wanted to be lawyers, artists, photographers, writers, and scientists. Several of the girls said that getting pregnant and fighting with the family would be setbacks to their dreams. One of the girls in one of the leadership groups I ran asked, "What about the boys?" I thought she meant leadership camps for the boys, but she was asking about educational workshops for the boys, because the girls don't get pregnant by themselves. She said that girls have dreams, too, so we needed to let the boys know that they need to take responsibility and be in control of themselves as well.

Sometimes, we would take the girls to the University of Hawaiʻi-West Oʻahu campus just to inspire them and let them know they belong there too. The girls had so many questions on financial literacy, careers, and were very excited about their future. It was a wonderful experience.

> Do you then create programs for girls or do you work to lift the community as a whole?

I see my work as helping people find their voices. For the girls, I helped to design a three-part mapping process, which I start by showing them a photo of the *Hōkūleʻa* from a helicopter and the craft looks tiny in the ocean. It seems counterintuitive in our modern thinking to navigate, as one of the things we are taught is to be able to see land or you will never get to your destination. But what we learn is that, when we are in the middle of the ocean that is not the time to discuss if the canoe is of the right size or if we have enough food or crew. You need to do all the planning on land and have a vision of where you are going—hence, the importance of the mind map.

I then ask them to draw their vision map followed by their kuleana map, which shows their responsibilities and duties, and then, finally, draw their place in those circles. In typical university applications, they do not ask the kuleana question and many students actually have a lot of responsibilities to shoulder between school, family, work, and other kuleanas. So educational institutions need to understand this about the students and adjust accordingly.

Finally, the third map is their resource map which is the people they can turn to when they are in trouble, so the institutions can build bridges to those resources that students can go to for kōkua.

What do you remember about Hawaiʻi growing up and how has it changed for you?

Growing up, I never understood poverty in the way that I hear it spoken about. When I was a freshman at the university, I took a Hawaiian geography class taught by Abraham Piianaia.[4] He would speak about the reality of ghettos in Hawaiʻi, and I didn't understand that I lived in a ghetto and started to cry in a class of about 150 students. So it was interesting that I had to come to grips that I actually grew up in poverty and, today, here I am. Maybe, because of that, I understand the kids, who come from this community that has a bad rep, and I can appreciate them.

What would you hope to see in the next ten years?

I wrote a poem called "Kākou"[5] which speaks of the universe and all the citizens of Hawaiʻi, including life that is not human. I hope we can do something inherently Hawaiʻi, which is to be able to see all these beings as equal to us, so we need to find people who communicate with that world and engage them in conversation to lead us in dealing with nature and natural resources.

There is now more work being done in sustainable farming and there's awareness about the foods we eat, as well as management processes for handling the ocean resources.

My way of working with this is twofold. I work with the coastal communities to organize ways to sit and talk. One of the strategies I share is the "weather ball." I ask these communities to share what the weather is within them and, through their stories, you begin to hear what they're going through. I also share the idea of co-management, which means that man and nature have to work together.

---

4 Abraham Piianaia was an educator, geographer, historian, seaman, explorer, and police detective. He was an early chairman of the University of Hawaiʻi program in Hawaiian studies and will be remembered by many for his work as an educator, beginning in the 1950s as a teacher of the Hawaiian language at Kamehameha Schools and continuing for forty years as a lecturer in geography, history, and Hawaiian studies. His work has helped to perpetuate the Hawaiian culture. In 1999, he was awarded the title of "Living Treasure" by the Honpa Hongwanji Mission of Hawaiʻi. He passed away in 2003 at eighty-seven years old.

5 Kākou is the Hawaiian value of inclusiveness. It means "all of us" and "we are in this together." Kākou is very unifying when applied to language, and all are taught to learn, speak, and practice "the language of we." Coupled with the value of lōkahi, kākou promotes synergy as a habit of creation which seeks additional solutions and alternatives. There is a definite *as-spoken-aloud-to-include* connotation within the *kaona* of this value, thus we'll often refer to kākou as our value of communication.

Is there anything else you would like to accomplish?

I would like to write a book of poems.

Who would you like to have a sit-down dinner with?

Obama. He is a very nice man and very intelligent.

You have so much energy. Would you ever retire?

I may want to retire to write a book. You have inspired me to do that.

If you met God, what would you say?

Hi. I know a lot of good people you put in my path and I am so appreciative.

Who are your role models?

I once had a chance to moderate a conversation between W.S. Merwin[6] and Maxine Hong Kingston as part of my work at *YES!* magazine. I was speechless the whole time, as they had an enormous wealth of experience and a combined capacity with words to express and share like you can never imagine. And Maxine's husband was my drama teacher and I loved his classes. I would also like to have dinner with them, again.

What pisses you off?

Donald Trump. His attitude toward people who aren't from the U.S. Hello? What do you think the country was built on? It pisses me off that he cannot see spaces for conversation with just about anybody.

---

6 W.S. Merwin was a prolific, leading American writer whose poetry, translations, and prose have won praise over seven decades. His first book, *A Mask for Janus* (1952), was chosen by W.H. Auden for the Yale Younger Poets Prize. Merwin eventually became known for an impersonal, open style that eschewed punctuation. Although Merwin's writing had undergone stylistic changes, a recurring theme was man's separation from nature. The poet saw the consequences of that alienation as disastrous, both for the human race and for the rest of the world. He was a practicing Buddhist as well as a proponent of deep ecology and lived, since the late 1970s, on an old pineapple plantation in Hawai'i which he had painstakingly restored to its original rain forest state. He passed away in March 2019, following the interview with Auntie Pua.

What is your life philosophy on a bumper sticker?

In sharing, everybody can have enough.

Finally, how do you want to be remembered?

Auntie Pua—friend to all.

THE WORKHORSE FIGHTER
Mazie Hirono

Democracy is not neat. It is messy, but give me another system that is better? Is there another system that gives people the freedom of speech? Democracy is aspirational and we still are fighting battles to provide equal opportunity and treatment to all, but we have fought and won some battles. I think someone once said that democracy is not perfect but it is more perfect than the other systems.

The Workhorse Fighter

Born in Japan in 1947, Mazie Hirono moved to Hawai'i with her family in 1954. She later graduated from Georgetown University Law Center in 1978 and briefly worked in the legal field before winning a seat in the Hawai'i state House of Representatives. She served in this capacity until being elected Hawai'i's lieutenant governor in 1994. After two terms as lieutenant governor, Hirono entered the Hawai'i gubernatorial elections of 2002, but lost. In 2006, she was elected to the U.S. House of Representatives, a post she held until she was elected to the U.S. Senate in 2012, thereby becoming the first Asian American woman, Buddhist, and Japan-born individual to be elected to the senate. She was sworn in on January 3, 2013 by Vice President Joe Biden.

In the 2018 senate election, Senator Hirono ran unopposed in her party's primary and was easily reelected, defeating Republican challenger Ron Curtis. Today, she is said to be more outspoken and decisive than ever—a champion of immigrants, women, health care rights, veterans, and the military. As a liberal Democrat, she has bluntly challenged President Donald Trump in the national spotlight and continues her fight for people who are struggling: immigrants, kūpuna worried about Social Security and Medicare, veterans, the environment, and the LGBTQ community. In February 2019, Senator Hirono won the first-ever Courage Award from the Hawai'i Comprehensive Cancer Coalition, a group that includes doctors, researchers, and advocates working on cancer prevention and treatment.

Throughout our interview, Senator Hirono laughs easily, speaks fast, is quick on the uptake, and offers quote-worthy answers swiftly and passionately. Her vast knowledge on policy matters, pulse for justice, and deep sense of empathy is palpable and it is indeed refreshing to speak with a politician that speaks her mind! That, and I am thankful we share a common bond on our love for our strong mother figures, cats, and the movie Crazy Rich Asians!

Good afternoon, senator.

Good afternoon. So you are from Singapore, where they did the movie *Crazy Rich Asians*?

Yes! A lot of my friends are in it and all of us in the industry are like one big 'ohana. My brother is an actor, too. He's fifty-seven now and the first Singaporean to make it to Hollywood, but the time wasn't right for him and Asians then, so he only played supporting roles in movies like *Street Fighter,* where Chun Li was played by a Caucasian. So we are collectively very proud of this CRA moment where we finally see Asian representation on the global stage.

It's a great movie. I watched it twice!

That's so heartening to hear! *(laughter)* I know you're incredibly busy, so let's jump right to it. You are a first generation Asian American, Buddhist, immigrant woman elected to senate. So many firsts! I also read your mother left her abusive husband in Japan to come to the USA. I am sure all of this must have shaped you.

I definitely did not have a typical childhood. I did not know my father and was raised by a single mother, which made me so aware of how hard life circumstances can be. That made me a lot more sensible at a young age and I did not spend any time giving my mother any grief. I also recognized how it is like to be vulnerable—to not have money or proper health care.

These experiences never left me—that combined with protesting the Vietnam War while I was in college. The moment made me realize that I could perhaps make a difference through political activism. Prior to that time, I fully expected that I would join the health care field and become a therapist or counselor. But protesting the Vietnam War made me question the government, and I also made friends that made me recognize that protesting and singing "We Shall Overcome" was not enough. That was the genesis of my political activism.

So that was the inspiration for you to give up psychology and study law?

Yes, I always knew I wanted to do something that would help people. With my background, I decided early on that making my own–little-self happy was not enough. I wanted to help people who had my kind of experiences.

Given your penchant for doing what's right …

And it was less about doing what's right than doing what would make other people's lives better.

: And you did much given your decorated career. You became a state legislator in the 1980s, worked on improving sexual-assault laws, pushed for the passage of the DREAM Act, fought for increased Asian American Pacific Islander (AAPI) data, shared your own personal #MeToo story, and recently pushed for bipartisan legislation to award Fred Korematsu the Congressional Gold Medal in recognition of his work to advance civil rights. You have done so much, but what has been the most significant for you?

People have always asked me what my biggest accomplishment is and I would say that it is being able to do the work that we do. Having my staff be able to answer our constituents is huge for me and it's a big part of what I do that doesn't get a lot of attention.

We have a lot of people who have social security and veterans' issues, or what we call constituency services. I am thankful that I am able to not just work on issues that are important to Hawai'i, but to Americans at large. Immigration is pivotal work for me. I also sit on the Judiciary Committee that decides on who gets these lifetime appointments in court, which, in turn, decides on health care, civil rights, women's rights, you name it. These are all important things for me to fight for and I am very grateful that I get to fight for these things.

: And given this administration, your job is that much more important today. What are some of the biggest challenges that you have to face as a political leader and what do you do to try to overcome them as they come?

I have to keep showing up, raise my voice, and speak up. These are not normal times under this president, as he comes up with outrageous lies on a regular basis. It is very important that as a woman and a minority person that I speak up. Everything is under assault—our courts, justice system, how women are treated, health care, the Affordable Care Act, the eliminating of the protection of pre-existing conditions. Those are things that, if Republicans had their way, they would want to do away with.

: You have been very vocal about what you feel about this president. Is there anything you would want to say to him?

I would like him to resign. That won't happen so we need to do all we can to protect the Affordable Care Act, for example. There has been a lot of divisiveness that he has sown, so I worry that even after he has left the stage, I don't know if we can put Humpty Dumpty back together again as he has unleashed all these anger and animosity. We are going to have a lot of work to do in our country to bring us to some sort of agreement as these disagreements under this presidency have really taken a harmful turn.

Could you lay out for us what would that path forward be given the huge gulfs that have been created?

We need to get more Republicans to distance themselves from this President. As long as they continue to kowtow to him and his desire to build a vanity wall, give tax breaks to the richest people in the country, separate children from their parents at the border, and attempt to get rid of the Affordable Care Act, it is going to tough for us Democrats to work together. That is not to say that we are unable to work together at all as I, for one, have been successful at getting a number of my bills passed with Republican co-sponsorship. We have worked in a bipartisan way for veterans and on some other issues.

Do you think that the constitution and the notion of democracy in itself has certain loopholes that has now come to roost? Is freedom of speech truly tenable because we see the rise of such angry, hateful rhetoric of late?

I do not think that it is a loophole. Democracy is not neat. It is messy, but give me another system that is better? Is there another system that gives people the freedom of speech? Democracy is aspirational and we still are fighting battles to provide equal opportunity and treatment to all, but we have fought and won some battles. I think someone once said that democracy is not perfect but it is more perfect than the other systems.

We see a lack of empathy and real connection to the people from the leader of the free world today. What is the role of empathy in leadership and what else do you think makes a good leader?

Empathy is paramount as that is what allows one to feel for another. How else can you make policy decisions that will affect the population if you do not see how they feel and what challenges they face? I think this president is particularly unable to feel any kind of real empathy for anybody. There are only two things he cares about, himself and money.

> **We are also seeing the rise of the strongman and playing tough. With the Democrats taking over the House and Nancy Pelosi reclaiming the gavel, will we see the rise in the "power of no" with the Democrats fighting back?**

Absolutely, because you are dealing with a president who changes his mind on a whim and his word is not good. He runs this country like he runs his business, where if the going gets tough, he just declares bankruptcy. He certainly does not know how to run a country, he does not know how to compromise, and he is fixated on things that are not even real, like the national emergency at the border.

So you cannot talk sense to one who makes no sense. That is why Congress needs to act like a separate branch of government that it is. We just need to ensure we keep the government running until the end of the fiscal year but we certainly cannot let the president do whatever he wants. He is so fixated on a wall and has declared this emergency which we will most certainly challenge.

I think that more and more people are coming to the realization that he should not be the person leading our country. But not enough Republicans have come to that conclusion yet and, once they do, hopefully Congress will start acting like that separate branch of government that they are. Now that the Democrats are in control of the House, at least that body is acting like a separate branch of government which is the beauty of the constitution, as it provides a system of checks and balances.

> **How do you think history will characterize this moment in contemporary America and this White House?**

I don't think history will be kind to Trump and we have already seen so many signs of this. Our own allies are wondering what is going on and if they can rely on us. We have definitely lost our leadership position in the world and are no longer that shiny beacon on the hill. History will also not be kind to all those who lied for, kowtowed, and enabled him.

> **How do you think history will characterize the Democratic Party?**

History is a moving target and democracy is always in the state of becoming, but I hope people will remember the Democratic Party as the party that cares for the people, families, and communities, but I have to admit that that is not a message that is unanimously felt and recognized.

Given what you have gone through and what is happening right now, what are some of the most poignant leadership and life lessons?

Whenever I speak to students, I always share that I have three life lessons. One, half the battle is showing up, not just physically but mentally and emotionally.

Another lesson is that one person can make a difference, as my mother did by bringing me to America. I like to paraphrase Martin Luther King Jr., who said we can all be great if we define greatness as being of help to someone else. It can be a small act of kindness to our parents, but we need to recognize that one person can make a difference. It is not just a lesson for people who are elected to office, but it is important for all of us to be engaged as a community to live together.

And the final lesson is to dare to take risks and to do things that we may not usually do, but we need to find ways where we make a difference, by doing by advocacy and working with other groups that you may not work with before.

In fact, I never refer to my work as politician as a "career" or a "living," because what kind of career is it if you have to put yourself out there and run for office every couple of years? It is definitely not comfortable; it is about taking risks, and stems from a commitment that I have to the community because it is necessary.

On that note, I am reminded of Fred Korematsu,[1] who fought for civil rights and was labeled a traitor only to have his name cleared after forty years. It takes a lot of courage to stand up against immorality. So standing up to this president is the least we can do compared to what Fred had to endure.

---

1 Fred T. Korematsu was a national civil rights hero. In 1942, at the age of twenty-three, he refused to go to the government's incarceration camps for Japanese Americans. After he was arrested and convicted of defying the government's order, he appealed his case all the way to the Supreme Court. In 1944, the Supreme Court ruled against him, arguing that the incarceration was justified due to military necessity.

In 1983, Prof. Peter Irons, a legal historian, together with researcher Aiko Herzig-Yoshinaga, discovered key documents that government intelligence agencies had hidden from the Supreme Court in 1944. The documents consistently showed that Japanese Americans had committed no acts of treason to justify mass incarceration. With this new evidence, a pro-bono legal team that included the Asian Law Caucus reopened Korematsu's forty-year-old case on the basis of government misconduct. On November 10, 1983, Korematsu's conviction was overturned in a federal court in San Francisco. It was a pivotal moment in civil rights history.

What sacrifices have you made in your decision to serve the community?

I don't consider what I do as a sacrifice and actually feel really grateful to be able to speak out at a time when people are looking for leaders who can empathize.

Life is really full of surprises, as who would know that a poor kid from Japan with a struggling, single mom would be able to be here today? It is hardly expected. There is not a day that goes by where I do not acknowledge the privilege that I have in doing what I do. And by the way, when I am not running for office or at work, I like to spend my time working on ceramics!

Which brings up the age-old question—do you think leadership is nurture or nature? You are an anomaly. As you say, your success today is "hardly expected." So do you think leadership seems to stem from the kernel of your core?

I think it really is both. I was raised by my mother, who was very kind and caring. She never forgot people who helped us by giving us clothes and furniture. But yes, the life choices that I made are not usual which is why I emphasize taking risks. All of us in office take risks, no matter what our political structure is. I remember, the very first time I ran for office, I was so uncomfortable as I was working behind-the-scenes to get other people elected. We need to do things that are not particularly comfortable.

Let's change tracks for a bit and contextualize for our readers what the climate was back then when you started in politics?

Women have to be much better prepared before we decide to run for office. When I started, there were only eight women in the state legislature. It was male dominated and I even had my fair share of men hitting on me.

We need to make sure that the #MeToo movement stays a movement and not a moment. I do my part to call attention to it. It is important that we shine the light on people who engage in sexual harassment and abuse.

It was definitely much harder for women back then who ran for executive or highest office in the state or country. When I ran for governor, I saw the strange ideas that people had about a woman in power. It was not just me, but this was the same for Heidi Heitkamp[2] when she ran for governor.

Women politicians who ran for the position will know what I am talking about. People will ask if you are able to make tough decisions, even if you clearly exhibited toughness throughout your professional career. Clearly, a lot of these attitudes still remain, but I can say much less these days, which is a good thing. This last election proves that the people do believe in women leadership, judging by how many women have been elected to the House. This is terrific, as the legislature is beginning to reflect the diversity of our country.

During the Kavanaugh hearings, you said that "men just need to shut up, step up, and do the right thing."

Yes *(laughter)*.

What other changes would you like to see moving forward?

I'd like to see a president who does not engage in divisive rhetoric. The Trump administration has unleashed all the fault lines in our country—the racism we never adequately dealt with, sexism, and the anti-LGBTQIA sentiments. He has brought it to the fore and even enforced it! I like to see him leave the stage, which would be the first big sigh of relief for everybody, and then we can much better get on with the things that we should be doing in a bipartisan way.

I am not being naive, and I am aware Democrats and Republicans have a lot of differences in the things we care about. I mean, if we were in charge, we would not be trying to repeal the Affordable Care Act and pass the trillion-dollar tax giveaway to the rich and screwing the middle class. There are differences, yes, but I hope we can work together to move the county forward in terms of infrastructure and job creation which we both agree on.

---

2 Mary Kathryn "Heidi" Heitkamp is an American businesswoman, lawyer, and politician, who served as a United States senator from North Dakota from 2013 to 2019. She was the first woman elected to the U.S. Senate from North Dakota and served as the 28th North Dakota Attorney General from 1992 to 2000 and as state tax commissioner, from 1986 to 1992. She ran for Governor of North Dakota in 2000 and lost and considered a bid for the Democratic nomination in the 2010 U.S. Senate election but later declined. In November 2011, she declared her candidacy to replace Kent Conrad as U.S. senator from North Dakota in the 2012 election and became North Dakota's second female senator and the first woman to be elected to the Senate from that state. In 2018, Heitkamp was defeated in her bid for reelection and became a CNBC contributor and a visiting fellow at the Institute of Politics at Harvard Kennedy School.

Do you think women have been or can be harder on women, judging from last election where white women voted like their husbands?

It used to be that women can be hard on women, but I think women of late have become very much mobilized. They became very engaged after the Trump election but were further mobilized by the Kavanaugh hearings and they stayed mobilized. All over the world, women watched Dr. Blasey Ford's testimony and they were shaking and scratching their heads and going, "What the heck is going on?!"

I have heard from so many women who experienced sexual harassment and assault in varying degrees and who have had to deal with unwanted advances and unsolicited comments passed on our looks, bodies, you name it. It was so rampant, it was normalized and it became a "thing" that we did not even think to report, nor could we afford to [because of the repercussions]. So many women could relate to Dr. Blasey Ford, and seeing it was highly mobilizing. The women have stayed mobilized and they came out in droves in the 2018 elections.

Obviously, we are very encouraged by this fresh cohort of congresswomen. What does it take to get more of us out?

We have more women running in the 2018 election than in the history of our country. When women become mobilized and engaged, they start thinking about running for office and that is what happened to me, too, but it just took me a heck longer! *(laughter)* So I think the key is to keep women engaged and have minority women step up so we have a pipeline at levels of office. All this is really encouraging. The year I ran for governor in 2002, there were literally only ten women combined from both parties running. It was considered the highpoint in [women's political activism equality] and "the year of the women governor!" Fast forward to 2018, we saw at least sixty women run for governor, which to me is significant progress.

Representatives Alexandria Ocasio-Cortez and Rashida Tlaib have gained significant public attention in their take-no-prisoners approach. They drop the F-bomb, use colorful language, and are adept at social media. Is this going to be the new norm? What are your thoughts?

(Laughter) I think we are going to see all kinds of people with all kinds of leadership styles. And we also need to get good with Instagram and so-

cial media, as that is not going to go away. I am very energized by this influx of young leaders and, particularly, by the number of women and minorities elected to office. It is significant that we have the first two Native American women elected to Congress, as that has been a group that has been basically screwed by the system.

> Sheryl Sandberg gained brickbats and accolades when she said that women should lean in and can "have it all." What do you say to that?

(Laughter) I don't even know what that means?!
We all make different choices, need to do what we can to stay engaged and make a difference. The reason I went into politics was one of the reasons why I didn't get married till very late. I do not see it as a sacrifice, as marriage was just not on my list of priorities as I was busy. Of all the things that I have done, I truly do not have any regrets, even when I lost the gubernatorial race. All of these experiences got me to where I am today.

> I got married late, too, and my mother never pressured and, in fact, encouraged me to pursue my own life.

(Laughter) My mother was the same and never pressured me to get married or have children.

> My mummy was the same and in fact told me to not have children so that I could have my own life. She said calling someone mummy is easy but being a mummy is difficult!

(Laughter)

> By your own admission, what were some of your biggest lessons learned when you lost the gubernatorial race?

I learned some very practical lessons. You have to raise money and hire people who can help you win these races because, when you are up against a Republican, they come with big donors and a professional team, while I was working with well-meaning volunteers. I learned from my 2002 election in time for my 2006 campaign. This time, I raised money and hired a team of professionals and ran to win.[3]

Let's change tracks and discuss your personal life and your battle with cancer. Can you share that journey with us?

The hardest part was coming to terms with the diagnosis, especially as I have always been healthy and have never been hospitalized. The closest I came to being ill was having appendicitis at seventeen, and it went away, thank goodness. It was a shock, so the first question I asked my doctor was if I was going to die anytime soon and he said no.

My second question was, "What kind of treatment should I have?" I am still undergoing treatment in addition to the two surgeries I had.

But it was important for me to let my constituents know. This was not something I wanted to hide from them, though it was only fair that they be concerned if I could do my job. It was not an easy decision, as I am a private person living a public life. So the first thing I did was to discuss with my partner who was concerned if it was too big a challenge to be hiding, so we decided to go public. The news has actually made my constituents and people in general feel more connected to me. I have people who come up to share with me their own battles with cancer or simply to check in with me on how I am doing.

Do you have any words of advice for anyone going through a similar journey?

They are not alone and we are all connected in so many ways. I sympathize and empathize and stand with them.

Some of your peers have shared in confidence that you have become more brazen in speaking your mind and also more colorful with your language since your illness. Do you agree?

(Laughter) I think that has a part to play, but for a long time now, I also decided I had to be more myself and be able to speak plainly. For many women

---

3 In 2006, Hirono ran for Hawai'i's second congressional district. Her advantage was that she was the only candidate who held statewide office and had the most name recognition. She also raised more money than any other candidate in the race and won with a plurality of just 22 percent of the vote. In the general election, she defeated Republican State Senator Bob Hogue, and later won reelection to a second term with 76 percent of the vote.

running for office, especially for me way back in the 80s, we had to break a lot of barriers to be heard and to be good in what we do.

A large part of my journey has been to eliminate as many of those barriers, especially when I chose to share my cancer story on the eve of the repeal of the Affordable Care Act in the senate. I really exposed myself in a way that is not easy for us in office. I have always been a fighter and can't do the work that I do if I weren't, but I never felt the need to be so noisy about it. This administration, however, has given me many opportunities to do so.

> Out of the mud blooms a lotus, so ironically, this president has spurred many women to find their voice and unleash their powers within. Let's talk a little bit about Hawaiʻi. How have things been for you since your arrival here as an eight-year-old immigrant?

Oh my goodness. My earliest memories were just of my mother working so hard. I was very close to my mother and did not hang out with a lot of people. I was always very self-contained and learned early on to make do with very little and not cause my mother any trouble. I would help with the chores and make dinner, as I was acutely aware of how hard my mother struggled to keep it all together for us. I did not fool around at all.

I am grateful to my mother for taking us here, as I would have stayed at the farm with my grandparents otherwise. We did not have running water there and drew water from a well. It was very rural and I would have had a totally different life. I would not have left the country and never gone to college. Even when I was little, I saw that this country provided all kinds of opportunities that required me to adapt, which I could since I was little.

My story is not typical for a person in office, which is why immigration reform is so personal and meaningful to me.

> You have an intimate and helicopter view of Hawaiʻi. What are some of its unique challenges and characteristics that you know through your years here?

I strongly recognize that Hawaiʻi people are very caring, and that concept of ʻohana runs through the community. It really is part of our ethos and there is a deep appreciation of different cultures that I don't see in many other places.

There are also a lot of intercultural marriages which is unique to Hawaiʻi. New York may have a multicultural makeup, but Hawaiʻi sees many interracial marriages. Our children here are hapa, and that is special.

From an economic standpoint, there is an over-reliance on tourism with tourist figures reaching ten million, so we do need to diversify. We also need to become more energy and food self-sufficient. We also need to look into affordability and the cost of living, and it has to be at a government level—all federal, state, and local.

Hawaiʻi also faces a major homeless issue that is not easy to resolve and it is going to take a concerted effort to see change.

From an economic point of view, how do you think we can balance this sense of aloha and increase productivity here? We see projects such as the rail stalling.

It is not just Hawaiʻi. Other cities have these issues, too.

What are your hopes and aspirations then for Hawaiʻi?

To have an education system that is not just supportive of teachers, but also creates an environment of learning so that every child can feel some measure of worth and success. I speak from personal experience as I saw my younger brother struggle in school, which very much magnified for me how every child learns differently, hence the need for an equitable system that does not merely benefit students with As and Bs.

I would like our public and private schools to be comparable, as I do believe that education is foundational and I am a huge proponent of quality education, universal preschool, and college affordability. That does not mean everybody has to go to college, but that it should be made available to them.

What do you do to relax?

I like to get creative. I got interested in making my own paper and ceramics. I also like watching Korean drama.

What pisses you off?

This president.

Who would you like to have a sit-down dinner with?

Ruth Bader Ginsburg, but I already got to meet and chat with her.

I have met a lot of interesting people, but I recently met Carol Anderson, the author of *White Rage*. She recently published *One Person, No Vote: How Voter Suppression Is Destroying Our Democracy* and I would like to meet with her, as her work focuses on discrimination racial inequality. I've been very concerned about the voter suppression that is going on in the country. The fact that she writes about it and wins national awards means she is able to get the attention of a lot of people. I would really like to get to know her better.

If you weren't a politician, you would be …

I would like to own a successful brick-and-mortar bookstore. Not one that has to close down because of Amazon. I love books and I love to read, so this will be perfect.

Any role models?

I don't have role models but I have people I admire, which is my mother who is my inspiration. And people who stay the course, like Patsy Mink, who ran so many races, picked herself up, and always stayed the course.

What does your mother think about all your accomplishments?

She is very proud of me, though she is now in a situation where she needs affordable health care, which is something many families face and need.

Favorite spot in Hawai'i?

My home, where I can just veg out and do whatever I want!

Happiness is …

I haven't mentioned him at all, but my husband. I hope that I can live healthy and long to be with him as he's a wonderful man.

Hawaiʻi is …

A unique, wonderful place that has its challenges, but I am lucky to represent a state like Hawaiʻi and be able to fight the battles that I fight for my constituents.

Describe yourself in three words.

I'm a fighter.

Your life philosophy on a bumper sticker?

Half the battle is showing up.

The title of your memoir will be ….

I'm Still Standing.

What would your epitaph say?

It is for someone else to write so I will leave it as that. *(laughter)*

THE POWER LISTENER

Connie Lau

I learned that getting at the real truth goes back to learning to listen and to be respectful of other people's views, because they believe in their own views as strongly as I believe in mine. It is not as if they are being disingenuous or advocating a position that they know is wrong. Somehow, if we are all not to end up in war, we need to learn how to be respectful and really try to understand where the other person is coming from.

The Power Listener

Constance Hee Lau, better known as Connie Lau, serves as president and chief executive officer (CBO) and director of Hawaiian Electric Industries, parent company of Hawaiian Electric Company, and American Savings Bank. Connie first joined the HEI companies in 1984 as an assistant corporate counsel and has served in many executive capacities including chairman, president, and CEO of American Savings Bank and chairman of Hawaiian Electric Company. Since 2004, she also serves as a director of Matson. Connie is a nationally recognized leader in the fields of critical infrastructure, resilience and physical and cyber security, banking and energy. Since 2012, Connie has chaired the National Infrastructure Advisory Council (NIAC) and was named 2011 Woman of the Year by the Women's Council on energy and the environment in Washington, D.C. She also serves on the boards of the Edison Electric Institute, the Associated Electrical & Gas Insurance Services, and the Electricity Subsector Coordinating Council.

In banking, Connie previously served as a member of the Federal Reserve Bank of San Francisco's Twelfth District Community Depository Institutions Advisory Council, and was one of American Banker's 25 Most Powerful Women in Banking for 2004, 2005, and 2006 when she headed American Savings. In Hawai'i, she was named Pacific Business News' (PBN) 2004 Hawai'i Business Leader of the Year, and in 2013, named one of PBN's 10 to Watch, for her leadership in clean energy and transportation. Additionally, Connie also serves on the boards of the Hawai'i Business Roundtable, the Asia-Pacific Center for Security Studies, Punahou School, and the Consuelo Foundation. She was a Trustee for Kamehameha Schools Bishop Estate from 1999 to 2007.

Connie graduated from Yale College with a BS in administrative sciences, and earned a Juris Doctor from the University of California Hastings College of the Law, as well as an MBA from Stanford Graduate School of Business. She is a consummate leader with great familiarity with management, corporate governance and financial oversight. She possesses expansive knowledge of the Hawai'i business community and the local communities, from her years serving as a director for various local industry, business development, educational, and nonprofit organizations.

Despite all her accomplishments, Connie remains a local girl at heart and is happiest at her late mother's homestead in Kāne'ohe Bay, being by the water and labouring in the yard!

You are just about the most powerful woman in Hawai'i. Share with us your background and how the granddaughter of a houseboy got to where she is today.

The real key to getting where I am today is education. That was something my parents really believed in. I was born in the 1950s, before the Civil Rights Act, and many people faced discrimination in Hawai'i. My parents saw education as one of the only ways that one could level the playing field and be able to change the trajectory of a family in a single generation. I was very fortunate that my parents had those beliefs even though my father barely even graduated from sixth grade.

My mother almost didn't graduate from high school either. She took the entrance test for Pearl Harbor, scored very well, and was offered a job in her senior year at McKinley. She was going to accept the job so she could earn money to help the family. However, her teacher stopped her and asked her to consider graduating before going off to work at Pearl Harbor. Thankfully she listened to her teacher's advice and graduated.

I was very fortunate, too, that they sent me to Punahou, which was one of those amazing institutions that care about the community and train their students to be socially conscious. As a result, I was raised with values, such as "to whom much is given, much is expected." Ideas of equality, diversity, inclusivity, servant leadership, giving back to society, and "leaving a place better than when you found it" are ingrained in us.

So this formed the backdrop of my formative years and learning. As a result, one of the early discussions between my husband and I revolved around the notion of whether life is fair. I grew up thinking life is fair, as that was what my school engendered in us. My husband, however, grew up in the rough and tumble public school system and was under the impression that life was not fair.

In our early years of marriage, he would always tell me, "Connie, how can you say that life is fair? Just look at all the terrible things that happen in this world?"

Over time, I ended up compromising, and my moniker became, "Life should be fair." That was also seminal to why I obtained the degrees I did and the educational background that I have today, as my dad always wanted me to know my rights. From the time I was a little girl, my dad wanted me to study law. He said it would equip me with knowing my rights and being able to not only speak up for myself, but for others who did not have that knowledge.

But being Asian, he also wanted me to go to business school, as he wanted me to learn how to make money and feed the family. And that was just what I did. After college, I went to law and business school before making my way out to work.

You will also notice that most people who come from Hawai'i have a very strong sense of social justice. They truly believe Hawai'i is a place where all people should be treated equally as it is a melting pot and a paradise, where all can live in harmony while celebrating diversity and respecting differences.

Speaking of diversity, you were probably one of the few women at Yale and Stanford. How was that like?

I was in the second class of women who studied for four years through Yale, as it used to be an all-male school. To set the context for you, in the year I entered Yale, the former president of the university, Kingman Brewster, promised the alumni that he would graduate a thousand male leaders a year. Meanwhile, he converted one of the buildings on the old freshman campus and accepted 125 women. The gender ratios were crazy as it was almost eight to one. By the time I graduated, it had gotten better and was four to one.

It was a very strange time to be in the university, as it was in transition between being all boys to coed. The legacy of the men's college was evident, especially in the mixer events and social traditions. I used to head to school with the boys on the weekdays, and, on Friday evenings, the buses would be full of women from all the colleges in the northeast coming to the campus for the weekend. It was a little unreal.

Do you think you worked harder because you were female or was that not a consideration at all?

I think it's true that women have always had to work harder. Having said that, if anyone were to ask me what the number one success factor is, I will say it is hard work. I was raised to be a hard worker. You could be a brilliant person but if you don't want to work, then you would be completely eclipsed by someone who may not be as brilliant or insightful but will get the job done. I was already raised to be a hard worker and it does help that I was aware of my gender and I did work even harder.

Given what you just shared, do you think leadership is nature or nurture? I hear, on the one hand, it is nurture as your parents have a huge part to play in who you are. But do you think you, too, are intrinsically motivated to work hard?

I don't really know. It sure has to do with nurture and this isn't just the period when you are growing up, but all the experiences in life that shape you. I believe that your environment molds you.

I know that certain experiences have shaped me. For example, when I was a trustee at Kamehameha Schools, I learned my first major lessons in leadership. I also think there is an intrinsic element, as there is diversity in performance levels in the workforce and there are some people who can just get the job done. Some are just better and faster than others. It is no different than if you're on the track and field team. I did a lot of track and field when I was young, and there were just some people who were faster and physically more capable than me. There are others who are better dancers and musicians, so I do think there is an element of intrinsic abilities.

You shared that some of your earliest leadership lessons came from when you were on the board of trustees at Kamehameha Schools. Share with us your learnings.

One of the biggest lessons I learned was from retired Vice Admiral Robert Kihune, who had been the head of the Pacific Fleet. Hundreds of thousands of sailors and civilians worked under him and he commanded hundreds of ships and huge multibillion-dollar budgets. Because of his military background, I assumed that he would always take charge of every situation that may arise.

There was a time when the probate court wanted us to do a new strategic plan for the estate. We had to do it with the stakeholders and the community in mind and with their input.

We were in community meeting after community meeting, sometimes lasting well into the late hours of the night. And after one particularly grueling meeting, I said to the vice admiral, "Bob, I just don't understand why you would let the meeting go on and on? Since you are an admiral, don't you military officers just command and take charge? Why didn't you take charge of the meeting to help direct the conversation and get us to a resolution faster?"

He responded, "Connie, if we were in war and we had to take that hill, I would tell the guys to go take that hill. But when you are not in war, you need to actually listen to everybody. It's really important to listen." That was one of the biggest lessons I learned. Even though you may be an admiral and have command of hundreds of ships and thousands of men and resources, you need to listen.

A key characteristic of leadership is learning to listen. I've carried that lesson with me throughout my life.

The other leadership lesson has to do with learning to discern between right and wrong and, more important, how to react, particularly with the media out there. We know the media is not the way it used to be where reporters subscribed to a code of ethics and thoroughly researched everything they were writing, and aimed for objectivity and balance.

Today, it is all about attracting attention and expressing raw views through social media, so the media has become more extreme than anything else. How do you begin to sort through all the information that is out there, particularly if you are a young person?

We faced the huge "Broken Trust" controversy at the estate in the late 1990s, and our group of trustees, who were brought in to clean up the controversy were on the front page of the newspaper for years. It really became just a question of whether we were going to be above the fold or below.

We would be sitting in the boardroom and reading the news wondering where the source of the information came from—many untruths were fabricated. That was when I learned that I can't just simply trust the media. I had grown up trusting the media wholeheartedly, and the incident made me realize that I had to develop an internal compass that tells me whether something is or isn't right, or at least gain an understanding of the context, instead of simply believing what I see or hear in the media.

My husband was recently at a lecture at the East-West Center. He told me there was a media expert there and he was recommending that we watch both CNN and Fox News and toggle between the channels, so you could actually make up your own mind about what is real and what isn't. So you know, in many ways the world is flooded with all sorts of fake news and you need to know how to sort through what the real truth is.

The other thing I learned from leadership at Kamehameha is that what I think is the real truth or the right thing may be very different from what someone else might think.

What is "truth" to you then?

For me, I learned that getting at the real truth goes back to learning to listen and to be respectful of other people's views, because they believe in their own views as strongly as I believe in mine. It is not as if they are being disingenuous or advocating a position that they know is wrong. Somehow, if we are all not to end up in war, we need to learn how to be respectful and really try to understand where the other person is coming from.

It is also funny and ironic how some of these leadership lessons are learned when I was a kid as my mother always taught me to put myself in the other person's shoes. Perhaps it is an Asian-woman trait. Did you grow up with that, too?

> **Absolutely. My favorite character is Scout from *To Kill a Mockingbird*. Atticus Finch told his daughter Scout that "you never really know a man until you walk in his shoes."**

Yes! My mom always told me to look at things objectively and to step outside of who I am or the position that I hold to see things from the other person's point of view. This has been an invaluable lesson. Today, I can say I am a competent facilitator because I will try to listen to everybody and make sure that everybody speaks up. You can forget about being heard if they don't even speak up, so the key is to get them to share, as many may have strong views, but they choose to not share them for whatever reason. So if I sense that someone has something to say or has thoughts that should be shared, I ensure I reach out to encourage them to do that.

The only way one can reach a resolution is to make sure as many views as possible get onto the table, find a balance, and enable everyone to come to an understanding, as there's never anyone who is absolutely right all the time. That, for me, is probably the best solution that most people can buy into and support.

> **I can see how this ability to listen and mediate is one of the secrets to your success. What happens, though, if you are faced with violent objections or obstacles and how do you deal with that? And how do you deal with negative press and being misquoted?**

Negative press and a hostile situation is quite different. For the former, what is key is for you to know where you stand and listen to your internal compass. I'm also a big advocate for not wasting a lot of effort or energy on things that you can't fix or influence. In my case, I accept the negative press and remind myself that the other person is entitled to their point of view and to not let it bother me.

But if someone confronts me at a meeting—and I have been present at occasions where people are shouting and waving signs—then as a leader, I have to stand there and take it. That is what people expect. If you are going to be in a leadership position and you're in a meeting where people are invited to share their views, then you need to turn on your listening ear no matter how angry they may be. You have to remain calm and receive that information openly, and genuinely want to understand where that other person is coming from.

> There is a recent McKinsey report that says a CEO's job starts out tough and gets even tougher. What do you say to that?

CEO jobs are always challenging. Sometimes they are tougher depending on what the entity is going through at that time, and sometimes they are easier. During the easier times, you have to celebrate those moments. (*laughter*) But when times are really challenging, then you just have to be there 150 percent for the organization.

So I don't know if I'd say the CEO jobs have gotten tougher, though I think where McKinsey might be coming from is in the area of governance. Governance has certainly gotten tougher in the sense that the expectations for leaders have gone up significantly.

Boards of directors used to be able to say, "It was the CEO's responsibility and the CEO will take care of it," but no longer. Lehman Brothers, Dodd-Frank, and the financial crisis have changed the face of corporate governance so much so that anybody in positions of influence, and particularly the board of directors, need to step up. The board has to function as an oversight mechanism. From that standpoint, yes, it is changing times and expectations have changed but, in general, the role of the CEO has always been tough.

> Speaking of changing times, what are your thoughts on the #MeToo phenomenon?

Standards and people's expectations are going to rise. Behavior and conduct that was tolerated previously is not going to be tolerated going forward. Everyone is going to have to adjust as the genie in the bottle has been released and can't be put back.

It's going to be interesting moving forward as the United States tends to lead change which is why, to a large extent, we all are very privileged to live in America. I don't know if the rest of the world will necessarily follow suit. I do hope that the pendulum does not swing too far, but will fall gradually into a rational place as some people on the other side may get hurt inadvertently.

In your own personal career, have you suffered discrimination or latent misogyny? Do you think being a woman has been a boon or bane for you and your career?

It is not a question I actually think about and I think that not thinking about it actually helped me. If I saw it as a bane, I might use it as an excuse for why I don't succeed. If I saw it as a boon, I might feel like I am getting something that I don't necessarily deserve.

Case in point is the affirmative action admission policies at universities that favor minorities and women. Whether you are admitted because you are a woman or a minority, you just are. It is a fact of existence that one has to deal with. This goes back to my discussion with my husband about whether life is fair and just. Was there discrimination? Likely, but fortunately, my gender didn't ultimately prevent me from rising to the level that I have, though I am sure there were both boons and banes along the way.

Do you think motherhood has changed you?

Definitely. I love being a mother and I think motherhood really helped me be a leader because kids don't report to you nor do you cut their paycheck. *(laughter)* So if you want them to do what you hope they will do, you have to influence them and figure out how to inspire them. That is no different from a workforce, you know. If I just wanted to order my employees about like a command and control center, it won't work. You can't get to an empowered organization that way. You have to be able to set a vision and inspire them to want to achieve that. Inspiration is what engenders creativity and my kids have definitely taught me how to achieve that! *(laughter)*

My kids have taught me a lot, particularly because I don't have perfect kids, but nobody does. There was a time in my life where I almost placed work as a priority and had to deal with some issues with my kids. That was when I learned a great deal on leadership philosophies and, thankfully, my kids came out fine.

> **If a young executive shared that she is on the cusp of choosing between her career and her family, what would you tell her?**

For starters, I would share that she should have thought about it before she started her family. I've always maintained that once you have a family, it's not a choice, as the time for choosing has passed. You need to decide before you start having kids, because once you do have kids, you have to take care of your family.

It boils down to time and personal choice. What I can do is to lay out for the person what the positives and the negatives are to becoming a mother and the impact it can have on one's career and she will have to make her own personal decision on whether she is willing to make the sacrifices and/or reap the rewards.

> **That is why I chose to not be a mom, so I can just take off and have my own independence and freedom.**

Yes, and that is OK, as it is a conscious decision. That has been one of my strong philosophies as a leader—to not judge women for the personal choices they make. There are so many women who have to take care of their families and turn down a promotion. It does not mean they don't want to move forward in the organization, but it just may not be the right time, as they have little kids at home. It may take two to four years when the kids go to school until these women choose to accept a promotion.

It is important we let them choose and not choose for them. Just because a woman has young children does not mean we should not offer her a promotion, as we must allow her to choose.

> **Do you think a woman can have it all? Sheryl Sandberg gained brickbats when she said women could have it all.**

It goes back to definitions. What is "having it all?"

I think people have to define what they are satisfied with. There are some of us who believe that we can have both a great family and a career. I would like to think at this point in my life that I've been able to do both. At times, I have had to make sacrifices on the career side and, other times, I've had to make sacrifices on the personal side. What really helps is choosing wisely who you marry, as the spouse is a big factor for most women. Many can make it happen or "have it all," when they have a supportive spouse.

> Yes, I read that your husband and you have that very supportive relationship.

Yes, we are fortunate that both of us are CEOs, so we understand the requirements of the job. We also understand that sometimes personal things have to give, though at other times, we ensure our personal lives are a priority and we take time off to spend time with the family.

> Women are expected to retire with over $1.1 million less than men. What are your thoughts?

I am a strong believer in financial literacy. We need to teach women how to manage their own finances early on, since they tend to end up with the family responsibilities, such as buying the groceries or ensuring the kids have books or computers. Financial literacy is all the more important for women, as they tend to have these additional responsibilities.

> Hawaiʻi has one of the highest credit card debt ratios. How do you suggest we can remedy this?

Financial literacy helps there, too. Credit counselors can sit with you and help you work out a budget to understand how much interest you pay when you pay it on a credit card versus when you refinance a personal or a secured loan.

> How do we encourage Hawaiʻi residents to save more?

Actually, Hawaiʻi has one of the highest average balances in savings nationwide, possibly due to the strong Asian influence. China and Singapore, in general, definitely have a higher rate of savings than the United States and, here in Hawaiʻi, we rank approximately fifteenth across the country, so there is a cultural factor at play, as Asians generally hold the belief that saving is good and they shore up a rainy day.

> What advice would you give to an aspiring leader?

Definitely learn to listen.

You were born and raised here on island. What are some of your fondest memories?

Growing up in Hawai'i is wonderful. I grew up on the Windward Side, which was country back then. I recall lying on the grass and staring up at the sky. I used to do that with my mother and she would talk about the shapes in the clouds—be it a dragon, a fairy, or a princess. How can one have a more idyllic childhood than catching grasshoppers and crabs and dreaming in the clouds?

What has changed over the years?

A lot has changed, but I still have the house that I grew up in on Kāne'ohe Bay. My mother left it to me when she passed on at ninety-six, so she had a long life.

You know, we had some elderly friends over last weekend and they had to take care walking down the long flight of stairs from our house at the street level to the bay. They were concerned that we didn't install a guard rail.

That did make me think and convinced me that my mother lived to ninety-six because she went up and down those stairs every day with no handrails! I recall us having to tell mom to be careful on those stairs. Yet every morning, she would take the stairs to head to the yard and rake the lawn. In fact, on many occasions when I visited, she would be by the bay just enjoying the ocean, so I guess some things don't change, like our old house and our stairs without the rail!

I also love being by the water and I'm a Pisces. For me, water is healing and I love to watch the tides come in and hear them crash on the shore. It's like watching life ebb and flow and that puts everything in context and perspective.

What changes would you like to see in Hawai'i? Or conversely, what do you not want to see?

Hawai'i is really special. I don't know if it's because of the host culture, the sense of 'ohana, community, or the aloha, which is very inclusive. I would never want to see this change. What is special about Hawai'i needs to stay special.

But, as the state grows and businesses develop, there are some changes that may be bad for the state. My wish is that we can come to a better equilibrium in the future where the economy can be strong; business can be good; and people can feel good about the good economy, that is done in a way that doesn't take away from that wonderful warmth of inclusive 'ohana and community.

You were one of the biggest advocates for Obama's Presidential Library to be built here.

There were many plans to commemorate the forty-fourth president here. I knew it would be a long shot compared to Chicago, but it was still worth a try.

During his presidency, Obama had been speaking about the pivot to Asia Pacific and the importance of that part of the world and he's absolutely right. It is the world's second largest economy and is growing leaps and bounds.

Asia is rising, so I am sure something will happen and he may have an office at the East-West Center. What the actual plans are remains to be seen, but I do think we should have something here because of his philosophy, his sense of home and place in Hawai'i. Having grown up here, I do think he is a strong ambassador for the unique nature of Hawai'i, and Hawai'i itself is a great symbol of that sense of interconnectedness and globalism.

How would you personally want Hawai'i to be remembered?

I would like it to be remembered the way it is remembered today. It is funny that I can travel all over the world, be it in Asia, Europe or the Midwest, and everyone I meet knows of Hawai'i. In fact, many dream of visiting Hawai'i. We are such a tiny little place in the Pacific Ocean with 1.4 million people and yet it is renowned all over the world. Many think of Hawai'i as being a paradise island with incredible beauty and phenomenal weather.

But I also tell them that in addition to that, what is special about Hawai'i is the spirit of aloha, where all races can come together. Just head out on the streets and you see all the hapa kids. *(laughter)*

What do you do to relax?

I still go out to Kāne'ohe! *(laughter)* I am happy just sitting on the bay and watching the waves. I also enjoy doing yard work and going up and down those stairs like mom. I always think about her.

They say, to age gracefully, you need to keep moving, though I don't know if my husband's definition is quite the same *(laughter)*, because over the weekend, he had to work hard at trimming our trees! *(laughter)*

There's a lot of yard work when you have a house on the Windward Side of the island, where it rains a lot and things grow a lot. That's a lot of yard work.

What is that your secret to keeping so graceful and lean?

I try not to worry about a lot of things. *(laughter)*

What gets you angry?

What gets me angry is not when people make mistakes, but when they refuse to listen to others. Some folks have made pretty significant errors at work, but I understand mistakes happen, as there is no ill intent or ill will. But it's not good when people won't listen.

What do you think has been your biggest mistake or regret?

Being too trusting. I generally will err on the side of trust. I have now reached this stage where most people don't take advantage of me and I've learned to not let them do so. But early in my career, I was much too trusting.

Who would you like to have a sit-down dinner with?

My husband! *(laughter)* And Barack Obama. I would love to have dinner with him, too!

What has been your best investment to date?

My kids. I'm very proud of them and I am so proud they all turned out OK. My oldest daughter, who is thirty-two, just got married last August, my middle one just turned thirty, and the youngest is twenty-seven. They are now all grown, forging their own lives, and are all good people.

What would you say if and when you meet God?

Hello.

What's your life philosophy on a bumper sticker?

Live life.

Suppose you are writing your memoir, the title would be?

It would probably have to revolve around the concept of servant leadership, because that is indeed what I think.

What would your epitaph say or how do you want to be remembered?

As a servant leader, though I certainly haven't thought that far ahead! *(laughter)*.

Some people think about leaving legacies, but I haven't really thought about it. And you know, this may sound funny, but I'm not sure I necessarily want to be remembered, except just by my kids and grandkids.

I just want to do good things while I'm here and there is really no reason to have to be remembered beyond that, as it is what you do today that counts.

THE RETAIL DOYENNE
Marleen Akau

Young people need to get into the real world and learn to see the big picture and not to lose the forest for the tree. I think planning is important, hence my saying, "Put your goals in cement and your plans in the sand" as you have to be flexible to change your plans in order to achieve your goals.

Marleen Akau is the vice president and general manager of Royal Hawaiian Center (RHC) in Waikīkī and has over thirty-five years of experience in the shopping center industry. While at RHC, Marleen guided her team through the $115 million revitalization of the property and the sale of the land improvements to RHC Property Holdings, LLC in 2014.

Prior to joining Festival Management Corp., the developer and property manager of RHC in 2004, her industry experience included management, leasing, financial investments, and real estate responsibilities with Kamehameha Schools. She also managed Windward Mall, Aloha Tower Marketplace, and Keauhou Shopping Center, and has experience in managing office buildings and industrial warehouse spaces while employed with Kamehameha Schools.

Marleen is a member on the executive committee of the Waikīkī Improvement Association (WIA) and the Waikīkī Business Improvement District (WBID). She is also a board member for the newly formed Waikīkī Beach Special Improvement District (WBSID), and a past chair of the WIA board of directors. A member of Hotel Lodging and Tourism Association, International Council of Shopping Centers, and Retail Merchants of Hawaii, Marleen received the Native Hawaiian Chamber of Commerce 'Ō'o Award in April 2018. In March 2019, she was selected as one of the honorees for the Pacific Business News Women Who Mean Business Award.

She enjoys being with her husband and family of five children, fifteen grandchildren, ten great-grandchildren, and four dogs. Her hearty, husky loud voice and laughter matches only the largesse of her personality, depth of her spirit, and strength of her character.

Yours is truly a rags to riches story. Share with us your humble beginnings.

My mom had eight children; three were put up for adoption and five of us remained. We had a really hard life back then. By third grade, I decided I had to help my parents and took on babysitting jobs. I would watch the janitor's kids at the elementary school as they had three boys. Every morning, my mom would drop me off at 6 a.m. and I'd watch the kids until 7:45 a.m. when the school bell rang. I did that Monday through Friday all the way until the sixth grade. This allowed me to have pocket money without having to depend on my parents.

I was the most responsible of my older sister and younger brother. My parents depended on me to watch them. I was always looking for work to get money. In the seventh grade, I got a job in a beauty salon washing towels and cleaning the salon. In high school, I worked at the cannery during the summer and then after work at a burger drive-in. Work was all I did. I thought it was the only way to succeed in life and not burden my parents.

I heard you also found time to be very active in volleyball?

Yes, we lived in veteran housing and all we had was a gym, so I started playing volleyball and became very good at that. I was a song leader my junior year. My senior year, I became pregnant and my parents weren't happy because they knew I had so much potential and drive and felt that having a baby would keep me from achieving my goals. They knew that my decision was to keep my child, and in May of 1970, I got married.

After having a second child in 1972, we ended our marriage. We both agreed to be good parents and respected each other for the sake of our children. My ex was a great guy but we were not compatible. We remained good friends from the time of our divorce until his passing a few years ago. By keeping a good friendship, we were able to set an example for our children and could attend all of the children's parties together. My current husband of forty-three years agreed with our decision and he, too, became good friends with my ex-husband and his wife.

Your focus and motivation to work became all about your children.

Yes. The deal was that my children would be a big part of my life. I worked different jobs and all I knew about life was to work hard and take care of my children. I always had faith that good jobs would come my way. Finally, I landed a job with Bishop Estate now known as Kamehameha Schools (KS).

I had applied as the file clerk but the job had been taken by an in-house employee, so the only position available was the messenger position. I gladly took the job and was happy because all I had was a high school degree. That position paid a little over $400 per month. As messenger, my role was to drive the board of trustees around which included Richard Lyman, Hung Wo Ching, Matsuo Takabuki, Frank Midkiff, and Pinky Thompson. Of course, I ended up having a good relationship with them.

Later, the position of file clerk did open up, and I became both the messenger and the file clerk, though I always knew I was not content and had to keep moving on to find the right job.

What part did your husband play in your career?

My husband was a very big part of my career. He graduated from KS. He said that from the minute he met me, he knew I was a diamond in the rough and saw my potential. However, he shared that in order for me to grow, I had to find a mentor or a role model and emulate them. This required me to change what I was doing and to watch my language and behavior. In order to accomplish this, I had to associate myself with positive people who had big dreams.

An opportunity became available to me when KS had to sell the land in fee to the lessees. This created the treasury assistant position which I applied for and was promoted two grade levels. The position required me to negotiate the best interest rates for KS from different investment bankers and local banks for the increase in funds they received due to the sale of the land to the lessees.

Did you face any sexual discrimination in your early career?

Most of my bosses were men who didn't have a lot of confidence in me. I had to rely on prayer and have faith things would work out.

But I would also ask a lot of questions and would look at creative or effective ways to get the job done. Some of my fellow workers were not interested in teaching me more because of the fear they may lose their jobs. I never felt that way because if I didn't teach another employee to do my job, I wouldn't have the chance to learn another position, and I would miss out on other opportunities. After being the treasury assistant for a few years, I wanted to do something different.

Eventually, I asked my boss if I could attend real estate classes. He declined my request and stated that going to real estate school had nothing to do with my current position. So even though I suggested that knowledge of the industry is integral to the job, he said "no."

At this point, I decided to pay on my own and attended real estate classes with my husband. We both were blessed and passed the school and the state exam. The next day, I was excited and told my boss that I had my real estate license and that I would be doing real estate part time with my husband. By then, my goal was to be a lady land manager so that I could eventually take care of Bishop Estate's lands, buildings, and homes.

Later, another opportunity for a land manager position became available. I was so excited I told my boss that I wanted to apply for the position. He told me that I was not qualified for the position and they wouldn't hire me. Although I didn't meet the qualifications they were looking for, I applied anyway because I felt that I had equivalent experience.

When it was my turn, I took the test which basically asked for a recommendation for a particular project and why we should or shouldn't do the deal. As I started writing my recommendation, I couldn't get past one paragraph. All I thought about were the other applicants turning in many pages. I kept trying to expand on my paragraph and couldn't do it, so I stayed with my one paragraph. I then went to the manager of that department and said, "I don't know what the other applicants are saying, but what I am turning in is right to the point."

Later, I learned the manager of that department had to submit the name of the person they chose for the land manager position to the board of trustees. My current boss attended this meeting. When the manager told them I was their selected person for the land manager position, my boss was shocked because he said I had no chance in getting the job. This position gave me a promotion of three levels above my current one. The hard thing for my boss was finding a replacement for me. It took them almost one month to find someone.

> I am so glad you proved your boss wrong ! As you scaled up the proverbial career ladder, did you have any mentors along the way?

Yes. About a year later, I was promoted to commercial land manager which is another step up and that's where I learned about the land under a shopping center, which is known as ground leases. Eventually, I started to manage and oversee the ground leases at Kapalama, Kakaʻako, and the University area. KS gave me the opportunity and paid for me to attend different seminars on land leasing, management, marketing, retailing, deal-making, and how to deal with people. I appreciate all the opportunities that KS gave and the investment they made in me to attend the different courses.

Later, the president of RHSC wanted to find out who ran all these properties at KS as the documentation was well done, up to date, and the accounts receivables were current. My name was raised. I was, by then, known to be the troubleshooter for KS.

Anyway, one of the trustees, Mr. Takabuki, always looked out for me as he knew I had the desire to grow and keep learning. The president spoke to Mr. Takabuki and shared with him that they wanted me to be transferred to RHSC. When my current boss came to me, I was reluctant to be transferred because at that point I had thirteen years with KS. I saw Mr. Takabuki buying lunch next to me and I asked him why they were sending me to RHSC. He said that I reached all I could at KS and he felt that I would be able to learn more by moving to RHSC. I said ok but asked, "What if I don't like the job? Would I be able to come back to KS?" He said yes, but in his heart, he knew that I wouldn't want to come back. Nonetheless, to assure me, he said he would keep my position open for ninety days.

And so you never did go back to Kamehameha Schools?

Yes, in fact I ended up taking over the management of RHSC in March 1988. At that time, many restaurants in Waikīkī started to close and were converted to retail space.

What do you think was key to the center's success?

We had a great cultural program that drew in the visitors. What I also liked most about our center was that we catered to the locals. The locals wouldn't shop at the center, but they would come and enjoy our restaurants and concerts.

You also had a brief stint at Windward Mall and Aloha Tower?

Yes, later, the board of trustees decided that I had to transfer to Windward Mall. My mission was to oversee the renovations and enhance the leasing of the vacant spaces. I was initially disappointed when they required me to transfer to Windward Mall because of the amount of effort I had put into RHSC which became the crown jewel for KS. But the trustees convinced me that they needed their strongest property manager to help with Windward Mall.

So I went there in 1993 and stayed for a couple of years. It was a learning experience being the general manager at Windward Mall because the locals were our main customers. At RHSC, the visitor was our main customer.

Previously, the owner of Aloha Tower approached me three times to join their team, but since I had seventeen years with KS, I did not feel it was appropriate to leave because of how much Bishop Estate invested in me and I wanted to give back. In June of 1995, the owner for Aloha Tower Marketplace approached me again to be their general manager. I said yes and took the position, even though I knew it was going to be short term. Knowing this, I negotiated a three-year contract.

I worked as hard as I could with the team, but I had to fire many people as we couldn't afford to retain everybody. I knew that eventually Aloha Tower would not survive because we weren't able to pay the mortgage and the ground lease rent. Eighteen months after I started, Aloha Tower Marketplace filed for bankruptcy and I was terminated. It was a sad day because of all the work that our team put in. During my tenure, we were able to increase sales and pay the expenses except for the mortgage and ground lease rent.

Wow. You had to start all over again despite how far you had come?

Yes, I had to start over again. I didn't have a job from January 1997. With all of my experience in property management, leasing, marketing, and retailing, I wasn't able to get a job. Reasons given to me were that I was overqualified, or previously making more money than the position was offering. So my only option was to fall back on my real estate and leasing experience.

I immediately went to Coldwell Banker and started to do real estate sales for a couple of years before transferring to Coldwell Banker Commercial for a year to focus on commercial leasing. I really enjoyed doing commercial leasing. The only challenge I had was that my husband and I were living on commissions only. I wasn't really comfortable with the situation and continued to seek full-time employment.

That's how you landed on the Big Island?

In December 1999, my previous boss from RHSC became the president of Kamehameha Investment Corp. and was responsible for overseeing the Keauhou area which included Keauhou Shopping Center. He needed a general manager for the center. I heard of this opening from my friend so I connected with my previous boss and he hired me. The condition was that I had to move to Kona. My husband agreed and we packed up and moved to Kona.

Once again, I was able to lease up the center and increase sales. This was another learning experience for me because this center had to deal with locals and visitors. Our marketing efforts were to satisfy all of our customers. I was very active with the development team when they started developing residential homes and condominiums around the shopping center. This was a wonderful community and I enjoyed being there.

In August 2003, I learned that RHSC was about to undergo renovations. We used to get the newsletter from KS and I noticed that they created a severance policy. That was a red flag to me. I knew at that point they would start letting employees go. They also hired a former director that was in real estate, so I had the feeling that Keauhou Shopping Center was going to be outsourced to a third party management company. This would require terminating employees. So being the trouble shooter, I figured out what was happening and spoke to my boss to confirm. He said yes and told me that Keauhou Shopping Center was the first to be outsourced. I asked if I had the opportunity to return to the RHSC. He said he would contact the president and get back to me.

Later, I heard great news that they would hire me back. On August 2003, I returned to RHSC. But by July 2004, RHSC was outsourced to The Festival Companies and I learned that I, along with my coworkers, would be terminated. I encouraged the RHSC team not to give up I said, "It isn't over until the fat lady sings."

What happened to you and your team at the Royal Hawaiian Shopping Center?

By sitting in board meetings as part of the exit team, I got to know the Festival team that was potentially going to renovate the center. The Festival Companies wanted to hire me and some of the existing employees. We explained to them that we were unable to work for the new management company for one year because of our severance package. The CEO of The Festival Companies said that was unacceptable and discussed this matter with KS. The CEO insisted that she needed to retain the core team at RHSC. A couple of executives from KS approached me to see if I would give up my severance package in order to work for Festival. I said no. I worked almost twenty-five years for KS and now I wouldn't get severance because another company wanted to retain me? That was unacceptable. The managers at KS came back and offered me 50 percent of the package and again I rejected their offer and insisted that if they wanted me to stay, they should offer me signing bonus instead of calling it a severance package.

KS finally agreed to allow Festival to retain a majority of the employees. We won that battle and that is how I ended up being here again. Anyway, by 2014, KS decided they were going to sell the RHSC as there were some fears after the last tsunami incident and KS felt they had to focus on running the school.

This was the third time that I might lose my job, but I knew I was not going to give up. I knew that my team had to show the new owners that The Festival Companies was the best in town, and I had faith since we made RHSC very successful. True enough, the new owners, J.P. Morgan, decided to retain our local team at The Festival Companies. We have now been here for fourteen years even though the initial contract with Festival was only going to be for two years.

What is your formula to making a mall successful?

It is a matter of asking questions. I observe what people do and listen to what they have to say. I also show them that I am sincere about what I do. Sometimes, I have irate tenants and I can hear them screaming from my office. I will talk to them and in a while, they come out smiling. I always try to turn a negative into a positive, and I think that's my strength. I am happy when I see people succeed. I gave many Asian tenants a head start here when some came with nothing from Korea or China. I would help them by leasing them a cart or a space. They are so grateful and many have remained here. They would thank me and I would tell them that the hard work is all theirs. I merely gave them an opportunity and they rose to the challenge. So yes, I think my strongest skill is dealing with people. I want to help them in everything they do and I don't care who, even it is a competitor. In fact, I am a mentor to one of the ladies in a competitor's center.

Is it fair to say you are focusing on creating an experience economy as brick-and-mortar stores face insurmountable competition from online retail?

Yes, a lot of our customers want to come in for the experience—touch, see, feel, do, taste. Being surrounded by hotels, we don't believe we will be impacted by online retail. Our visitors enjoy coming to the center to experience all that we have to offer.

Our CEO got it right in 2005 when she said she wanted this to be a place that people would remember. When we started renovations, we got rid of a lot of concrete and created a "gathering place" in paradise. Many locals love the revamp, and I think nobody can compete with us because of the uniqueness of the center.

You keep saying you are a hard worker, so what is your work ethic?

Believe it or not, I only work eight hours a day as I know exactly how to get all my work done and what can wait until the next day. I refuse to be the employee that is the "first in and last out." I used to work overtime but realized that if I wanted to climb the ladder, I had to ensure that my managers could do their jobs well, so I made sure I trained them well. I knew that to be a leader, one has to create leaders who can follow in your footsteps. If all you do is get bogged down with the day to day, then you cannot grow. I also always try to look at people's strengths and weaknesses and try to see if they are happy, because if they are not happy, they're not going to enjoy what they are doing.

Do you think leadership skills are innate or cultivated?

I had a very tough life so I just always wanted more, especially for my kids. I don't want them to live the tough life I lived.

I also like learning so I guess that's cultivation. I like going to conferences, seminars, and workshops as I could share what I learned with my team or the owners. That's why I always tell young people they need to get into the real world and learn to see the big picture and not to lose the forest for the tree. I think planning is important, hence my saying, "Put your goals in cement and your plans in the sand" as you have to be flexible to change your plans in order to achieve your goals.

How did you balance family and your career all those years?

All in all, we have five kids, fifteen grand kids, and ten great-grandkids so we have a huge family. Many have asked how I climbed the corporate ladder with kids and I always said that it was because I had help from my mom and my sister. Having people to depend on and support you is important.

At one time in my life, my husband was managing a bar. I would work all day at KS and would go help at the bar in the evenings, but still I made sure that I spent quality time with my children when they were growing up which meant no phones and no interruptions.

How do you feel about the #metoo phenomenon? When you started, you faced quite a bit of sexism from your male boss so how is it for you now as a female leader?

Yeah, I'm a very strong person so even the men are afraid of me! *(laughter)* Even my boss who is male will tell everybody that I'm the boss.

I'm so proud that more women are tired of being put down, stepping up, and demanding equal pay. I'm just proud to see females rise to CEOs. As I am nearing retirement, it is very important to hire young people to take over. The younger generation is so energetic, have totally different goals, and are focused on their careers. So when I do see very driven young staff, especially the females, I encourage them to go for courses and seminars to advance their careers as that was what helped me.

What would you tell a nineteen-year-old young mom who comes to you for a job as you did years ago?

I would tell her it is going to be challenging as a young mother, having to raise and support children at the same time. But what is exciting is that she will realize quickly how to balance both work and family life and still achieve her goals.

Where do you see yourself in the near future?

For now, I am happy to be here at RHC with The Festival Companies for another couple of years. We have so many great things happening now.

If God lets me live long enough, I'm going to retire and open my own leasing company since my daughter and husband are already in the industry. I have always worked for companies and made them successful. My daughter said, "Mom, you need to start your own business and stop working for others." I enjoy leasing because when I help a person find the right location for their business and they succeed, it brings joy to me.

Traveling is another one of our goals. We like to take cruises, and the great thing about being retired or working for yourself is that you can make quick decisions to travel and get the best deals.

What are your best memories of Hawaiʻi?

I don't remember how many states I have been to but the people in Hawaiʻi are special as they give so much aloha. I call this a melting pot and it is our aloha spirit that keeps people coming to our lovely state.

What would you like to see in the future?

I think we need more things for families. We don't have enough on the island. We have the baby boomers that have grandkids and the millennials, which are a huge market, who will also have kids in the near future. But we do not have enough things to do except for water activities. We need Disneyland or Legoland like they have on the Mainland, especially since we have the perfect weather for it.

Hawaiʻi is missing the entertainment component for families. Most people visit for outdoor activities but they all need to be enhanced. We also have these great beaches but there's nothing to do once the sun goes down, unlike in California or the other parts of the world.

How do you want Hawai'i to be remembered?

As the island of aloha. You can never find people that you find in Hawai'i any place else in the world. As long as you live here, the island grows on you and you see the change in people.

Since you are the Grand Dame of Malls, which is your favorite mall?

Right here at Royal Hawaiian Center because we are unique! (laughter) No one will find this center anywhere else in the world. This is a first-class international destination offering the best in dining, shopping, cultural activities, and entertainment.

Who would you like to sit down with?

I am sure many of the women here will say Barack and Michelle Obama —me too, and I also love Oprah Winfrey because she is successful, she loves people and is not afraid to fight and stand up for her rights.

What will you say when you meet God?

Thank you Lord for all the blessings and for giving me beautiful children, grandchildren, and great-grandchildren. Without you in our lives we wouldn't have been able to achieve many of our goals. Even if I died tomorrow, I'll still be a happy person because I know I am going home to a great place and have accomplished so many goals in my life because of Him.

What is your life philosophy in a bumper sticker?

Kamakawiwo'ole which means "fearless leader." It's engraved on my Hawaiian bracelet from my team at Windward Mall.

Finally, how would you like to be remembered?

As a caring and truly loving person.

THE FILMMAKER
Leanne Ferrer

You don't need a professional-grade camera, as it really isn't the camera but the person behind the camera. I want more of our authentic stories to be preserved so we can share them with a larger audience. The more stories we convey the more we can grow as a society. Pacific Islanders are an integral part of the global tapestry so we must get our voices out there.

Leanne Ka'iulani Ferrer is the executive director of Pacific Islanders in Communications (PIC). She has been with PIC for ten years and is responsible for the overall health of the organization, while building networks and strategic partnerships, nurturing relationships with funders and increasing the annual budget.

She is an award-winning producer who has over thirty years of experience in the film and television industry, and previously worked for Disney Films, PBS Hawai'i, and 1013 Integrated (formerly known as Pacific Focus Inc., Hawai'i's longest running full-service production company). She was a fellow in the National Arts Strategies' chief executive program, and is board president of Hawai'i Women in Filmmaking. In fact, Leanne was a PIC-funded producer, whose film, I Scream, Floats, and Sundays, *was aired nationally on PBS.*

Leanne's biggest accomplishments are her two children, Ka'iulani and Keolala'i. They are her driving force, source of inspiration, and joy. Her strong, caring maternal energy is evident from the minute you set foot in her well-appointed office, covered in artwork by her children. She shares with me the tears and joys of raising a child with autism and wishes to use this platform as her way of sharing her learnings and journey with any parent or guardian similarly gifted.

Tell us a little about you and your background.

My maiden name is Kang and it wasn't till I was in college when I realized it was a Korean surname, not Chinese, as I am ethnically a quarter Chinese. It turns out my father was adopted by his Korean stepfather, and my father took on the name when he was about sixteen years old. When he married my mom, we all took on his last name that is apparently a rather popular last name. It was funny as it wasn't till I was in college that a professor called me by my Korean last name and I was oblivious to the pronunciation. He taught me how to properly pronounce my Korean last name! It was a learning lesson. After that encounter, if people were to ask me if I am Korean, I would simply reply yes, even though I actually don't have Korean roots because I didn't want to explain the entire backstory.

I am ethnically Hawaiian, Chinese, Filipino, French, and German. My mom is the Hawaiian Chinese and my dad is Caucasian Filipino. My dad's mom was from Manila but she met an American serviceman and they got married, which is how she and my dad's family came to Hawai'i.

My maternal grandparents were both full-blooded Chinese businessmen, who married full-blooded Hawaiian women. Growing up, we always had more Chinese influence than Hawaiian. In addition, I was born in 1967 and grew up at a time when being Hawaiian was suppressed and not an identity you were made to feel proud of. We moved to Waiʻanae in 1973 where many Hawaiians lived, but it was not until my mom bought us a shirt that said "Proud to be Hawaiian" that I realized my mom had a bit of an activist streak. My two brothers, sister, and I would wear our shirts all the time as it gave us a new sense of pride in our cultural identity, but we never wore it outside of the Waiʻanae Coast because my mom told us that people on the "outside" would not get it.

My mom gave birth to me at nineteen while my dad was away fighting a war in Vietnam. I was pretty much raised by my mother's parents in the Hawaiian tradition of hānai. In retrospect, my multiethnic upbringing was terrific, as I got to experience Hawaiʻi in Waiʻanae and Kailua, both sides of the spectrum, and experienced different lifestyles.

I was spoiled by my grandparents and treated as their youngest child. My parents were sort of hippies and very laid back. When I stayed with them, I stepped into the role of eldest child and was frequently told I was the example for my siblings. I think that was central to my psyche. I also remember lugging a little suitcase or duffel bag going from my parents' home to my grandparents. I had essentials at both homes so it wasn't confusing, but I had to constantly change my identity for each household.

As for my education, I went to the Kamehameha Schools from kindergarten, and used to catch the bus from Waiʻanae, or my papa would drop me off from Kailua.

I was very fortunate to be a part of Kamehameha Schools and received a wonderful education. I knew going to college was inevitable, but I also knew I loved Hawaiʻi and I didn't want to leave, so I ended up going to Leeward Community College. I loved the fact that I could still live at home while seeking out my path in life. As luck would have it, on the very first day of school, I had to stand in line for the classes I wanted to take. I had no clue what I wanted to do. Just then an instructor, Ms. Kay Yamada, called out to me as she could probably tell I was lost. She told me I had to take her communications class and proceeded to interest me in telecommunications and TV production. I was already exposed to theater and band in Kamehameha Schools, so it seemed like a good fit.

This was in the 1980s?

Yes, 1985. Kay told me she was starting up a new weekly news program called *Leeward News*, and she was looking for anchors and thought I would be great. That was how I became a part of a small but strong team for the closed-circuit campus news program that was broadcast live every morning. After a year of being in front of the camera, I decided to go behind-the-scenes so I didn't have to keep buying blouses, put on makeup, and be told to get my bangs out of my face. That was how I got into television production.

And that was also how you met your husband?

Yes! I met my future husband, Frank Ferrer, whom I am still married to now, through the Leeward news program. He was also an anchor who made the jump to the back of the camera as well, so you can say we started our career together.

How was the news industry like for you as a young artist?

It was a cutthroat, dog-eat-dog type of world, and everything was an emergency. You are made to feel as if everything is life or death, and it isn't. People were constantly stressing out, yelling, throwing pencils at monitors, and screaming. I remember the screaming most and that would freak me out. I think the culture of local network news, at the time, gave people an excuse to act immature, throw tantrums, and disrespect others. I didn't like that and left when I got hired at PBS Hawai'i. My husband got a job there, too.

PBS opened my eyes to a different type of television production at a slower, more meaningful pace that was less cruel. It was, overall, more nurturing, though there were some that had the same newsroom vibe. I worked there for quite a while, going to school at the same time. I eventually graduated with a degree in speech and a minor in political science; my main interestes were women's studies, Hawaiian studies, and language. My interests intersected and so began my awakening as an advocate for Hawaiian rights and women's rights, and I became aware of how to use media as a tool.

You also worked on Disney films?

I did. Charlotte Simmons, a producer at PBS HI, connected me to a television series that was coming to Hawai'i. Shortly thereafter, I went to work for the new CW Network as a production secretary, which was completely different from my technical background. I learned that they moved at a very fast pace, filming an episode a week while also writing the upcoming episode and editing the previous. This went on for more than a year, before the series *Marker*, starring Richard Grieco from *21 Jump Street*, was canceled.

During this time in the 1990s, the movies started coming back to Hawaiʻi. In the late 80s, film production slowed down in Hawaiʻi because of some union issues. Fortunately, the new STARZ network was just starting up and decided to film a pilot here; I was blessed to be hired by Hawaiʻi film coordinator Jeanne Ishikawa as her assistant coordinator. During the filming of that pilot, Disney executives starting coming around looking for locations for several new movies and Jeanne and I were chosen to work on them. We worked with crews from L.A., organizing hotel accommodations and getting offices set-up.

I eventually ended up at the longest operating video/film production company in Hawaiʻi, Pacific Focus, Inc. (now known as 1013 Integrated). I worked as a coordinator and producer. While I was there, the company I work for now, Pacific Islanders in Communications, would bring films in to edit or for other services and that's how I was introduced to the organization and the great work they were doing.

Which leads to the question, how did you end up as the executive director of PIC?

One day, producer Leah Kihara told me PIC was starting up a short film initiative and asked if I would be keen on working as a producer on an all-Hawaiian-women project and I jumped at the opportunity.

So in 2000, we created the short "*Ice cream, Floats and Sundays*" and we were funded $25,000 by PIC, which was huge for a short film. The funds were still barely enough to pay everyone, so we still had to ask people to work pro bono. Most people agreed to as they saw it as a chance to work with an all-woman crew and be part of a visual piece of art. That became my first experience as a producer and it was a meaningful endeavor. It made me feel a sense of ownership as well as made me proud of my culture and my being a woman.

The film made me realize that I built all these relationships in the film making community and I wanted to work with as many people as possible. The commercial projects made me feel trapped in the daily grind and I decided I wanted something more fulfilling. It so happened that one of my friends, Nālani Blane, told me that a grassroots Hawaiian nonprofit is looking for a marketing director and that I was suitable as I had my experience in producing. I decided to take on the role. It was leap of faith because all I knew was the film industry.

The nonprofit is called the Nānākuli Housing Corporation[1] (NHC) and is also known as Base Yard. I worked on the marketing and, soon, got them press and media coverage. Later, the NHC wanted me to teach classes on fiscal responsibility, which I did, and I even ventured into teaching construction classes! I took charge of event coordination for the workshops and made a deep dive into the nonprofit world.

By 2003, I realized I wasn't getting pregnant, and after ten years of trying, I figured I had to slow down to see what was going on. My husband, Frank, actually reminded me that we had planned to have a family, but I had let work take over. Eventually, I went to see an ob-gyn. Within four months of seeing Dr. Thomas Kosasa, I got pregnant. My daughter, Kaʻiulani, was born in 2005 and I was already thirty-seven then. Honestly, I did not expect it to happen so quickly and had to figure out babysitting arrangements. My nonprofit work was sometimes not conducive for a new mom. I also wanted to enjoy motherhood as I had waited so long.

Frank and I decided that I would be a stay-at-home mom and we would make it work on his paycheck by living very frugally. It did work and I ended up staying home with my daughter for three years. Kaʻiulani was the smartest baby and, even at four months, she could say, "Hi, Dad!" We were so proud. But soon, it was time for her to attend preschool, which meant it was time for me to head back to work so we could afford it. Leah told me PIC was looking for a program manager, so I interviewed for them and started the day after! I was indeed very lucky, as PIC did not view my being a stay-at-home mom as a liability but as an asset, and so I started with them in 2008.

This is your eleventh year anniversary!

Yes. I can't believe it. I worked my way up from program manager to program director to interim executive director to being the current ED now.

What have you learned about leadership all these years?

I learned there is no single leadership style. Mine is democratic and nurturing. My experience as a mother helps in that. I like to build leaders and I

---

[1] This was a nonprofit organization dedicated to making affordable housing and homeownership a possibility for all Native Hawaiians. Programs provided by NHC include classes on financial literacy, homebuyer education, post homeownership training for self-help home repair, foreclosure prevention and default intervention, and affordable housing options.

want my team to feel as if they are their own leaders and that I am just here to work right by them. People have their own ideas of what a leader should be and sometimes want you to tell them what to do, though I'd really rather have them make their own decisions. I want my team to be happy with what they're doing and feel that their work is meaningful for them.

What are some of the biggest challenges you've had to face and what did you learn?

I had to learn very quickly when I took over as ED how to create a strategic plan, a business plan, craft policies, and standard operating procedures. In fact, I'm still working on these even though the organization was founded in 1991. Each successive ED had their own management style so there was no continuity, and I had to learn how to create all that from scratch. It really is like charting my own voyage while learning how to paddle and steer.

Do you think your gender has been a boon or bane in your career?

My gender helped me reach out to other women and fight harder for their acknowledgment. Coincidentally, every ED of PIC has been a woman, though I don't think gender played into it. Passion, dedication, and belief in the mission certainly did. But when I did take over, I did feel that we had drifted off from the original mission.

What have you done to get the organization back on track and what do you think we need to do to cultivate passion for the filmmaking industry?

I started with a new staff and promoted junior members of staff that have been here for a long time. I would ask them to find out what drives them. Having belief in your passion is huge and is what makes people go out and do what they do. We fund documentary filmmakers and they go in knowing they're not going to make a ton of money. They can, either, be ego-driven and just want to see their name as a director, or they're very passionate about getting that story out. I see more of the latter, thankfully.

How do you see social media impacting the film industry now that anyone can be a content creator?

I see this progression as a boon, as a lot more people are interested in creating content. There are a lot more stories getting told and I also see the technology trying to keep up and get less and less expensive. Before, you had to have thousands of dollars in equipment just to be a filmmaker. My husband has a great quote, "Everyone has a kitchen but not everyone is an executive chef." There are the professionals, self-starters, and the very talented ones that will rise to the top. Even with the advancement in technology, filmmaking is still about the storyteller and their ability to create a good story.

How do you hope to get more Pacific Islanders to share their stories?

We tell them exactly what you just asked which is to use any medium or smartphone. You don't need a professional-grade camera, as it really isn't the camera but the person behind the camera. I want more of our authentic stories to be preserved so we can share them with a larger audience. The more stories we convey the more we can grow as a society. Pacific Islanders are an integral part of the global tapestry so we must get our voices out there.

What do you think is the future of filmmaking here? Are there always going to be 400 people using Hawai'i as a film hub and leaving, or are we building an industry?

We are on the same wavelength! (*laughter*) Right now, the film industry is a hub with 400 people coming in for three months and then leaving. So what we need to do is to change our mindsets. We need to own it by working together, and help create jobs so much so that anything that comes from the outside is ancillary. That is why I am keen on helping people to stay, work, and create here. I have helped put together the Hawai'i Media Makers Conference as a way to bring media makers together and promote networking collaboration opportunities. I really want all of us to recognize that we are the film industry and need to be a show of force.

How do you deal when you are faced with criticism and pushback?

I go into it knowing I'm going to have criticism but I keep telling myself, if it wasn't difficult, it would already have been done. I remind myself to keep plugging away.

You shared that motherhood and raising a child with special needs has really transformed you. Can you please share with our readers?

Yes, I wanted to share that at age forty-five I had a second child, as my daughter had been asking for a sibling. My husband and I tried again, and I went with Dr. Kosasa, but I gave up after six months. I was on an emotional roller coaster with my hormones in flux. Somehow, two months after that I stopped medication, I felt him in my uterus and, by that time, I was actually six months pregnant. So we had less than three months to wrap our heads around the fact that we were expecting a miracle baby. We named him Keolalaʻi, as he was tranquil in my womb.

I was program director at the time he was born, and it was such a different experience from Kaʻiulani. I kept my job and he went to the sitters. He was also a very different baby. He was very easy at the beginning and would hardly cry at night. If he wanted to drink, he would pat me, I would turn over to breastfeed, and go back to sleep. However, fast forward a year later, we knew he was not like other babies, as he would not babble, but would occasionally utter a random "bird" or "cat" and never say it again. We decided to take him to his pediatrician, who wanted him tested for autism. He was diagnosed at about age two. He is eight now and it has been a difficult but rewarding journey.

How has it been raising an autistic child? Can you share with us your experiences, obstacles, challenges, and the joys?

I personally thought it would get easier as he got older but it has been harder on him. He struggles to be understood and be independent. I feel that the way we are communicating with him may not be the best way, so we are finding alternatives such as learning sign language. Our whole family will learn together so that may make it easier. For now, he will bring us a loaf of bread and cheese if he wants a grilled cheese sandwich. But he is also at the age where he is exploring and wants to do things himself which can freak me out. For example, he will try to use the toaster but he doesn't quite understand the nuances, so I would find several packets of cheese in our toaster with the cellophane on.

I have to remind myself constantly that he is coming into his own, though he is developmentally about age three. It is hard when he throws tantrums as he can't understand why he can't have every DVD he wants, and we can't reason with him so it can be a constant battle. He does do quirky things that we don't understand and I don't think we will ever understand. For now, I try to go with the flow. He has taught me unconditional love. He is also teaching me to learn to let go, not coddle him, and to see him as an individual and a big boy.

> What advice would you give to any parent raising a child with disability or autism?

Read up, learn as much as you can, then take away what you want. Everyone has their own opinion of what you should do or how you should do things but, ultimately, you know your child best.

> Thank you so much for sharing. This means a lot to our readers who may be going through similar challenges. Let's turn our conversation to Hawai'i. What are your fondest memories growing up in Hawai'i and what do you think has changed?

My fondest memories are of seeing children play outside and going to the neighbor's house. It is not the same growing up today. I have a thirteen-year-old and I don't put her on a bike and let her ride around like we did before, and that makes me so sad. When I was growing up, I could leave the doors open, cars unlocked, and the children would be playing everywhere without a care. Now that we have become a big city, we have to be very mindful of our surroundings.

> If you could do any film on and about Hawai'i, what would it be about and why?

It would be a small, personal story of the strength of women and girls with Hawai'i and Hawaiian culture prominently featured.

> What do you want people to remember most about Hawai'i?

That without the Hawaiian people (nā Kanaka Maoli), Hawaiian culture, or language, there would be no Hawai'i.

> Where are your favorite hangouts?

Home and at the beach with the kids.

What is your favorite movie and director?

Whale Rider is an indigenous story that has gone global. My favorite director is Kathryn Bigelow, who broke the Hollywood glass ceiling on action films.

Describe yourself in three words.

Nurturing, patient, and empathetic.

What is your best and worst trait?

Being too lenient. It takes me a while to get angry when provoked and it also takes me a while to calm down.

What would you say when you meet God?

Thank you for everything.

What would your epitaph say?

Thank you to all who believed in me. Or not.

THE PLACE MAKER

Mary Philpotts McGrath

If you know why you're doing something, then proceed, but if you don't know why you're doing something, then that is dangerous. If you make conscious decisions, then you would have established some guidelines.

As a premier designer with a national and international reputation, Mary Philpotts McGrath has navigated the firm she founded through both rough and affluent times with a sure and steady vision. Her design aesthetic has always been to give the client a firm connection to their environment.

In her bestseller book, Hawai'i: A Sense of Place, *she shows in detail the progression of island design, from its cultural roots to the needs of today's contemporary spaces. Her atelier, PLACE, located on the Waikīkī side of Philpotts Interiors' headquarters in Honolulu, is a stylish resource for furnishings, accessories, and art.*

She is not only a distinguished designer, but an accomplished fine artist, printmaker, and dedicated community leader. In 2010, she was included in Architectural Digest's *worldwide list of the Top 100 Designers and, in 2013,* Pacific Business News *named her one of the most influential persons in Hawai'i in the past fifty years.*

Her atelier is a quiet sanctuary away from the hustle and bustle of the streets and it is where I find Mary most at home and relaxed, eager to show me her latest print creations. It seems beauty follows her everywhere she goes as each square inch of her atelier is dripping with style, grace, and quite demonstrably, Mary's very own sense of place.

Share with us your background.

I am very fortunate to be part Hawaiian, as the culture treats women and men equally. In fact, women have a power of their own and it's empowering. This allows women to achieve great success here. This ideology seems to permeate most of the Pacific Rim.

Is that how you were raised?

Yes, my grandmother[1] was very influential, as she was a senator during

---

1 During the territorial period (1900–1959), Senator Alice Kamokilaikawai Campbell was a notable force in Hawai'i and the strongest Hawaiian opponent of statehood. In these difficult territorial years, Kamokila's actions continued to breathe life in the spirit of aloha 'āina. Her statements against statehood would foretell kānaka voices today seeking greater rights and autonomy for kānaka maoli, who—through historical injustices—have been forced to live in the construct of the state of Hawai'i and the United States. Kamokila Campbell, in many ways, could be hailed as one of the last true ali'i—an elite woman, born into affluence and high social standing, who used her position to give voice and strength to her people. For more, log on to https://www.kamakakoi.com/hawaiianpatriots/kamokila.html

World War II, representing the island of Molokaʻi. She would fly to Molokaʻi every week to deliver a speech.

During that time, I was in San Francisco, as my grandmother had us evacuated right away, but she remained on island which was a really brave and risky thing to do. Growing up and seeing her take on leadership roles in the community was very inspiring to me and she was my role model.

In fact, her voice is still heard on the radio today. She is the one who says, "This land of aloha." She used to record with the legendary musicians of Hawaiʻi.

How did your family become involved in design, given their background in politics?

We were less politically involved than culturally and philosophically. It was always about the Hawaiian culture and that has fueled our design mentality, an environment, and a unique Hawaiian legacy that has been our success. We love designing spaces where we can come home to, feel comfortable, and love. We balanced outside influences, including Asian and Western aesthetics, and found ways to appropriately blend them with the Hawaiian lifestyle.

How did you start your journey?

I was always drawing since I was a little girl. Later, I majored in art at the University of Colorado and then transferred to the University of Hawaiʻi. Teaching at that time, we had a gifted international staff, which included renowned artists, such as Jean Charlot, Harue Oyama McVay and Dr. Gustav Ecke. They all had unique backgrounds and stories. For example, Dr. Ecke fled the Communist Party in China. His father was the curator of a museum and a noted scholar of Chinese history, while Dr. Ecke, himself, was an art scholar and lived next door to me. As he didn't drive, I got to drive him to school every day and had private sessions on art in the mornings on the way to the university.

What key elements did you learn from these scholars and artists that most influenced your sense, place, and beauty?

I guess a lot of it is me putting it all together. Scholastically, you're doing one thing, and then there's living the culture. I always wanted to go to the lūʻau or society events with my grandmother. We would go to the Halekulani with many older tūtū, and I would participate in these rich, cultural events.

How did that shape you when you decided to start design?

I watched Hawaiʻi copy the outside world, rather than creating design from within the cultural resources. I was drawn to interpret and differentiate what is real and what isn't. I recognize the nuances of subtle aspects of the culture.

How would you describe your aesthetic?

I was taught through my fine-art education that good design is artful and timeless.

Do you remember what your first project was?

During college, a significant early project was the first Hawaiian Furniture Exhibition that was later released as a book.

One of our professors, Kenneth Kingery, took us all under his wing and mentored us individually. He was primarily a graphic designer but he was practicing interior design on the side, because he brought a keen aesthetic and was in high demand. He pushed me in that same direction and I fell right into it as he paved the way. We would work with him on exhibits to showcase our culture.

Which takes us to—what do you think has been the secret of your success? Being at the right place at the right time, innate talent, hard work, or a combination?

It is all of that. You obviously need to have talent, but hard work is important. I was very fortunate that the people I engaged with, whether accidental or deliberate, all had a great impact on the scene.

Not too long ago, I was cleaning up my files and saw my birth certificate, and it said my father was an interior designer. I had to laugh as I never heard of that before! *(laughter)*

But, the story goes, my father had worked with Walter Lamb, who was a Californian interior designer known for his creation of the brass tubing furniture, which is still a sought after collectible—and my father was doing that with him!

What was the design scene like when you first came on?

Everything was done locally, from furniture to fabrics, as this was prior to statehood. Small workshops were scattered throughout Honolulu with fine craftsmen in every service industry. In those days, no one threw anything away. It was refurbished and reused and often passed to the next generation.

So how did people here start to engage in design?

It was statehood. Before, there weren't a lot of options. You either had things handcrafted or you had things passed down in the family, but the aesthetic reflected the eclectic culture—Japanese, Chinese, Hawaiian, and cherished koa. We had great designers and craftspeople of furniture, fabrics, and artists here, and we were not into throwaway culture. Everything was handed down from one generation to the next, even if it was from Sears.

Today, we seem to throw things away after two years these days. Back then, there was a sense of value and people respected these timeless designs.

Of all the projects you have undertaken, which is the most memorable?

My book entitled *Hawai'i: A Sense of Place*. I am so glad Kaui and I did the book, as I don't think it would be possible to do it today. We were so fortunate then to be allowed into the homes of these kama'aina statewide. They were so gracious. David Livingston, a seasoned photographer based in California, patiently did the shoot and spent many hours diligently waiting for the right light.

Our goal was to accurately record the local lifestyles, values, and timeless design, which brought architectural freedom. The climate gave way to our sense of indoor-outdoor living legacy.

I remember one particular shoot with a family friend on the Big Island who had an extensive collection of koa furniture. David was in the room photographing something, and I happened to walk down the hallway heavily clad in beautiful koa paneling. There was something about the way the sun lit the room and the lighting was just perfect, so I asked David to shoot it and he told me, "You go shoot it yourself!" So I did, and that photo is in the book!

The book projects some very fun experiences in expressing the freedom of the lifestyle of multicultural expression. For instance, the last few photos in the book show outdoor living. My son's wedding was by the stream, so David decided to go across the stream to shoot. My son's wife is Tahitian, so the family was present and all seated on the rocks. As the couple were being pronounced man and wife, the band started and, all of a sudden, we see David rolling from amongst the bamboo across the stream. He was so excited that he fell, and his camera almost landed into the water! (*laughter*)

Doing the book was a lot of fun, as we went all around the island.

> You speak so fondly of these classic, heritage, handcrafted pieces. Do you think we are in danger of losing this sense of culture and history, and where do you see a place for these nostalgic artifacts?

I think there is always going to be a sense of place for these interiors, as the islands have always attracted people of different cultures and interests with the strong presence of the Hawaiian culture combined.

Although there is a sharper, more minimalist sense to design today, it still incorporates a lot of the native and Pacific Rim-inspired geometric patterns and motifs. This imagery shows up in numerous aspects which are applied to the design of carpets, lighting, wall coverings, and numerous other applications.

> What do you think we can do preserve the roots of Hawaiian design when everything is beginning to look like IKEA or Starbucks?

It still goes back to the environment and the climate. We just need to take control of the rain, but otherwise, it's the perfect climate, so we keep that same indoor-outdoor aesthetic and "design philosophy." We reinvent as the design climate changes.

> Let's change tracks and chat about your roles as a wife, mother, and designer. Was it hard trying to juggle all that?

No, having my own business probably made the difference, as my kids each found their place within the trades. Between my original business partner and me, we had seven children and I still have a photograph of us posing in front of our first shop on Beretania Street. The seven children were mentioned as our staff in a holiday card. (*laughter*)

We also had an old sink at the back and we filled it with water lilies and fish, and that became a children's swimming pool.

It definitely sounds like motherhood was not an impediment in your career.

No it wasn't. There are many stories of family businesses where the families and kids are part of the second-generation ownership.

By the time my children were ten years old, they were pretty much in the business.

Are all your children in the business?

Yes, my daughter is one of the three partners, another does the finances and the other is an artist we use frequently. These days, I am not so much part of the design company but am more involved in the gallery, called PLACE Hawaii, with my youngest son.

What about gender norms? Typically, the male is the architect and the female is cast as the interior designer. What are your thoughts on that?

If you are good at your profession, then you have to be a people person regardless of gender, as you need to understand the customer.

How has being a designer evolved over the years?

Technology has changed the way we work. We can now visualize and access products and information at the click of a button.

What would you say has been your most challenging project to date?

It would be the Hawai'i Convention Center, because it was a big project and it had an impact on the island. It was actually part of a competition and one of the judges was Vladimir Ossipoff. We had to design from scratch, and I was the primary interior designer. We were part of an international competition and we won it over internationally-renowned architect I.M. Pei. Julie Walters was our landscape architect and she came up with the signature aspect of the building—the sails. It was based on Hawaiian elements, but feels wonderfully contemporary, incorporating thoughtful and timeless spaces for art, provided by the State Foundation for Culture and Arts.

The design team met along the banks of the Ala Wai with a picnic lunch. It was there that we accepted the idea that this facility should not have a "bad" side to the building. This meant even the service entry had to be well-designed and downplayed. So the building stands as it does today. You can't tell how the trucks get in, but they do.

We had wanted the Ala Wai Canal to be the main feature and saw it as the corridor of the building.

Every great piece of art will have its lovers and haters. How do you deal with criticism?

I ignore it and I learned that from Val Ossipoff. He always told me to be true to myself. If you know why you're doing something, then proceed, but if you don't know why you're doing something, then that is dangerous.

If you make conscious decisions, then you would have established some guidelines.

What do you look for in a young designer?

Someone who listens, as he or she would need to absorb. Usually if they don't listen, they will shut off and not smell the roses.

If a young designer is torn between her career and her family, what would you tell her?

That it doesn't matter. We have babies here all the time. Often, our designers come to work with their kids, as well as meet their deadlines.

What did you do to educate yourself and to keep going?

I make sure I have time to read all the newspapers and all the magazines from all over the world.

You are only as good as your ability and your tools to deliver, so we need to keep learning. This is what we encourage here in the office—just look at the size of our library.

What can we expect from you in the next couple of years?

To keep making more art! *(laughter)*

What do you see as the future of Hawai'i design?

We are not the only ones that are working with imagery. Most of us in the interior design field are ambitious, as we've always been like underdogs in the architectural world. We have to work a lot harder, as everything we do is so visual.

Let's change tracks and talk about Hawai'i. You were born and raised here and only left for a short while.

Yes, I left briefly when I was about five years old, shortly after Pearl Harbor was bombed. As shared earlier, my grandmother had breakfast with us and left about a half an hour before the bombing started, and she was on her way to 'Ewa Beach when she witnessed all the burning. My mother wrote about it later, as she was a writer.

Anyway, my grandmother got me on a destroyer away to San Francisco, together with my mother and sisters, and I remember our week on the destroyer. I remember us playing cards, talking about the reservoir being poisoned, and the sailor that fell in love with mother, as he would help her change my sister's diapers every morning! *(laughter)*

What are your fondest memories of Hawai'i and what would you like to keep?

Keep life slow and keep the country, country.

How can we then keep the country, country?

Because of our balance between nature and our built environment, we need to decide what is enough and then stop giving out building permits.

There is a point in life when you need to say no, though I could never say no to an extra bowl of ice cream. *(laughter)*

What are your hopes and aspirations for Hawai'i?

That we strengthen our government and protect our resources.

What advice would you give to someone who is visiting Hawaiʻi for the first time?

Go to Waikīkī and put your feet in the water.

Whose home would you most like to be able to design or have designed?

Every home I worked with is special, as all the clients placed their hearts in their home.

Who is favorite designer or architect?

Vladimir Ossipoff.

What would you say when you meet God?

Where have you been? *(laughter)*

Where's your favorite place?

My own home.

What is your life philosophy in a bumper sticker?

Aloha.

How do you best want to be remembered?

Laughing.

How would you describe home?

My grandmother at her death bed said, "I am Hawaiʻi," so Hawaiʻi will always be home to me.

THE PEOPLE'S ADVOCATE

Kymberly Marcos Pine

Seeking the friendship of other successful women is new to us but it is what men do with fellow men. They help each other to succeed. We need to do that, too, because it is just naturally harder for us. As much as I would like to believe we are equal, we are not there yet.

Kymberly Pine never imagined she would be an elected official. Seeing her community neglected by government leaders in the areas of traffic relief, school funding, and crime motivated her to run for office to ensure that the Leeward Coast would not be left behind. Since her election to the Hawai'i House of Representatives in 2004 and now as a member of the Honolulu City Council, her district has received over a billion dollars in funding for new roads, schools, parks, beaches, and various community improvement projects. Tougher crime laws were also passed.

Kymberly has a strong work ethic and a passionate desire to succeed. She graduated from the University of California, Berkeley, where she obtained a bachelor's degree in English. She was the youngest staffer to be appointed as director of the Minority Research Office in the State House of Representatives, where she ran a team focused on cutting waste and mismanagement in government spending and created new solutions to Hawai'i's problems. Her work in policy has received extensive coverage in local television, radio, and print media, and has also been used by the governor's and lieutenant governor's offices. She currently serves as the First District city council member, representing the areas of 'Ewa, 'Ewa Beach, Kapolei, Honokai Hale, Ko'olina, Nānākuli, Mā'ili, Wai'anae, Mākaha, Kea'au, and Mākua. As the chair of the Zoning & Housing Committee, Kymberly is committed to addressing Hawai'i's critical need for affordable housing.

Unbeknown to many, Kymberly is an avid athlete. She completed the forty-two-mile Nā Wāhine O Ke Kai outrigger canoe race from Moloka'i to O'ahu and the 2.4-mile Waikīkī Rough Water Swim. In fact, she once even impersonated a boy so she could play in Little League baseball, an all-boy sport in Mānoa at the time.

How did you get started in politics?

I trained to be a journalist in college and running for office was never part of my plan. My involvement in politics started when I saw my community in 'Ewa Beach being neglected by government. Politicians had approved all these new home developments, but didn't think about the roads, or, more importantly, job creation in the area. Getting to the freeway from my house was just under seven miles and yet it took an average forty-five minutes every day, seven days a week. Then, there is the traffic on the freeway getting to town, which is forty-five minutes to an hour, at least. After a long day of work, commuters in my community get to do it again driving home. Our schools were not getting enough funding. There were so many examples of unfair treatment. 'Ewa

Beach, then, was one of the older, working-class communities on Oʻahu. People work hard to provide for their families. They deserved better. That's why I ran for office—to bring equality back to government service and let people know they have the power to change anything.

What do you think is the secret to your success?

I live to serve others and just love everything that I do. I wake up with so much joy because I know I'm bringing the voice of my community to the legislative process. In my heart, I want so much to improve their quality of life. I really believe in what I'm doing and know that my constituents trust that I will work very hard for them and ensure they are not taken advantage of. I am very sincere about how I feel about my community. They are a part of my family.

How do you deal with negative criticisms?

Many years ago, I had a campaign volunteer who made inappropriate advances toward me. I banned him from the campaign and from contacting me. Because I rejected him, he made up stories about me, hacked into my websites, emails, and harassed me every day by sending out fake stories about me by fax and email to every single person that worked at the State Capitol. Since he was a designer, the fake emails and documents looked real, so real that even the news covered it as fact until they realized he was a psychopath and pathological liar. I finally did some research about him and found out that he had done this to many people before but no one ever stood up to him. One day, I decided that I was not going to let him victimize anyone anymore. I spoke out against him and took him to court and won. Before I fought back, this incident nearly destroyed me. Can you imagine reporters reporting what your harasser says about you as if it was true? It was like they were helping him to harass me over and over again. I was reminded of it wherever I went and almost quit politics because it was so intense.

The day that I finally said I am not going to let this creep control my life, was the day I no longer cared what he or anyone else said about me. There was an incredible freedom that came with that. That is the key to dealing with criticism. Criticism is good if it is meaningful, but if it's just meant to cause pain then ignore it. In the end, no one really cares.

Today, I no longer make decisions based on whether I'll get re-elected or whether I'll lose my donors. I make my decisions based on what I feel is best for my community. The message I tell young girls and other women who are being harassed or facing a difficult tragedy is to view the circumstance as a test of your strength. Fight for your own survival and live a good life. Ignore what people say about you. Be proud of who you are. This was one of the most challenging experiences I had in my political career but it was also my greatest teaching moment. I am a stronger leader because of it.

How has your gender been a boon or a bane in your career?

It's complicated. I don't think my gender has ever helped my career. I certainly had to work harder because of it. My parents raised me to believe I could achieve anything I wanted to. As a result, I was blind to gender discrimination. If I didn't achieve something, I would just work harder. I think my mom prepared me for the real world by ensuring I overcame any obstacles that would arise by allowing me to do what the boys did. In fact, she gave me my favorite shirt as a kid that said, "Anything boys can do, girls can do better." She taught that to compete with the guys, you just have to be better. If my older brother and his friends climbed trees, I climbed trees. If they played soccer, I played soccer, and if they played baseball, I played baseball.

My parents' teachings were put to a test one day when I told them that I wanted to play Little League baseball, an all-boys sport in Mānoa at the time. My dad told me that boys play baseball and that girls play softball. I said, "What's that? I only know how to play baseball." My parents were in a dilemma. In the end, I argued my case and my dad went to sign me up. The league rejected me because I was a girl. He said he would sue and they let me try out. At the time, the Mānoa Baseball Little League was the most prestigious league to play for. Everyone tried out just to get on a team, and many boys were cut every year. The league leaders knew I would have a very difficult time making a team.

On the day of the tryout, my mom and grandma helped me to do my hair into pigtail braids. They tucked my hair into my hat so I could pass as a boy on the field. I remembered everyone in my family was very nervous. As the day came to an end and numerous cuts were made, I was still there. A man was hitting balls to players from home plate and it was my turn to step up to the shortstop position to catch a ground ball. He looked at me and shook his head, irritated that I was still there. Instead of a ground ball, he hit a pop-up ball close to home plate. No one thought I could catch it. I ran toward home plate, caught the ball, rolled, and my hat came off. The audience and players erupted yelling, "It's a girl! Why is there a girl here? Oh, my God!" and so forth. My grandma later told me she thought the family was going to get kicked out of

Mānoa. I played in the shortstop position for the Giants and made it to the league's all-star team. We placed third in the state. It was a wonderful time with meaningful lessons. But this shows you my parents raised me to be gender blind to what society expects of a girl. I think it made me not focus on the injustices and instead focus on just being good at what I do.

When I go into a meeting, I make sure I am prepared. When I am debating an issue, I make sure I know more than others. When I am campaigning, I make sure I work harder than my opponent. This way no one can deny your desire or effort to succeed.

What are your thoughts on the #MeToo movement?

I applaud the very brave women who started the #MeToo movement. While it did bring back memories that I had locked away in my mind for a very long time, it has also brought many professional women and I together. We realized that we have lived in silos for too long and some had to survive through some very tough experiences alone. Women, especially high-level professional women, need each other because oftentimes, they are the only female executives in their company. Seeking the friendship of other successful women is new to us but it is what men do with fellow men. They help each other to succeed. We need to do that, too, because it is just naturally harder for us. As much as I would like to believe we are equal, we are not there yet.

Most importantly, we need to mentor and protect young women so that they don't have to go through what we have. More and more women will become leaders because of this and that will be good for everyone.

What advice would you give to younger women in your shoes?

You just have to be yourself and be proud of who you are. Don't try to change who you are. Be real and focus on the work you have to do for your community. Love what you do. Work ten times harder than everyone else, so when you do experience discrimination, your success and results will speak for itself.

You are very much involved with the Blue Zones Project. Share with us more about your environmental outreach.

When I became a mother to my three-year-old girl, something changed in who I am as a woman and as a leader. I was always passionate about the environment, but now that I had a child, I really started to think thirty years ahead. I've always been a very healthy person; a triathlete and long-distance canoe paddler. I was also a soccer player, ran track and cross-country; rarely ate candy, only granola bars, and my parents were hippies. I was very blessed to be raised with a very healthy mindset. When I saw many in my community suffering from medical problems because of their diet and lifestyle choices, it really troubled me. Someone gave me a book about the Blue Zones Project[1] which is a study started by a group of archaeologists, doctors, and anthropologists, together with the National Geographic Society. The group studied parts of the world where people lived over one-hundred years of age in very large numbers. They studied what they ate, their happiness levels, their families, outlook on life, careers, and physicality. These researchers found out that DNA only constitutes twenty percent of your lifespan whereas the rest are lifestyle choices. We have a lot of high blood pressure, heart problems and diabetes in my district, so I decided that we have got to fight this. We competed with communities statewide to secure free staff support and other resources for Kapolei and 'Ewa Beach. Now, our community is on its way to getting healthier.

> **You have also been very vocal about the rail as well as issues on homelessness and affordable housing. Share with us your thoughts.**

When I was in the House of Representatives, I voted against the rail because I felt it was being rushed by certain interest groups. Many were not pausing to think what the true cost would be. There was a lot of estimation with no real calculations and something didn't sound right. I was not against the rail per se but I felt the decision was rushed.

Sadly, many things I had concerns about has rung true as the finances don't make sense and the project is over budget. Nevertheless, I serve my community, the people are my boss and they want to see it completed. The government pushed us all out to live on the West Side, but never thought about our commute. One of the reasons I ran for office was because of the traffic issue. At this point, this is all we have. Should rail fail, my community will have nothing. We need to get this project right or they will suffer even more for many

---

[1] What began as a *New York Times* bestseller by National Geographic Fellow Dan Buettner has evolved into a global movement that is inspiring people to live longer, more active lives with lower rates of chronic disease. From Sardinia, Italy, to Okinawa, Japan, to Loma Linda, California, people are living vibrant, active lives well into their hundreds. Buettner calls these areas Blue Zones and they are the inspiration behind his book, *The Blue Zones: Lessons for Living Longer from the People Who've Lived the Longest*. Buettner's research, along with a global longevity study, have led to a program that helps people live longer, healthier, and happier lives.

generations. That is one of the main reasons why I continue to be a staunch advocate for the rail.

Regarding affordable housing, I'm very blessed and honored I get to chair the Zoning & Housing Committee. I'm looking at all these projects and I get to see the big picture of what we're trying to do in the future. What's exciting is that we passed legislation that will provide a lot of housing for our constituents in the future.

It sounds like a steep learning curve indeed. So what skills did you have to master along the way?

I learned that anybody can be a political leader if you love your community. You will figure out real quick who the good and bad leaders are and how to get things done. I've met some wonderful leaders who don't have college degrees, but they are phenomenal because they really care about their community. They demand results.

How would you deal with a crisis of leadership, or what if what your leaders say is at odds with what you believe for your community?

This happened to me in the House of Representatives when I voted against enabling legislation to build the first rail system in Honolulu. Throughout the entire legislative session, I supported the concept. The new tax for rail was supposed to just go to rail but then legislative leaders added a skim on the tax for their own pork barrel projects. Three-hundred million dollars! The financial plan didn't make sense and the vote felt rushed. You were looked down on if you asked tough questions. On the final vote, I voted no. A strong, fully funded special interest candidate was running against me and, at first, my constituents were angry with me. Because this system would benefit my constituents the most, other leaders said I would not survive the next election. As I explained my vote to my constituents, they started to understand my thinking and realized I wasn't a rubber stamp of anyone and had their best interests in mind. I won reelection by a large margin but it was certainly painful.

Do you think your ability to rally people together is the secret to your success or popularity?

They know that I love them, will fight for them and do what it takes as they are my priority.

The other reason for my success is the support I get from my husband, Brian. He is a phenomenal husband, who has no ego and is very supportive of everything that I do. He is non-judgmental and trusts me fully. There have been times when I am so busy I forget to call but he understands I must be busy. I am very thankful for my husband and my daughter, who is sweet and kind. Brian serves in the navy and, in the beginning of our relationship, he was usually gone for long periods of time, including a year in the Middle East when I was pregnant. He now serves on shore duty and I see him a lot, and that is the reason I have so much support now to serve others. My mother also has been incredible. After my daughter was born, I had to get to work right away. She helped me keep things together at home while my husband was still in the Middle East. I honestly would not be able to continue my public service without both of them.

So it is true you are running for mayor?

Yes. That is the plan should the people have me. I feel that many people in power make government harder than it really is. We just need the city to do what it is supposed to do and do it well.

I know I don't look like, act like, or speak like anyone who has run before. But it seems people are ready for a change. Politics is a tough profession. You can be subject to scrutiny, critique, and harassment, but many people remind me every day why it is important for me to keep serving. After I won my first election, I went to the elementary school in my district, which receives the highest amount of government subsidies for serving low-income students. Many of the children were from immigrant families or were new to the U.S. themselves. I was invited to their inauguration ceremony for the elected officers and the student leaders were almost all boys, except for a couple of girls. The next year I went back, and it was almost all girls, except for one boy. So I went up to the student president of the school and asked her what happened, and she said, "You happened, Miss Pine. You showed us we could do this."

So I think of my daughter and I think about all the things we are seeing in the women's movement. I just want to show that we as women can be strong, intelligent and be whoever you want to be. I want to inspire boys and girls to see they shouldn't allow society to tell them what they can or cannot do.

How do you manage to balance your career and motherhood?

I balance it with a lot of help from my mother, husband, and my neighbor. I work hard at everything that I try to do, but I have given up trying to be perfect at everything. You have to accept that you just can't fit everything into one day. Get the important stuff done first and let the small stuff go, or ask someone to help with it. All that I strive for as a mother, now, is to ensure that my daughter is happy and loved. If I could send one message to mothers, it would be to raise your little girls and boys with love. All else doesn't matter.

I ask my daughter every day, "Do you feel loved and happy?" and she says, "Yes." That's all that matters.

How do you think motherhood has changed your style of leadership?

It's helped me to think long-term, say thirty, forty, or sixty years ahead, whereas before, I would think about the here and now. It's why my team and I created the Hire Leeward initiative. Creating job opportunities on the West Side for future generations, and connecting leeward residents with leeward jobs is a priority of mine. I want to improve the quality of life of my constituents, as they are spending three to four hours in traffic.

It was hard initially, as employers thought our leeward residents weren't motivated. But we had the job fair and surprisingly thousands of people came. They already had jobs, but they wanted a better quality of life and to not have a household of latchkey kids. The idea of being able to have breakfast with your kids, drive to work down the street, and come back in time for dinner really appealed to them. And our residents were highly motivated, as these were individuals who were used to leaving their homes at four or five in the morning just to get to work. If families didn't have family to take the kids to school, some would bring their kids with them and they would go to school in town. They would still be in their pajamas, eat breakfast in the car, change, and then go to school or work. So when a parent gets a job close to home, entire lives can change. They are happy and employers report to me that they have never had such dedicated and happy workers.

There's a story of a Makakilo woman, who used to go all the way to the Ala Moana Hotel in Waikīkī for twenty years. Today, she has a job as sales manager for the Hampton Inn, and is able to have dinner every night with her husband for the first time in years. So people's lives have changed in so many ways and all for the better.

What are your fondest memories growing up in Hawaiʻi?

I grew up on the north shore in the country in Pūpūkea, so we played in the forests. We had these tall pine trees and we were latchkey kids, as our parents worked far away. I didn't have many toys growing up, so we spent more time in nature or on the beach. We never had much money but I was happy. I also spent a lot of my time on the soccer field and was always running. I was a very busy kid. *(laughter)*

What do you think has changed over the years and what changes would you like to see in the years ahead?

The biggest change that makes me sad is the high rate of homelessness. It has happened so rapidly just in the last fifteen years, as the cost of living has skyrocketed. It really goes back to not having enough housing for our residents that matches their income. There are so many families in my district that are homeless. Rents in town have gotten so expensive, so the people who normally rent in town move to ʻAiea, and those who are in ʻAiea can't afford their rentals and move to ʻEwa Beach, and those there move to Waiʻanae, so those in Waiʻanae have their rents double, and there are now entire families who have gone to the beach.

What do you think we need to do to solve this crisis?

Government needs to step up and invest in affordable housing but it also needs to get out of the way of innovative builders. We need to support and partner with developers who want to build affordable housing by giving them more density and incentives so their projects are more cost-effective. I recently passed legislation that for the first time requires larger projects to build affordable housing in their plan, but in exchange we give them more density and incentives to help their projects pencil out. The city also needs to completely overhaul the Department of Planning and Permitting (DPP) as there are serious delays caused there for affordable housing builders. One family is building an affordable home without government money and yet it has taken a year to get their permit. They say, if they wait any longer, they will have to sell the land. DPP is understaffed and the staff is underpaid for their talent, which is why we keep losing good people. The city must fix this problem. We also need to get rid of old building codes that add more to the cost of building a unit but is no longer relevant today or needed in innovative construction.

The city and the state need to partner with these affordable housing developers. We need to keep the costs of government land down and help with the water and sewer connections to lower the infrastructure costs. We need to pool our money and resources together to be very successful but we need to work together for the next twenty years.

On that note, what would be your hopes and aspirations for the next twenty years?

We need to build housing that people can afford. When parents aren't home because they have to work two to three jobs, this can cause serious consequences at home. I think the most successful communities are the people who aren't always stressed about their finances and are spending more time with their family. The family unit is strong. This has been my main focus. I strive to wake up every day to improve the quality of life of our constituents. The other is to reduce the time they spend getting stuck in traffic because that is time away from their family and it is physically, mentally, and emotionally stressful. So my goals are to alleviate these two issues as everything else is related to them.

I also want to ensure we preserve the Hawaiian environment with her dense, thick, green areas and beautiful ocean. We need to make sure we have more trees and not too much concrete and all of this is all related to happiness which is ultimately what we all seek.

What do you foresee are some of the challenges with trying to maintain wellness and happiness together with increasing pressures to succeed and demands on productivity?

I look at my constituents to answer and make their own choices. They need to decide how much money they want to make financially and know what their breaking point is.

From the Blue Zone statistics, we see that over sixty-eight percent of my constituents love their family, they are happy with things as is, and appreciate that I am helping to make them more competitive by bringing jobs to them and making it easier for them to get those jobs, as their priority is to be with their children.

As a leader, we also see the bigger picture that we can't let New York or Tahiti beat us too much in terms of tourism. We have to make sure that our taxes are not so high that we lose our touristic charm as that is our biggest bread and butter. At the same time, we cannot have too many tourists that locals no longer can to enjoy Hawai'i, and where our resources get overused and destroyed. We need to make sure that we keep our culture intact. It is what makes us who we are.

Our second largest economy is construction. Half of my constituents work in the construction industry and so we need to see how we can keep building but not destroy Hawai'i with all the concrete and the upscale, luxury market, which upsets our local residents and leads to the homelessness we spoke about.

The luxury market is about to cool off so many will lose their jobs. Switching to building affordable housing will keep people working and house people who can't find a place that they can comfortably afford.

On that note on tourism, how do we draw the line in cultural preservation and yet make Hawai'i an attractive tourist destination?

It is very difficult. Case in point, we have our smaller beaches being discovered by tourists, so we as leaders have to step in and limit the number of tour buses that are going to small beaches. We cannot let the tour industry upset the ecosystem. These are things I have to look into as a leader. We also should focus on keeping tourism to certain areas. For example, we allow resort areas to flourish and attract big hoteliers and smaller chains so local families can also have staycations at more affordable rates. But we need to ensure that our environmental laws are strong. In fact, we are the first to ban plastic bags[2] and harmful sunscreens. We are also looking at the styrofoam ban, as my constituents know it is bad for the environment. It is also key that we preserve our water and don't overbuild O'ahu. It is all very complex and I can talk for hours on this issue.

Now for some trivia. You are so incredibly busy. What do you do to relax?

I'm Catholic as well as Filipino, so I am very spiritual. This morning, I drove and walked along the Ko'olina coast. I went out to the rocks and I did my spiritual practice by just sitting in the sun for a little bit to help me cleanse my spirit. I also love spending time with my husband and we canoe paddle together.

---

[2] The City and County of Honolulu which covers the entirety of Oahu, Hawaii's most populated island enforced a ban that prohibits stores from handing plastic bags to customers at checkout, making Oahu the last populated island in the state to give the bags the boot. The state is the first state to have a complete ban on plastic bags.

Nature is how I center myself. From a spiritual perspective, no matter what religion you believe in, all spiritual leaders say you can't get closer to God than through nature, which is the purest form of God.

What would you say if you met God?

Wow! Finally! And thank you. I have had many tough lessons, but I am thankful for them all.

So what would you say is your toughest lesson?

My toughest lesson was the most needed lesson, which is to not be ashamed of who you are, what you believe, and what you look like.

What pisses you off?

(laughter) You are asking a Filipino Irish girl what pisses her off?!

Actually, I found that to really have peace, one needs to learn to forgive instantly. But if someone hurts someone else who doesn't have a lot of resources, then that can really bring out a part of me that will fight for them. Injustice upsets me. Ever since I was a kid, I was always getting into trouble defending the nerd or the kid that was bullied. These trigger my courage to fight for the underdog.

Who would you love to have a sit down dinner with?

Mother Teresa, as I have read a lot about her and I've tried to incorporate the things that she has said about helping the less fortunate. When my third term in politics was up, I was about done. I was overwhelmed by the politics and I was no longer happy, so I prayed to God to give me my sense of purpose. I was so blessed to wake up the next morning with a vision of Mother Teresa and was filled with a sense forgiveness. That filled me with resolve and I told myself I'm going to love my job, forgive every person that hurt or harmed me, and wake up every day with amnesia. *(laughter)* I have had joy ever since. I would love to meet Mother Teresa so I could learn to be a more selfless leader, as I think she's ten times better than I could ever be. I would also love to learn what kept her going when things seemed hopeless.

What is life philosophy on a bumper sticker?

Forgiveness and amnesia equals happiness.

The title of your memoir would be?

Hope.

How would you want to be remembered?

That I inspired people to be their best.

What can we expect from you in the near future?

It is important as parents that we embrace our differences for our own little girl and I also wish to step up as a leader and inspire other women, so it would be wonderful to be the first Hawai'i-born female mayor of the City and County of Honolulu.

THE CONTROVERSIAL STORYTELLER

Lois-Ann Yamanaka

"Until you see yourself in literature, you don't exist." That is the power of the written word. We believed our geographic isolation and pidgin would not be understood but by only us. I learned through reading the works of other writers who used voice and decided that the shores that surround us and isolate us touch other shores. And that the human experience is universal no matter how you say it.

Born in Hoʻolehua, Molokaʻi, Lois-Ann Yamanaka is a Japanese American writer, raised by her teacher-parents, together with her four younger sisters, in the sugarcane plantation town of Pāhala on Hawaiʻi Island. Following in her parents' footsteps, Lois Ann went into education and received her bachelor's degree in 1983 and completed her master's degree at the University of Hawaiʻi at Mānoa (UHM).

Jennifer Harris writes that "Lois Ann's writing is uncontrovertibly controversial," but she however, did not set out to be controversial. In fact, she didn't even set out to be a writer, but discovered creative writing while working as a schoolteacher and became a vocal proponent of speaking pidgin. Her works typically explore the sense of alienation and difference against a predominantly white, mainstream urban culture. For Lois Ann, writing about Hawaiʻi, and in pidgin, is a fundamentally political act.

These themes of alienation are seen in her novels Saturday Night at the Pāhala Theatre *(1993),* Wild Meat and the Bully Burgers *(1996),* Blu's Hanging *(1997),* Heads by Harry *(1999), and* Father of the Four Passages *(2001).*

Blu's Hanging, *set after the death of the mother figure, tells the story of three siblings who attempt to negotiate a world of severe poverty, violence, racism, and exploitation. As their father struggles to make ends meet, twelve-year-old Ivah attempts to assume her mother's responsibilities, but fails and her brother, Blu, is raped by their Filipino neighbor. In 1998, the Association of Asian American Studies awarded Lois Ann a fiction award for her novel, but the award was abruptly rescinded when claims were made that Lois Ann's characterization of an abusive Filipino man was racist. Widespread controversy ensued.*

In Wild Meat and the Bully Burgers, *Lois Ann explores the idea of cultural alienation through the protagonist, Lovey. Through a series of vignettes, the readers witness Lovey's comic and poignant struggle to establish a sense of self-worth as she moves into adolescence. Lois Ann later became the recipient of a 1998 Lannan Literary Award and two Pushcart Prizes. Her last publication is* Behold the Many: A Novel, *published in 2006.*

Lois Ann's works have been staged as plays by Kuma Kahua Theatre and she remains committed to the use of pidgin, and writing about the experiences of her community no matter how unpopular those experiences may be.

Share with us your background.

The Big Island and Molokaʻi, I call home for me. On the Big Island, we lived in Pāhala, Keauhou, Kona, and Hilo. My father, Harry Yamanaka, worked for the state and also as a taxidermist, photographer, stone sculptor, hunter, multimedia artist, musician, environmentalist, world traveler, and author—a true Renaissance man.

My family made enough for us to have a new pair of shoes at the start of each school year but never traveled past Molokaʻi. However, I did not feel deprived or without. What my father and mother, Jean Narikiyo Yamanaka, made known to my three younger sisters and me, I came to understand as God Manifest. Because of his taxidermy, my father befriended many ranchers and landowners, who allowed us access to pristine sites on the Big Island, where I experienced the once-in-a-lifetimes in nature, which is God's expression of himself.

How and why did you start writing?

Writing began with the foresight and vision of Debbie Ziemke, the language arts department chair at my first real teaching job at Kalākaua Intermediate School. She spent a sizable portion of our budget on a Poets-in-the-Schools residency with poet Eric Chock for all of our students who were placed in X, Y, and Z homogeneous classes according to SAT scores. Her vision that poetry belonged to all of our students, not only the gifted and talented became a gift to them and me.

My students wrote such heart-wrenching, guttural poems about their lives in a way that astounded me. Then I thought, if thirteen year olds can do that, and I have a master's degree, and I wrote such crappy poems, then I needed to go back to school.

Faye Kicknosway at UH became my mentor by fire—intense, brutally honest, and so very compassionate. She scared the hell out of me at first. My big break came after she gave me the permission to be me: pidgin-speaking, Hilo-hillbilly, kick-ass-at-the-man me. I remember giving Eric Chock the poems I wrote under my mentor in a plastic supermarket bag. Eric Chock walked away with my entire being in his hands. Faye submitted poems for me that I never imagined I'd do because it was never my intention to be published. Eric selected the first poems for publication in Bamboo Ridge Press: a Literary Journal.

What inspires you?

Somewhere, I read, "Find appreciation in life's contrary experiences." That sums up my inspiration.

My best friend, Shari Nakamura, who passed in 2013 always said, "How come this kind crazy shit only happen to you, Lois? Only you. But that's why I love you."

And it's been a puzzling, complicated, mystifying, disturbing, complex, and miraculous ride. I fricken suffer—all of us— life is about suffering; no one is spared.

But in time, I appreciate these experiences. I used to think to myself even as a child, "There is a reason for this. There is a reason for this." I was right. Everything inspires me. Even road kill.

Which is your favorite work to date and why?

My favorite work to date is the work I am currently working on called *Up the Rabbit Hole*. My foot-washing, Southern Baptist Grandma Narikiyo, who was the last surviving founding member of Kaunakakai Baptist Church on Molokaʻi, told me when I was a little girl that God gave each and every one of us a gift.

Our job is to listen for our calling to use this gift. This book represents the true beginning of my answer to my original calling. In my other books, I used the gift that God gave me; in my current work, I answer my true calling.

Which is your favorite character to date and why?

Tita from *Saturday Night at the Pāhala Theatre* has to be at the top of the list of my favorite characters. She is raging, fucking mad at the world and courageous enough to speak it her way. I also understand her as the most fragile and hurt of my characters, yet one who will not let the world kill her ferocious spirit. Tita resembles me.

I show bravado and am perceived as an extrovert, but those who know the real me understand the shy, anxiety-ridden, broken child repairing herself piece by piece, who takes things hard and over thinks every little remark or facial expression or tone of voice; the me, who can be fractured easily, the shards of broken bones embedded into my own flesh for decades.

> **You are an advocate for pidgin and learned the importance of taking care of the language. Share with us your thoughts on this.**

What I understand now after reading the many voices of women of varying ethnicities and places they call home is that language is culture. If we are not allowed to use the sound of memory, then we become cut off from the place where all learning exist—family, community, culture. Language and culture are skin and flesh to me, so when my teachers told us that we had to speak standard English, or face the labels of stupidity and ignorance, I believed them.

What we faced here in Hawai'i can best be called institutional racism. We couldn't name the racists or why we felt less than. Chinese American poet Li Young Lee once told me that he understood racism because he could step outside his door and point to the neighbors who despised him for being Chinese. I told him that the prejudice we faced came through like an invisible, slithering puhi.

I didn't know why I felt inferior to my kotonk cousins on the Mainland who spoke perfect English or why I couldn't raise my hand to ask a question in five years of undergraduate study. Shame of being inarticulate. I could speak standard English, but the sound or lyricism of what came out of my mouth still had the music of pidgin.

> **You have chosen to take on darker themes in your writing, so much so it is described as being "anything but paradise." Why is that so?**

Images and books of the Hawai'i I knew—shoved in my face through movies, like *The Hawaiians* and *Blue Hawai'i*, or TV shows, like *Hawaii Five-O*. Tourist propaganda. White male writers told me about me in the works of James Michener, Robert Louis Stevenson, and Jack London.

But none came close to a depiction of me or my family. The co-founder of Bamboo Ridge Press, Darrell H.Y. Lum, once said, "Until you see yourself in literature, you don't exist." That is the power of the written word.

We believed our geographic isolation and pidgin would not be understood but by only us. I learned through reading the works of other writers who used voice and decided that the shores that surround us and isolate us touch other shores. And that the human experience is universal no matter how you say it.

I'd tell about me from the inside out, not be told by others from the outside looking in. Li Young Lee also taught me about writing as motion from heart to hand; too many writers take a detour from heart to head to hand. That motion affects the power of process.

> **You have gained accolades and brickbats for your work. How do you deal with the controversy and criticism?**

Controversy and criticism taught me to put my big girl panties on and realize that what people say or do has really nothing to do with me or my work. Each critic, academic, journalist has her own agenda. I notice a kind of cannibalism of our own kind by academics who vilify our works—Latino, Black, Asian American—like crabs in the proverbial bucket pulling the ones who challenge the canon back down to feed on them.

Another metaphor, instead of making the spokes on the wheel move forward, they choose to pull us off.

I say to them: be a spoke on the wheel. Tell your own story.

Add to the forward momentum of the wheel.

> **Do you suffer from writers' block? If no, how do you keep the juices flowing and, if yes, what do you do?**

The act of writing became only a part of the being a "writer"—the part of the process where I sit down at my desk and actually put my hands on the keyboard. Every moment, breath, utterance, spilled tea, broken pen, smeared lipstick, traffic jam, trade wind, monumental wonder, tragic loss, fresh eggs from my pet chickens is writing.

In the life I inhabit, good and bad have no differentiation; good and bad are indistinct because, in the end, it's all writing that leads to the sit-down time. It's not mine to say, "Now. Write. Help. I'm stuck."

Process means time for the gathering. Time for the Experiences that need to happen. It is patience, seeking, and peace in God's plan.

> **What sacrifices did you make to get to where you are today?**

Sacrifices include looking at and examining fear without fear. Accepting shortcomings in myself and others with gratitude. Forgiveness of those who attempted to catastrophically hurt me, my family, and even my autistic son. Risking the breaking. Risking the fragility of cell memory. Letting go of my own truths. Sanity. Sobriety. Sleep.

What are some of your biggest failures and successes?

My biggest failure was at my first-ever public reading with The Folder Poets, students in Faye Kicknosway's poetry workshop class. All of my former professors, several of whom thought I was retarded because I never spoke in class, sat in the audience.

I had zero relationships with most of them except that of reverence and awe. I drank three plastic cups of cheap wine and smoked twelve cigarettes on an empty stomach after running around doing errands all morning to prepare for my reading.

I got up to the podium and looked at all of their faces then began reading when my voice trailed off to the right of my head, farther and farther away as the frame of my vision shrank like our old TV that turned black until only one white dot remained then bleeped off. I fainted.

When I opened my eyes, the orientation of the room had shifted to ceiling which was odd and toes. Faye helped me up, and I insisted on continuing because it meant so much to me. Then I fainted again. I invited only one friend, and she fanned my face when I opened my eyes. I finished reading my poems from a chair. My friend said she thought that poets took a rest between poems by lying down. I was lucky when I twirled the first time I went down as my skirt didn't fly over my head.

My biggest success is always finding my way home in the big and small scheme of events and the healing that writing brings.

What are some of the most enduring life lessons learned?

The most enduring life lessons include knowing that:
  Time does not heal all wounds.
  There is such a thing as a dumb question.
  Wear big girl panties as needed.
  Good and bad are the same in the spirit world.
  Retain some affection for hometown scars, courtesy of
    William Burroughs.
  Surrender.
  Gratitude.
  The universal law of cause and effect, or karma's a bitch.

What advice would you give to an aspiring writer?

Real writing takes the utmost courage. Here's a metaphor: you stand at the edge of a cliff. You jump not knowing whether you will break every bone in your body. If you will survive as a quadriplegic or if you will get up and dust off your boots. Jump even if you will die.

Here's another. You make a fire. Do you write about its warmth? Do you write about the flames? Do you write about s'mores? Do you write about the 'ono steaks you grill? Or do you jump in with full knowledge of first, second, or third degree burns, or of burning into ash and rising up phoenix-like or simply a pile of dust.

If you cannot take those risks, then your time as a writer may be best spent on writing the Christmas card of family events month-by-month to send to your relatives, and everything you do comes back to you tenfold.

Suppose you are writing your memoir. The title of and the abstract to your memoir would say …

The book is called *Up the Rabbit Hole*. How light from the beginning of time infinite is born from darkness.

You were born and raised on Molokaʻi. Share with us your fondest memories growing up on the island?

Though born on Molokaʻi, I spent my life both there and on the Big Island. I would not call Molokaʻi "home," but Big Island is home.

However, whenever my mother kicked me out of the house, I lived with my Grandma Narikiyo on Molokaʻi. I begged her to take custody of me and consider her my true mother—the nurturing mother I longed for.

My fondest memories include picking kiawe tree seed pods in the gully, then Grandma boiling the small, sunflower-sized seeds for us to sew into lei to give to newcomers at her church; gathering ogo in the waters of East End.

Grandma used to tie Calrose rice bags around our waists and showed us how to gather the seaweed without pulling out the root so more could grow. I remember helping her make namasu for Grandpa and bottling the remainders for her church friends. The only fast food place was the Dairy Queen by the church, so Grandma bought Chef Boyardee pizza kits from Friendly Market, and we made our own pizza before Pizza Hut even existed in the islands.

When the halalu ran, we went down to the Kaunakakai Wharf with our bamboo fishing poles, chummed the water with the cheap, big cans of Ligo sardines that she opened with the key, and caught the silver halalu that we took home. Grandma cleaned the fish and fried them crispy-brown; we ate the whole thing even the bones from head to tail.

For Vacation Bible School, we caught the little yellow school bus to the west side of the island. We made Bible newspapers with headlines and by-lines with illustrations and ads, carved crosses out of Ivory soap, which I never wanted to Grandma to use. The best was when the church ladies made their homemade specialty cookies that we never heard of, like snickerdoodles and Russian tea cakes, which we ate with the cold Kool-Aid from the big yellow Igloo in tiny Dixie paper cups on snack break. *(laughter)*

What book would you say is a must-read for someone visiting Hawai'i for the first time?

Any book or all books put out by Bamboo Ridge Press are must-reads for visitors to Hawai'i. Watch the new *Hawai'i Five-O* as a comedy not a police drama.

Who is your favorite author?

My favorite author as a child are all the books written by Ruth Tabrah. She was the only writer I could find who used names and places I knew.

My life-changing authors are Darrell H.Y. Lum, Sandra Cisneros, William Faulkner, Dorothy Allison, Cathy Song, Jerry Kosinsky, Carolyn Chute, Yasunari Kawabata, Allen Ginsberg, William Burroughs, Kenzaburō Ōe, Eduardo Galeano, John Steinbeck, Paul Auster, Louise Erdrich, and Jessica Hagedorn.

What would you say when you meet God?

When I meet God, I will ask Him to let me meet my angels, spirit guides, saints, holy men and women, Him in all his manifestations in all cultures.

Where is your favorite spot in Hawai'i and why?

Punalu'u Black Sand Beach, where at Kolea Bay I saw stones give birth to stones.

What would your epitaph say?

Be wild. Tita out. Ack up.

THE AD-VENTURE CAPITALIST
Catherine Ngo

We need to adopt the mindset that it's OK to fail. It can be challenging for those raised in the Asian culture, like myself, where we were taught not to "lose face." While this is a great virtue, it should not stop us from embracing new challenges and taking some risks to improve ourselves.

Catherine Ngo

Catherine is the president and CEO of Central Pacific Bank, since 2015. With over twenty-five years of executive experience in the financial services and private equity industries, Catherine joined Central Pacific Bank (CPB) in November 2010 as executive vice president. She is also the director of the holding company and bank board. Prior to CPB, Catherine was a founding general partner of Startup Capital Ventures, an early-stage venture capital firm established in 2005, with investments in Silicon Valley and Hawai'i, as well as in China.

A graduate of the University of Virginia School of Law, Catherine started her career in a private law practice, focused on banking and securities law. After seven years, she joined Silicon Valley Bank (SVB), a financial services company focused on serving the needs of venture capital in 1993. In 2002 and until leaving SVB in 2005, she served as chief operating officer of Alliant Partners, an investment banking subsidiary of SVB.

Since Catherine's appointment as president and CEO of CPB, the bank has been named as one of Hawai'i's Best Places to Work by Hawai'i Business magazine in 2016, 2017, and 2018. Under her leadership, CPB also received the Hawai'i Small Business Lender of the Year (Category II, Mid-Size Lenders) Award in 2016 and 2017, amongst others. The Girl Scouts of Hawai'i honored Catherine as one of their 2016 Women of Distinction and, in May 2018, Catherine was one of four honorees at the YWCA Leader Luncheon celebrated for their commitment to the community.

It, thus, came as a pleasant surprise to me to find out that Catherine was as athletic as she was, preferring to spend her weekends on a stand-up paddleboard and being active. Her sense of 'ohana, camaraderie, and eagerness to help others is palpable, as she quickly got me connected to the CEO of the YWCA upon knowing that I was new in town and an active women's advocate and volunteer. It is little wonder that she has made Hawai'i her home and taken it upon herself to promote entrepreneurship here on the island.

I know I am pronouncing your last name as it should, with a silent G. I am from Singapore and Ngo is a fairly common last name.

That's right. Not many people know it's a silent G, so I go by "No" here, literally. But it's actually my parents who decided this when they migrated to the United States. People could not pronounce the G between the N and the O, so they decided to keep it simple.

Both of your parents are of Chinese descent?

Yes. While both their families are from Xiamen which is in the southern part of China, they, themselves, grew up in Manila. They decided to come to the United States to complete college with the idea they would eventually return to Manila to be with their parents as most children do. But my father ended up getting a wonderful job opportunity with a chemical company in Virginia and decided to make a life for himself and, later, his family there. But what has always been special for me is that I spent all the summers of my childhood and teenage years in Manila surrounded by my siblings, grandparents, and friends.

It was a wonderful experience being exposed to different cultures, foods, and people in my seminal growing up years. I think, in some regard that has a part to play in who I am today as I have a deep appreciation for different cultures and ideas and am open to learning about values in other cultures.

How and why did your parents end up in Manila?

It was my grandfather who moved to Manila to start a business. There is actually a small group of Chinese in the Philippines even today. These were the entrepreneurs who took a chance and left China to start their own businesses. There are many stories like that. Even in my family, entrepreneurship has always been integral.

As I look back, I think about my heritage, reflect upon my life, and know that it's ingrained in me to influence entrepreneurship, as it has always been a big part of my family and me.

We will certainly speak about that later on. How was it for you being born and raised in Virginia?

Our family was the only Chinese family in the neighborhood, and my brothers and I were the only Chinese in our school. Actually, we were the only non-white family in the neighborhood and school. So, in that regard, we were different, even though we were born in the United States, and I always identified as being American.

On the other hand, we always felt we stood out and knew we were seen as being different and that made me feel special, particularly on festive occasions like Chinese New Year. Every year, my parents would keep us all up late into the night and we would celebrate. These instances made me feel very special in a very nice way.

Having said that, there were times when I was younger when I didn't like the fact that I was different and did not want to stand out.

How did you get your start in your career?

I went to law school and started my career in a large law firm in Dallas that represented larger financial institutions. In fact, for most of my career, I always worked with banks, which was why my transition into a bank was rather smooth. My move to banking per se happened when I was in California. I was recruited by the largest client of my then law firm to be their first in-house legal counsel. I was only thirty years old then and could take a chance. So I grasped at the incredible opportunity to work as the first lawyer for this financial institution and to help build the division.

In time, I was given the opportunity to take on other divisions and eventually took on a role very similar to the one I played when I first started at Central Pacific Bank, where I oversaw most of the support divisions in the company.

Was it difficult being this legal eagle overseeing a huge task?

Because it happened over time, it was not very difficult. While I was at Silicon Valley Bank, I oversaw the legal department and began to learn more about the business of the company. I was gradually given more responsibilities in adjacent divisions.

How was it like being in Silicon Valley in the '80s?

It definitely was another instance of standing out and being different. There were very few women in leadership positions at Silicon Valley Bank, or in the technology companies and venture capital firms in Silicon Valley.

I soon grew accustomed to being the only woman at the table, be it in my own company or in business discussions with technology companies or venture capitalists. In fact, following the time at Silicon Valley Bank, I joined four other men as partners and founded our own venture capital firm. I was used to being the only woman or one of just a handful of women at the table.

In my earlier years, I felt I had to work harder than the men. I remember, very early on in my years at Silicon Valley Bank, I was sought out by a woman who was on our board of directors. She owned a very successful business in Silicon Valley. She founded her own temp services firm that supported many of the very large technology companies in Silicon Valley. I remember her sharing with me an adage that I still bear in mind: "Get in there and just do it, but you do need to work harder." I've always remembered that. By nature, I'm a very hard worker, so it was natural for me to do whatever it took to stand out and get ahead to the next step in my career.

That lady must have seen something in you.

I like to think so. I think she saw a person who was willing to take that step forward. Someone who dared to go beyond the job or the task at hand. I wouldn't say I'm aggressive but I am definitely proactive, assertive, and ambitious.

What would you say have been the biggest obstacles in your career?

I will say it is less obstacles than challenges. These challenges can come in the form of changes in the market, both unexpected and expected, and even changes in the team. But for me, it has always been about being resilient and about being willing to step up to these challenges.

One thing I like to share when I mentor is that we must learn to become comfortable with discomfort. I think back on how I have progressed and recognize that it has always been important for me to step outside of my comfort zone. I always know that once I start getting too comfortable with my current position that it is time to be thinking about the next step, and to start stepping into a new challenge.

How do you deal with criticism?

I frequently remind myself that I must not react too quickly to any given situation. So if I am facing criticism from a naysayer, I will tell myself to step away, and take the time to reflect before responding, if there is even a need for a response.

I also make it a point to surround myself with people who share my values and passion. In my days as a venture capitalist and working with entrepreneurs, I always sought out passionate entrepreneurs who shared similar values in leadership. I found that even if they had the right skills and technology, but did not have the right person or team chemistry, then it was not going to be a successful venture for us.

As a venture capitalist, what did you look out for in an entrepreneur?

The first thing that I always look out for is the kind of person the entrepreneur is. Then, I look at the team. Of course, there also has to be a good idea, good technology, and a good opportunity with suitable market barriers to entry—all the typical things an investor would look out for.

But, the most important is the team itself. The reason is that there will be challenging times for that young company, so the team must have the ability to come together, which means there must be trust and communication in the team.

Is this what you look out for in your team here as well?

I would say that is true of our team at Central Pacific Bank. We are not going to succeed if we don't take on opportunities and deal with challenges. We must have trust and communication to be able to do the things we do.

In fact, our managing committee goes off-site for our retreats so that we can do team-building activities to build strength and solidarity. I believe this starts with us becoming vulnerable to each other. It can be a very difficult thing for most as it's only human to want to protect ourselves. Yet, I think it's very important for the team to become vulnerable to each other so as to eradicate barriers and build trust. Our team has been together for a few years now so these exercises are becoming less threatening.

As part of our retreat, we also share our mistakes, learning, and feedback with each other. I think it's always important for teams not to take our camaraderie for granted. We stay humble and always enable ongoing dialogue, so we can see where we may have fallen short and find areas for improvement.

What would you say has been your most challenging encounter in your career?

I'd say the most challenging experience I've had was in my prior life in Silicon Valley, where I was the chief operating officer of an investment bank, which Silicon Valley Bank had purchased. One of the biggest mistakes in the acquisition was not recognizing that the investment bank had a different mindset and culture (from our bank's). At the onset, I did not see these differences and failed to appreciate how important shared values and mindsets were to the success of an organization.

I would say that from that encounter, I've learned that, if at any time, I had to pull together a group, distinct divisions or different companies, I would have to ensure that we have common values and shared mindsets right from the get-go. Otherwise, trying to achieve even the simplest task is going to be very difficult.

What is one of the biggest leadership lessons you have learned?

I would say that we need to adopt the mindset that it's OK to fail. It can be challenging for those raised in the Asian culture, like myself, where we were taught not to "lose face." While this is a great virtue, it should not stop us from embracing new challenges and taking some risks to improve ourselves.

In order for us to succeed and build an innovation economy here in Hawaiʻi, we have to be comfortable with failure as long as we learn from the experience.

This is a perfect segue to our discussion on how to encourage entrepreneurship in Hawaiʻi.

Yes, I believe that in order to build an entrepreneurship culture here in Hawaiʻi, we need to start in the schools. It starts before the university experience and should actually begin in elementary or high school. It is important for schools to inculcate the importance of thinking outside the box and being creative. The university plays a very important part later.

When I first moved here, I actually taught a graduate entrepreneurship class at the University of Hawaiʻi at Mānoa. There were about twenty-five students in the class, all of whom were very bright. Almost all were aspiring entrepreneurs. We spent much time in class brainstorming ideas, but what I learned through that experience was that we did not seem to have the necessary infrastructure and support system here in Hawaiʻi for those entrepreneurs to be successful.

Many had very good ideas, but we don't have the ecosystem here, whether that be professional advisors or funding sources. Yes, we have an angel community, but it's not a very organized and well-established community.

We also have a lack of the other supporting services entrepreneurs need to build their business, such as lawyers, accountants, and advisors, who can help the entrepreneurs in their pitch to the investors. We do need an entire ecosystem to promote and support entrepreneurship.

Having said that, I think we have made a lot of progress and are headed in the right direction, whether that be in the form of government funding or university programs. It is important that the business community enables these conversations to support young entrepreneurs, either as mentors or even have the willingness to be better customers to them.

In Silicon Valley, entrepreneurs had the luxury of being able to knock on any doors as most companies had the willingness to try a product or new service. I think if we are serious about building an innovative economy, then everybody here needs to play their part.

I would say the business community is coming together. Nowadays, we appreciate that we need to diversify our economy and are having these conversations. We must all see that we have a responsibility in cultivating this innovation economy and need to play our part from time to time.

Personally, I do have entrepreneurs who come to me for advice. One of the key pieces of advice I give is to instill the importance of a business plan in a successful pitch to an investor. I would also say, it is vital the entrepreneur surrounds him or herself with the right team. The founding team is integral to building the company.

Have you made any sacrifices to get to where you are today or do you think a woman can have it all?

I think for anyone, male or female, there are sacrifices. For me, I will say that I have put in hard work and very long hours to get to where I am today. You can't have all the time you want with your family and yet spend all your time in the company. It's impossible, but yet, I look at it positively and say that it's all about balance.

And yes, I do feel I can have it all. I have the good fortune of being married to a great husband and having a wonderful, supportive family. I am also very thankful for my job here at Central Pacific Bank.

I do not have children but I don't see that as a sacrifice. I look at others who have young families and know that they must aim to strike a balance and find the support they need whether at home or in the office.

As a leader, I recognize that this culture and mindset starts with me, so I aim to provide flexibility and hope to working mothers so that they can balance their diverse interests. But yes, I do agree that there is an element of give and take to enable them to do what they have to do.

What advice would you give to a young woman who is torn between her family and career?

I would say that she can have it all but she has to be sure to surround herself with a strong support network, both within the family and her work organization. This should ideally give her some flexibility to raise her family, as well as continue to progress in her career.

Share with us some of your most memorable mentoring experiences.

There are a couple of people who come to mind. There's a lady at Silicon Valley Bank. When I first met her, she was a member of one of the departments I oversaw. Over the next few years that I mentored her, I saw her grow from a brilliant individual contributor to someone overseeing a division of over 100 employees.

The second person that comes to mind is a young man that I met in China during my time as a venture capitalist. I was investing in companies in Silicon Valley but also doing work in China, where I met this young man who asked if I would be willing to mentor him. While it was a significant time commitment on my part, I also saw it was an opportunity for me to practice my Mandarin.

I give him credit for approaching me to be his mentor as I know it took courage on his part. I gave him the same advice that had been given to me over the years, which is to get out there, meet with other entrepreneurs and financing sources. After I left China and moved here to Hawaiʻi, we kept in touch. He reached out to say that he was grateful for the advice that I had given him and that he had taken the advice to heart and eventually did make his way into a private equity firm.

Share with us your learnings from your time spent in China.

Yes, I realized that in order to be successful in China, I needed to speak Mandarin. While I had a tutor in Silicon Valley, I felt that, unless I immersed myself in the language, I was not going to become fluent. So I went to China for four months in 2009. I was working but I spent time studying the language and did become conversational in Mandarin. I was able to carry a conversation over dinner, which was really my goal, though I didn't learn to read and write.

I was able to learn at a deeper level from my observations in China. There was a spirit of ambition and the innovation economy was taking off in a big way in China. It was relatively new compared to Silicon Valley and the rest of the U.S., but what I appreciated about Chinese entrepreneurs was that they saw this as a real opportunity.

They knew that they had to build that ecosystem we spoke about and had no qualms about attracting top talent from Silicon Valley. They realized that they need not reinvent the wheel and decided to learn from the U.S. and others who have done so successfully. They were happy to accept money from the U.S. venture capitalists to learn how to build great companies.

By extension, I think Hawai'i should recognize that we don't need to reinvent the wheel either. There are plenty of places including Silicon Valley that have done this successfully. Many successful venture capitalists have their second homes here in Hawai'i or would love to visit Hawai'i. Hawai'i does attract a pool of these types of people and talent, so we can certainly leverage on that and build the innovation economy we spoke about earlier.

Speaking of second homes in Hawai'i, were you one of those, too, that did not think you would settle in Hawai'i but ended up doing so?

Yes, absolutely. When I first came here with my husband, we were not planning to stay. My husband, Bob, is from the East Coast, but has lived around the country. I came here to lead a recapitalization of our company and was planning to return to the Mainland after we succeeded in recapitalizing the company and turning it back to profitability.

What we didn't expect was that we would fall in love with the culture, the people, and the state. I certainly fell in love with my own company as well! In fact, it did not take Bob long to get involved with the community and he was quicker than I was to call this place home. At one point, he even joked with one of the members of our board of directors and said that "Catherine can return to the Mainland but I'm staying here!" (*laughter*)

Within a couple of years, my husband and I decided that this is home, where we will live and eventually retire. We have since sold our home in Silicon Valley, knowing that this is where we belong. It is remarkable, as we didn't set out to move to Hawai'i but it happened. We feel very lucky and blessed that it happened.

What do you love about Hawai'i?

There is a saying that people come to Hawai'i for the beauty but stay for the people. That is so true. It is indeed the people, the humility, warmth, caring, and concern that keep us here, and that we feel we fit in and are accepted here. We also, now, feel that we can contribute to Hawaiʻi, so I look forward to being able to give back.

I also love the view. I live across from Ala Moana and look out from my window every day and am filled with so much gratitude that I am living here in Hawaiʻi.

What is the secret to your happy marriage?

I would say it is good communication. Bob and I have very deep conversations, ranging from the issues and challenges I face at work to the fears I have. And similarly, he shares with me, too. He has been all the support I need and I could not do what I'm doing without him. It helps that we been together since law school. We've grown together and seen each other through some of the best and worst times.

What were some things you had to get used to when you moved from the Mainland to Hawaiʻi?

The first thing to get used to is being so far away from family, whom I'm very close to. Mom and Dad are still in Virginia. The second thing that takes some getting used to is the traveling.

We have the good fortune of having many people come to visit, and we, too, have the flexibility to travel. In fact, my parents, my brother, and his wife just visited over the summer.

What are some changes you like to see in your new home?

The change I'd like to see is the one I can contribute to, which is a more diversified economy. I do think that for Hawaiʻi to continue to be relevant in decades ahead, we have to think about innovation and strengthening the other legs of our economy, in addition to tourism, military, and real estate.

What does this diversified economy mean in concrete terms?

I would, first, look at our strengths. What we don't want is to make Hawaiʻi another Silicon Valley. So we need to take stock of our strengths and leverage those. For example, we have the good fortune of having clean energy sources—solar, wind, and geothermal power. We can leverage that strength and create a competitive advantage for ourselves in the energy industry.

You're incredibly busy. What do you do to relax?

I love stand-up paddleboarding. I get out every week and enjoy being active, just another reason why I appreciate living here. I know many people who have been here all their lives, but don't even go to the beach. I go to the beach every weekend.

What gets you angry?

Even if I get angry, I stay pretty even-keeled. But if I had to pick the one thing, I would say it is unfairness and indecency in others' actions.

It takes a lot to get me angry, but when I do, I want to do something about it. But I don't react instantly as well, as I know it doesn't pay off.

Who would you like to have a sit-down dinner with?

Sheryl Sandberg. Even before her years at Facebook, she was already a trailblazer for women. She has taken a lead role in trying to change the lives of women. She has faced a lot of hardship, challenges, and I would like to understand how she deals with personal hardship, while successfully running a company. I think I could learn from her and would certainly enjoy the conversation.

What would you say when you meet God?

Thank you for the many blessings that have been bestowed on me. I hope I took those blessings and made a difference in the lives of others.

What is your life philosophy on a bumper sticker?

Being successful requires being comfortable with discomfort.

If you are writing your memoir, the title would be ...

The harder I work, the luckier I get.

How do you want to be remembered?

Always caring, always loving.

THE PEACEMAKER

Maya Soetoro-Ng

While it is important to think about these incredible women as inspiring leaders, I think it is also important that we do not ask them to be perfect. Mom was not perfect. She was incredible, but she was also imperfect. There is so much power and beauty in seeing a woman who strives and ultimately succeeds in building a connected life that matters to not only those who are near but also in others.

Best known as the maternal half-sister of former U.S. President Barack Obama, Maya Kasandra Soetoro-Ng has come into the spotlight, since she took part in the U.S. presidential campaign in 2007. However, Maya is a well-established researcher and educator in her own right. She has worked in a number of established centers and colleges, and she has proven herself as an academic. In addition, she is also an author and wrote Ladder to the Moon, *a children's book. She is currently working to publish more of her works soon.*

Known for her quick wit and humor—a trait she shares with her brother, Barack Obama—the mother of two describes herself as philosophically Buddhist, and actively participates in charity. She has spoken against racial discrimination and the need for introducing cultural diversity to students at an early age. She speaks fondly of her Indonesian heritage and also of her husband's Chinese roots, and is a loving auntie to her nieces, Malia and Sasha. Given her multicultural heritage and education, Maya supports cultural diversity and is a promoter for peace. She is co-founder of Ceeds of Peace, a nonprofit peace-building organization; co-founder of the Hawai'i-based Institute for Climate and Peace, which focuses on the three pillars of information, collaboration, and policy transformation around the intersection of climate change and positive peace building; and is also a consultant for the Obama Foundation.

When she invited me to her home for the interview, I was struck by just how down-to-earth Maya was. Our conversations ranged from our appreciation of Southeast Asian culture to our deep love and respect for our flawed but oh-so-strong mothers. Maya's deep strength stems from her willingness and ability to accept her vulnerabilities, which makes her all the more compelling, approachable and human.

How would you best describe yourself?

First, I am a mother and family woman. I am also a teacher and a sojourner. I'm also the director of the Matsunaga Institute for Peace and Conflict Resolution, and that is an important part of me. I wake up feeling grateful every day to be able to live and work in accordance with my most cherished values. I don't think many people can feel that kind of synergy between their work and their life's purpose and internal landscape.

I co-founded a nonprofit called Ceeds of Peace, which works to bring together schools, families, and community leaders in a 360-degree approach to develop action plans using backward mapping. Each participant, or cohort, envisions their beloved community, names the changes they would like to see, and then creates action plans to bring their vision to fruition with the help of our facilitators. We offer professional development credit for the teachers and help the family members, community leaders, and educators to implement the action plans together, building bridges of communication and collaboration with one another.

In essence, we aim to mine each person's leadership potential. Both these projects are focused on participatory leadership—getting young people to think of themselves as budding leaders and to see peace as an action oriented, pragmatic activity that is really about making the lives of others better and making the community stronger. The innovative action plans help individuals to develop a sense of personal resilience and empowerment, allow them to enact change, and to feel valuable in their positive peace work, regardless of their profession.

I love teaching my leadership and peace studies classes at the University of Hawai'i as well. I love to see my students work to impact public policy, solve problems in the community, and engage in service leadership. They are transformed with increased confidence and desire to participate. They begin to understand their own mettle and develop moral courage; they develop a stronger sense of responsibility to others and take pride in what they accomplish on behalf of others. That to me is a true education; it is not just about learning discrete bits of information, but about students putting the learning to use in their own lives, both for their personal development and the betterment of the community.

You are a huge advocate for servant leadership. How did you become this person that you are today?

I think that we all go through a pretty selfish period in our youth and that's necessary, as we do have to consider our own development, our own opportunities for advancement, at a time when we generally have very little. That said, I did grow up with a mom, who, in spite of my self-absorption (*laughter*), emphasized service to others. She worked with women in cottage industries, helped to develop rural credit programs and microfinance, so that villagers were empowered to take care of their families, maintain a sense of fortitude in rapidly urbanizing Indonesia or other places where she worked, like India, Bangladesh, Pakistan, Thailand, Ghana, and elsewhere.

My mother was a woman who delighted in human creation and community, and who found a great sense of satisfaction in helping others. She fed her curiosity, was able to relish the beautiful artistry of so many places, and enjoyed life as a great adventure. No one was a stranger to her. She wanted very much to help others, so Barack and I had a good model for the kind of servant leaders that we should become.

I think a great value of servant leadership is actually that it helps us to heal from traumas, especially in the absence of perfect faith and universal order. It is also the way we steady ourselves in the storm and retain a sense of optimism and buoyancy when things around you are not going well. I feel I can withstand almost anything, as I have healed and bound my own wounds through loving and giving to others, and receiving abundance in return. That is something I want to encourage people to understand. Yes, what we do when we serve is about making the world better, but it's also about making ourselves feel stronger as we try to make sense of the world and connect to culture and community. My kids are made stronger by spending time weeding and planting in the farms, or cleaning beaches and fishponds.

You definitely sound as if you have healed from your earlier wounds. What would you say were your coming-of-age or aha moments?

Not many people know this, but I did experience a period of depression when I was younger in my last years of high school and my first years of college. I had just left Indonesia to come to Hawaiʻi, where I went to Punahou. There was a lot going on then. My first high school romance ended and my mother was traveling a lot. My father died, and I had a delayed reaction to his death. I didn't necessarily have the support I needed from my teachers, and my friends didn't really know what I was going through.

This period of depression lasted for about four years and made it very hard for me to succeed in school and other endeavors. I ended up doing a lot of self-destructive things during this time. I had insomnia and would stay out late and walk alone in empty NYC streets at 4 a.m. I would put myself in precarious situations. I didn't do well in school. An overwhelming sense of sadness descended upon me.

Later, I went back to Indonesia for a year and worked for a travel company as a tour guide, which got me interested in the culture of my birth—Indonesian temples, history, and arts, like gamelan and shadow puppetry. That, I guess, was probably one of my first teaching experiences. These experiences allowed me to translate the beauty of the world and enable others to experience it. It was probably the starting point for my transformation into the much more contented woman that I would become. This was my first aha moment.

After completing my MA at NYU in my mid-twenties, I started teaching at an alternative, public middle school on the Lower East Side of Manhattan. It was very much a community school and set the standard for community engagement and connected learning. It was an imperfect place, and I was an imperfect teacher in those first years, but I cared for my students a great deal, engaged with their families, and worked to extract meaning from the subject matter that my students could use in their daily lives. In spite of coming from beautiful families, communities, and cultures, many of them struggled with the broader realities—with limited options, poverty or violence, bigotry and cruelty, illiteracy or hopelessness. This was another aha moment for me as I began to see the tragedy of an urban education that was too often disconnected and that failed to honor the lived experiences of the children. I became determined to teach in a way that was student-centered and that built bridges between school and community so that teaching and learning could feel truly meaningful.

Do you think you are a product of your multiethnic heritage, international worldview, and global perspective?

Yes. My mother gave me the gift of travel when I was young. We lived in Indonesia and we also spent time in India, Pakistan, and Bangladesh. We traveled to Singapore several times a year for mom to get her visa and we also traveled extensively through Asia, especially Thailand. I have also been to Egypt, Morocco, the Caribbean, and Europe. We took trips with my grandparents through Belgium, Germany, Lichtenstein, Greece, and Turkey.

My brother took me to Italy, France, England, and Scotland. That noted, I still think there are huge swaths of the world that are unknown to me. To date, I've never been to South America and I've never been below the Sahara desert. Last summer, I went, for the first time, to Kenya, Tanzania, and South Africa to commemorate Nelson Mandela's 100th birthday.

Even with the places we did not visit, we were given a robust, multifaceted education through books, music, philosophy, theology, and poetry. Mom was really adamant that we explore other cultures fully. That was the curious anthropologist in her. We explored and had a sense of belonging and connection to places we had never been. We weren't so arrogant as to assume we knew places in which we had never lived, except in a superficial way, but there was certainly this sense of expansiveness in our exploration of the world.

It certainly sounds as if your mother left your brother and you an indelible sense of curiosity, empathy, and humility.

Yes, she did but she died way too young. She wasn't ready. She had a great sense of curiosity and desire to see more of the world, experience more in life, and to give back more. She really wanted to be a grandmother and she didn't get to see any of her four granddaughters. That is profoundly sad to me. My mother would have loved so much to bear witness to her incredible granddaughters' lives, the opportunities she enabled through her work advocating for women, and her son becoming president.

You know, I have to remember to take better care of myself because I don't always, to be honest. Finding a way to prioritize oneself is difficult. I am in this place in my life where I try to focus on teaching and nourishing others, as well as being a mother. Self-care can be a challenge and I know it's not one that is unique to me. I am sure, most women, whether they are parents or not, want to be and do too many things—to embrace the bounty and complexity of womanhood—so self-care is essential to prevent burnout and illness. I'm still working on it.

I don't want to limit anyone in their ambitions, but it is hard in this day and age to not be burdened with career expectations. Add mothering and homemaking, and being a woman is athletically demanding. There are women who do it exceedingly well, but I am not one. I make small bits of progress. I try to eat healthfully, though I still eat too abundantly *(laughter)*, and find opportunities to meditate. I am not an anxious person, in general, and do feel very peaceful, which is helpful, but I am just too busy.

The logistics of my life are complex. I exercise only once or twice a week. But, reflecting on the early demise of my parents and what my mother missed, offers a constant reminder for me to be a good role model of health for my own girls and those whom we teach and mentor. There is so much illness and disease in our world that is tied to our diets, lifestyle choices, urban stress, and the seemingly insurmountable weight of the present moment. I think, therefore, we as feminists of today, need to strategize thoughtfully.

Has it always been just your brother and you? Even the years when you were both apart?

Yeah. The three of us—mom, my brother, and I lived just down the street from when I was three to six. Thereafter, in 1976, mom took me to Indonesia, but my brother remained here in Hawai'i with my grandparents where he spent his high school years. Granted, those were important years, but it wasn't like he spent his whole childhood apart from her. I think, had she had been able to do it all over again, she would not have allowed the separation to happen. My brother really did need her, though he often says that he did not feel the sting of that separation so much because she was so good at expressing her love for him. I know she felt some regret herself just being away from him.

My brother met his father once, and he wrote the book *Dreams From My Father* to explore the hollow spaces made by his father's absence. He has said, though, that it was really our mom who made him who he is. He was understandably preoccupied with the image, visage, and mystery of his father, and pursued greater understanding there, but when he won the Nobel Peace Prize, he said that everything that was good and kind about him was from mom, and he reiterated this again during a David Letterman interview.

Do you think a woman can have it all—to have dreams, aspirations, a career, a happy marriage, and children? Or, perhaps, perfection is overrated and that the best is to be the best version of us?

Yeah, I think that's a very astute statement. I think it is not impossible to have it all, but it is difficult. I haven't met many perfect people. I think "pretty great" is close enough, and mom was that, but she struggled with her health and got very overweight. She wasn't always able to have this pioneering career in microfinance and protect us from the destabilizing effects of movement, distance, and travel. She was not always able to protect us from harm, insult, or injury, whether physical, verbal, or psychic, but she tried. I think she did her best.

And so, while it is important to think about these incredible women as inspiring leaders, I think it is also important that we do not ask them to be perfect. Mom was not perfect. She was incredible, but she was also imperfect. There is so much power and beauty in seeing a woman who strives and ultimately succeeds in building a connected life that matters to not only those who are near but also in others. My mother was certainly all of those things. When we went back to Indonesia, people remembered her giving them their first loan. They are so grateful to her and her impact on their lives.

What are your thoughts now that you're a mom? What are your biggest challenges?

Yes. I am a mother of two and parenting has been quite extraordinary for me. I have a number of friends who have chosen not to be parents and not everyone needs to be a parent. That being said, I have to say it has been a remarkable journey for me. I didn't know that it would be such a transformative experience. I was always interested in kids but I was always more interested in the creative volatility of teenagers. I was not the sort who was very interested in babies.

But when my first child, Suhaila, was born thirteen and a half years ago, I instantly fell in love. I had been sold an incomplete picture, as no one told me about the fear that comes with the love of a parent, yet I also really understood the selfless love that people talk about—it was a very different love from what I had experienced before. I felt for the first time that sense of full certainty that I would run in front of a bus to protect this child. It was so absolute and clear.

Both my children, Savita and Suhaila, have given me great gifts. They both fill me with an overwhelming sense of gratitude and tenderness, but they've also taught me different things about myself as they are such different people. Suhaila is my calm water, and with her birth, I could feel the development of that part of my identity as a mother. Things that used to matter to me didn't and that was surprising. I saw how my priorities shifted.

Later, we adopted Savita from China and she was challenging in the early years, but became perhaps my life's greatest teacher. She tested my patience and endurance in helping her to get to where she is today—a happy, charming, lovely ten year old. Savita definitely helped me understand the depths of the human heart and the immense courage of which we are capable. If I look at her too long, sometimes I start crying because I know how far she has come and how strong she has become. I am so very proud of her.

Has your life changed since your brother became president?

Yes and no. Before I was the president's sister, I had a PhD, I was a teacher, and I worked in the communities in the same way as I am now. I was also wife and daughter, so nothing there really changed. It also helped that my brother protected and allowed me to establish a certain distance from his political life. He urged me to find a way to remain in Hawaiʻi because he knew that that was what I wanted.

In fact, my husband was in D.C. for a long time for his work and, even then, I was never attracted to life in D.C. I was never attracted to politics or politicians, preferring to lead from below, beside, behind, or through grassroots and educational means. I wanted to impact policy but I was never interested in governance or political leadership, so these choices kept my life from changing too much. That, and the fact that Barack and Michelle were so consistently themselves throughout the process of his presidency. While some things became harder, they still made it a point to come back here every year for Christmas for nearly two decades, for instance. The ways we interact and engage are the same, so I forgot that they were the First Family.

There are some smaller ways that I have changed. I worried at the start that there would be a lot of pressure on my brother and his family. I worried about their safety and happiness. I have also become a better public speaker from campaigning for him. I had always been a teacher and assumed I was a capable public speaker until I did a couple of events. I recall a speech I planned with talking points for a big Bishop Museum event, and I was just awful. I wish I could tell you that I handled it gracefully, but it was a train wreck. I forgot things and was clearly so nervous. That incident made me realize that I should stop having talking points or memorizing my speech and, instead, focus on telling stories that other people can't tell.

Today, I find it very easy to go out to the community and share the story of the work that we do. It is also no longer unpleasant to do the morning TV shows, as I have become more comfortable with being a community leader and public person, whereas before I was just teaching within the four walls.

That being said, I'm still me. I get excited about bringing a bunch of kids out or getting asked to participate in a community roof-thatching activity, as that is how I still prefer to live. I would never in a million years run for office, as it is just not in my nature.

What areas of advocacy and activism are most needed now?

I think in our globalized era, we need to be building more connections and reduce divisiveness. We need to practice nonviolent communication and learn negotiation, facilitation, and mediation skills. We should also find a way to build grassroots movements, diplomacy, and participatory leadership. We need to empower active youths to get them to be engaged civically and vote. I think we need to work on women's and civil rights and social justice, and we need to do that in a very deliberate way and develop skills and tools that can be used in professional spaces as well. We also need more intercultural exchange and international communication.

This is a powerful time to endeavor to do all of these things as we have access to one another and can connect and collaborate using technological tools like social media, podcasts, vlogging, blogging, distance learning, YouTube, and self-publication.

> What would you do if someone, or a leader of an organization, continues to be confrontational? What would be your best advice?

Let's say we have leadership that is, in my view, contentious, misguided, confrontational, and exacerbates violence—first, let me just say that I think protest is really important and we need to protest that leadership, though protest is not typically my personal modus operandi as I don't really believe on focusing on the bully. I would rather turn my attention to what is called positive peace—what is it that each of us can do? What can we do to raise the tone, texture, and relationship between us? We need to think about other ways we can choose to participate, be it as an up stander, educator, mentor, activist, or artist.

We can offer solace to those in need, give compassion, develop a caring community, and inspire others to live well. We need to see how we can work together to prevent the negative decisions of certain leaders from ever becoming solidified. In other words, if certain leadership isn't working very well, say, on environmental issues, then we need to see what we can do as a citizen activist to work toward alleviating the negative impacts both in our own homes, communities, schools, and public spaces, and find innovation to address these issues.

If environment is not the priority of the current administration, let's engage innovators, activists, artists, educators, scientists, and engineers, as well as people who are going to push policy and protect the environment. We need to get folks together to collaborate and forge consensus on a few priorities that are actionable that will allow us to move the needle forward. We need to neither feel silent or discouraged, but rather ignite our own capacities.

> You spent half your life growing up in Asia and the latter half in the Mainland and also Hawai'i. How and who do you identify with?

I feel sort of like I identify with all those places and I can't really choose. I would say that Indonesia has captured a lot of my heart. But I don't think I can live there anymore, even as I feel a lot of gratitude for it. My childhood cultures and communities in Indonesia helped to raise me and make me who I am, but today I feel very American.

> What does feeling American mean?

For me, that means the presence of a lot of choice in terms of how I name myself and how I walk the world. It means a strong sense of irreverence, as there is not a lot of cultural hierarchy in America. I find America, on the whole, is a lot more informal and I like that. New York, for example, where I lived for nine years of my life, is so irreverent

When I go back to Indonesia, I find myself thinking about protocols and whether I have the right to do something or speak to someone. I find myself bowing a lot and I'm hyperaware of whether my head is above someone else's and am sensitive to my tone and am mindful of being deferential or reverential.

In contrast, I find American culture to be a lot more liberating and I can lose sight of all of that. Having said that, Hawaiʻi is different, as it has quite a bit of that Asian value but it is my forever home, even if I don't live here forever. I think I will live here always and by that, I mean, even if I move to the continent to be closer to my kids when they go to college, I know I will want to keep a home here on the island. I want to retire and die here.

When I was younger, I remember mom asking me to reconnect with my Indonesian side. She reminded me that I had access to this part of the world that she was never going to be fully able to access. She wanted me to engage more with Indonesia, but I was more interested in the Spanish language and Latino culture and emphasized the fact I looked Latina. (*laughter*) It was not till much later that I realized the impact and importance of Indonesia on my cultural identity and sense of self.

Maybe, my daughters, too, will need to journey far before they come to embrace their Asian roots. But that, too, is a quintessentially American immigrant journey. I have no doubt the many gifts of culture and heritage will, in their own time, shape them into being more magnificent and thoughtful people.

You've been here now for twenty years. What changes have you seen?

Yes. I spent four years here in high school and then I came back in my early twenties for three years. I have now been here, in total, for almost twenty-five years, which is more than half my life. I've seen a lot of changes and I think one of the significant changes is how schools, both public and independent, have begun to acknowledge and honor Hawaiian culture. It has also started to think and take advantage of its weather and global positioning, by really embracing alternative energy and disaster preparedness. The art scene has also gotten really interesting. There is more urban planning, community organization, and citizen activism that I didn't really see before.

Hawaiʻi has some of the beautiful, messy cacophony of Southeast Asia. In the early years, my connection to Hawaiʻi was very loose and superficial.

It was not until recent years that I started to get to know the communities through my work with the schools. I have developed a stronger bond with the host culture and am now trying to study the Hawaiian language and honor the beautiful dimensions of Hawaiian culture. This has given me a much deeper, richer connection to Hawaiʻi and, now, I see Hawaiʻi as the place I feel most deeply connected to and it is where I want to raise my daughters.

Much as I loved New York, it's a hard place with a lot of jagged edges which Hawaiʻi doesn't have. Hawaiʻi is not only really beautiful, it is also a bridge between Asia and the continent, and it is ultimately just a deeply loving place.

Children and youth are now approaching a space with more reverence and I see them asking permission for entry and understanding protocol, which contrasts with the general attitude and expectations twenty or thirty years ago when I was in high school. I am so grateful to Hawaiʻi for accepting me and allowing me to raise my family here. I have learned now that I have to step back to ask Hawaiʻi what she wants of me and how I can be of service to her and not engage without asking for permission first. I feel like I belong to Hawaiʻi now, but don't know that it can belong to me.

What changes would you like to see in Hawaiʻi?

I would like for the organizations and individuals that are cultivating our community to heal, foster resilience and awareness, and improve education. I would like for the schools, especially public schools, to feel empowered to allow young people to do more culturally sensitive learning and purposeful play.

I would like to see our public schools becoming vibrant with many interesting programs and empowering initiatives in urban and public spaces, where people from multiple worlds get together to find a shared voice and purpose.

I would love to see some interesting leaders emerge with innovative practices that have traction. I would like us to make better use of alternative energy and improve our recycling. In general, the things I would like to see all amplify a deep cultural awareness and community engagement. I see new solutions for building resilient and viable neighborhoods that are sustainable, healthy, and peaceful.

Now for some trivia. I hear you are philosophically Buddhist. What does that mean and what gets your goat?

I practice mindfulness and try to live up to the Buddhist philosophy of nonviolence. I believe in trying to reduce suffering in myself and in the world and try not be too attached to particular outcomes. I have also learned to set my ego aside when I feel embarrassed or slighted in the things I don't get.

Having said that, my husband and daughters probably have the ability to get me agitated more than most. I say to my husband, "This is a compliment, as this means I clearly have high expectations of you, and I don't expect as much from the rest of the world." (*laughter*) With the rest of the world, I'm pretty calm and it takes a lot more for my tempers to flare.

You have traveled extensively. Which country or culture do you delight in most?

All of them. I especially love hybrid spaces like Mexico or Morocco, where multiple cultures collide, but I think that each of the places I've been have offered something special and powerful!

Who would you like to have a sit-down dinner with?

I'm still a really a huge fan of Gandhi and [Martin Luther] King Jr. Yes, there are some questions raised about Gandhi's laying with young women to test his celibacy. King wasn't the perfect husband either.

Still, I admire their everyday practice and commitment to equity, peace, and community building. I also admire their ability to overcome challenging situations by winning over hearts and minds without violence. I admire deeply their ability to get others to surrender their oppressive intents. They were willing to sacrifice everything for truth and justice.

Now that I am a mother, I really want to survive to watch my children grow. So the idea of people being willing to risk their lives for a cause is really extraordinary to me.

What would you say you met God?

That is a tough one. I think I would just listen. I'd be curious to see what God has to say. I'd probably ask him or her why there is so much suffering in this beautiful world or ask about the rationale for some creatures, like the mosquito. "Why mosquitoes, God?" I'll say. "Please explain, God." (*laughter*)

: **I love that! What's your life philosophy on a bumper sticker?**

Cuci Mata in Bahasa Indonesia, which literally means "wash eyes." This implores us to clear our visions and try to see things from different perspectives, as well as to always see the potential of a moment.

: **I know you are writing a memoir. The title is or would be …**

I have no idea yet, though I have written an outline under the encouragement of my agent. But I just wrote a young adult novel called *Yellowwood*, which contains peace and conflict themes, and the protagonist is called Savita, since the lead character in my earlier picture book was named after my other daughter, Suhaila.

The memoir will be based on my experiences of womanhood, family, and all the complex facets of living as a woman. I guess you can call it an impact memoir. It's not meant to be a reflection of my entire life, nor will it be about my brother, though I may mention Michelle and my brother's efforts in the administration to improve the lives of women. Mostly, it will be about what it means to be a mother, daughter, sister, teacher, and a woman. I hope people won't be too disappointed, as they may be more interested in my brother instead of me!

: **Finally, how would you like to be remembered?**

Without being too corny, I would like to be remembered as a loving person. Love is a very strong word and concept. It is not always easy and it is frequently messy. The definition of love, for me, extends to our community, environment, ourselves, our family, and the entire world.

THE JUST DEFENDER
Crystal K. Rose

I tell women to have their own personal business plan. Businesses have it, and so should they. There must be a strategic plan and tactical plan. Ask yourself, "Where do you see yourself in three years? What skill sets do you need to get there? How are you going to accomplish that and move that needle?" Don't allow your career to happen to you, but chart your course and be in charge.

Crystal Rose is one of the founding members of Bays Lung Rose Holma, and one of Hawai'i's most accomplished and creative business litigation attorneys. Her cases over the past two decades have helped shape the face of Hawai'i business, transforming the state's largest private landowner and the state's banking industry.

Crystal's diverse practice includes counseling clients and litigating disputes involving real estate, construction, trusts, and commercial transactions, and she is well-versed in corporate governance and related legal and compliance issues. She has served on the board of directors of Central Pacific Bank, Hawaiian Airlines, Hawaiian Electric Company, and the Gentry Companies. She also has served as a commissioner to the State of Hawai'i Department of Hawaiian Homelands.

Despite her hectic work schedule, Crystal believes in giving back and is active in the community. Her community service includes serving as a trustee of the The Nature Conservancy; a board member of the Blue Planet Foundation and Child & Family Services; a member of the board of advisors to the chief executive of Kamehameha Schools; a member of the board of Assets School, Catholic Charities Hawai'i, and Boys & Girls Club of Hawai'i; as well as a member of the circuit court civil rules committee for the First Circuit Court of Hawai'i, and a hearing committee member of the disciplinary board of the Hawai'i Supreme Court.

Previously, Crystal served as the secretary and treasurer of the Native Hawaiian Chamber of Commerce; and was a member of the State of Hawai'i Board of Engineers, Architects, Surveyors and Landscape Architects. She has also published extensively, and is a graduate of the Hastings College of Law, University of California. Her sense of justice, doing what is right, and serving the community emanates from our conversation held in her well-appointed office overlooking the Aloha Tower. Her razor sharp, succinct responses never skip a beat—even as she multitasks during our interview to clean the spilled coffee in her tote bag!

Share with us your humble beginnings on the Big Island.

I was born and raised on the Big Island. My family has been there for multiple generations. My father retired as a captain in the police department and my mother did administrative, secretarial work. When I was eleven, my parents sent me to Kamehameha Schools. That was when I came to O'ahu as a boarder and lived there from seventh grade till I graduated in 1975. It was a very transformative experience for me, especially when you are that young. I lived in the dorm and my roommates are like my sisters till today, even after fifty years. I, then, went to college on the Mainland and, later, to law school in San Francisco.

After graduating from law school in 1982, I came back and worked for what is now known as Carlsmith Ball, one of the larger law firms here. I worked there for a little over three years and, in 1986, eight of us left to form what is now Bays Lung Rose Holma and we've been in business for thirty-three years. I was twenty eight when I left Carlsmith Ball to form this firm, so I was probably too young to appreciate the risks involved, though I am very happy with what we've done. I got married in 1986, the same year I started the law firm and, subsequently, had two sons, who are twenty-seven and thirty today.

What made you decide to start a career in law?

I think it had to do with my father who was in the police department. I have a longstanding family history of law enforcers, so I always had a sense of justice and doing the right thing. I also wanted to help people, so it was a logical progression.

During my summer experiences in law school, I learned that I didn't want to do criminal law and ended up doing civil law through process of elimination.

How was it for you in law school then?

Hastings was very progressive. We must have one of the first law classes to have a 50:50 ratio men and woman. Of course, this was San Francisco and not the case when I returned to Hawaiʻi.

Our law school had 1,500 students with about five-hundred students in class. It was part of the University of California system but it's not associated with any undergraduate campus, so this law school was standalone in the Tenderloin district, which was pretty rough back then. We stepped over all kinds of things going to school, but it is gentrified now.

How was it leaving progressive Hastings in San Francisco and returning to Hawaiʻi?

The law scene in Hawaiʻi was pretty male-dominated. There were women at Carlsmith, and we had just had our first female partner, which was a big deal. By 1980, women were allowed, for the first time, to be members of various country clubs. But it was still a different culture then and very male-dominated. People drank and lunched, and the dining halls would be filled with smoke, so a woman would have to find her own way and make it work.

What are some of the things that you had to do in trying to "find your way?"

I remember thinking that I can never be the one serving the coffee, as everyone would think I was the assistant because I was young and female. Today, I would offer anybody a coffee.

How has the climate changed in Hawaiʻi over the years?

Today, having women in the boardroom and courtroom is second nature. No one thinks it's odd to have a woman attorney. When I first started practicing, I would be the only female in a room. Today, you will find women on both sides all the time.

Do you see a rise of latent misogyny starting with the Hilary-Trump election season?

I felt it but I just I dealt with it and worked around like it. That said, there are things that are considered inappropriate today. Back then, everyone had more bad behavior. The #MeToo movement has brought to the forefront what would essentially have been unacceptable behavior.

Did you have any personal #MeToo encounters?

Nothing that affected me personally, but I have witnessed things that I don't think would happen today, such as men touching or picking up on professional women in a work setting.

The current legal system is fraught with inequities toward women. What are some of the imminent inequities that you hope to change or see changed in your lifetime?

It is hard for me to see how women work really hard for that degree, then work hard to practice law, and then give it up for the family, as they can't manage all aspects of family life. It's not expected of men to do that.

Today, women have choices and they're not forced to stay home, which is great. I honor all women and their choices but I can't help but feel a little sad to see them forego their law career for the family.

You had the support of your husband and family?

Yes, definitely.

I would say to women that there's not one right way and to find that balance. In fact, there's no such thing as balance. Sometimes, you are pulled in one direction or another, so it is important to constantly strive to make it as best you can. There is more than one way to peel an onion.

Sometimes, I had my mother or my husband, and sometimes, I paid help. Whatever it is that you need, don't be afraid to get it. No one else can decide for you. If you need live-in help, get it. If you need someone to come clean your house, do it.

There was a time when women judges were being criticized for having paid under-the-table for somebody to take care of their kids or clean their house. I think nowadays you can do it above board and no one thinks it is a huge cause for concern.

I am aware you do civil law, but what are your thoughts on the statistics that one-in-three women are incarcerated in the United States and that many of them are driven to crime by mental health issues, substance abuse, sexual and physical abuse?

I can say that these issues of sexual and physical abuse all stem from an issue of power. It is not about sex. It's about men having power.

What have been some of your most difficult cases?

My toughest cases have been those that fundamentally challenge the organization's mission or its purpose. I'll give you an example. I was one of the lawyers that represented the Kamehameha Schools. I've had two major cases for them. Once, I represented one of the trustees in a broken trust issue. If we didn't prevail, the school would not be in the position it is in today. We had to go in and get the school to establish a CEO management system and ignite a whole transformation of the organization. People put their life on the line for this. Teachers had to testify and, if they lost, they would lose their jobs. These are tough cases, as you are fighting for the essence of the organization.

I, then, represented Kamehameha Schools again on their admissions policy. They give preference to Native Hawaiians and that was challenged as being racially discriminatory. As they were a private institution, we fought all the way up to the Ninth Circuit. Supporting the Native Hawaiians was the founder's intention, so we felt we had to do what it takes to win. It is not just about the money, but that this organization plays an important place, has a legacy, and specific commitments we had to honor and fight for.

Have there been cases where your core has been challenged?

Yes. And they're so unpleasant for me personally. I now have my own moral compass, and because I am at the point in my career where I can pick and choose, one of my criteria is that my values are aligned with my client. So, as much as they are interviewing me, I am also interviewing them to see if our views and values are aligned. When that happens, I can become more than just a hired lawyer but a counselor and adviser. I don't like to be hired gun.

What used to happen when you were a hired gun?

I would take a deep breath and work through it. When the client and I are not aligned, we are in constant arguments. I will suggest this course of action, and they want to do something different or they have a different thought process. Sometimes, it's not always honest and, instead, it's conduct that I call revisionary history, where they give a different account of what really happened.

Thankfully, we have a paper trail today and we are able to piece together a chronology and show them what was said and what is going to get presented. They can argue that they didn't say this back then, but we have documentation and we tell them that it is always best to be truthful.

So for those hard cases, I manage it the best I can, but they're not happy experiences, which is why about twenty years ago, I started to pick and choose my cases. In my first decade, I took on everything and represented everyone, but now, I won't do it if it's not worth my time as I just want to be happy.

What would you say has been the most consequential piece of legislation that's been passed for women?

Title IX.

If you could change any law, what would it be?

I don't come up against that in civil law but I would like to see that it is somehow easier for women to advance in business.

A Derridean conundrum. What came first? The crime or the law?

As a society, we need rules to live by. So that becomes the law, whether it's documented or not. Even within a family, we have rules and consequences when things aren't done appropriately, so you may send your children to timeout because they broke the rules, right?

So I think to answer your question, the law comes first, because, as a society, we have to establish rules that we can agree on.

A proposed end to sex trafficking bill was recently put forth by the Hawai'i State Commission and gained a lot of controversy. What are your thoughts?

I truly think we need to work hard to stop sex trafficking. It's very prominent in Hawai'i and just horrific what happens to these girls.

The Trump presidency has doubled down on reproductive rights for women. What are your thoughts on that?

I am obviously not a Trump supporter. What he's done for women is to, on the one hand, create open debate, and, on the other, create tragic consequences for women from the way legislation and rulings are coming out of these conservative judges.

Your thoughts on legalizing marijuana in this state?

It should be legal and we should tax it.

How do you cope with all the responsibilities and directorships you hold?

Once I make a commitment, I take them very seriously. I would not do anything I don't think I can do 100 percent. So I won't say that I cope, but that I manage.

As for my directorships, I work my calendar carefully and make our meeting days a priority. The calendar usually plans ahead for two to three years, so those days that we meet are sacred, and I work around them and don't schedule other meetings on those days.

Again, I maintain life is never perfect. There are times I am off-the-charts busy and, other times, I can pick up the slack and manage.

How do we get more women on boards?

It starts with getting them engaged. These days, boards like diversity, and studies show that having women on boards increases productivity and profits. Women bring along different mindsets and perspectives which are helpful.

This also depends on individual boards, which do a self-assessment to see what the board needs. There is always a need for a financial adviser, as the board will have to face an audit committee, so the financial advisor has to be able to meet the qualifications of an audit committee.

Increasingly, most boards need an IT or technology advisor, who understands cybersecurity, as these are high risks for a company. Boards also need to ensure they reflect the shareholders, the customer base, and the goals of the company, so I think women need to get involved beyond nonprofit boards so that they can then be qualified to sit on larger boards as and when needed.

What are some of the biggest obstacles in your career?

In the early days, it was my own lack of confidence and my willingness to say, "I can do it." I don't want to say it's the fear of failure but I lacked the ability to feel as good as anyone else in the room. I acquired that, but it took time.

What were some of your biggest failures?

I lost a case that cost my client and his business a lot of money and I still think about it. I learn from my mistakes and failures and don't learn from my wins.

What did you learn from that incident?

I was working as a partner on that case and had an instinct that we weren't doing it right but I did not speak up. I have now learned that I have to trust that instinct in me.

How do you deal with criticism?

I take criticism pretty well, as I know my strengths and weaknesses. I think, as women, we all carry a little bit of insecurity around us and that's a good thing, as it makes us self-aware. I also listen and don't react right away.

What have you learned about leadership over the years?

That it is important to engage and make sure that a decision you're making involves getting as much input and impact from people. If people feel heard, then they can understand the decision, even if they don't like it.

I also think leadership is making tough decisions and having the courage to make it. If it is an easy decision, then it is not leadership.

Leadership also entails listening because somebody screaming at you may be telling you something important and you need to know how to filter away the noise.

Do you think leadership is nature or nurture?

Both, and I think a lot of it starts from family.

As I came from a very humble upbringing, I also learned resilience and drive, which is not taught but acquired. I definitely gained grit, as I wanted to make sure I provided for my children a better life than I had.

What advice would you give to an aspiring legal eagle like you?

I tell women to have their own personal business plan. Businesses have it, and so should they. There must be a strategic plan and tactical plan. Ask yourself, "Where do you see yourself in three years? What skill sets do you need to get there? How are you going to accomplish that and move that needle?" Don't allow your career to happen to you, but chart your course and be in charge.

What sacrifices have you made to be where you are today?

Nothing I regret, except my house and closets are not as clean they need to be. (*laughter*) Marie Kondo!

As an attorney and a woman, what were your thoughts watching the Kavanaugh-Blasey Ford hearing?

I was disgusted. The thought that our senate men could support him was just disgusting. I obviously believed her and don't think she made it up. I think their personal attacks on her are just unbelievable and un-American. As a lawyer, the Supreme Court is probably the most important job we have.

What are your thoughts on the current state of the Supreme Court?

I hope Ruth Bader Ginsburg hangs on as long as she can. The real tragedy is that the administration was able to hold up appointments below the Supreme Court, and they're running them through pretty quickly now. The number of federal and appellate judges that, for lack of a better word, have different ideology is pretty substantial. That's very scary.

Let's change tracks and chat on motherhood. Did it change you?

Yes of course. I don't think I ever understood unconditional love until I had a child.

I also had a deeper appreciation for my parents because I know their love for me transcends into their love for my sons and then into love for their grandchildren. I want to say I understood this before I became a mother but I only truly understood unconditional love when I became a mom.

What can we expect from you in the near future?

That I will always work hard and always try to do the right thing. I am also working toward giving back more in the community because I now have the time.

Do you think women can have it all?

Yes.

What are some of your fondest memories of Hawaiʻi?

Growing up and playing in the California grass in the ditches. I wasn't a girly girl. Now, we have twenty-three acres of land where I live, and I call it a farm as we have dogs and cats.

I'm not a city girl. I'm a country girl who can be in the city in thirty minutes. *(laughter)*

In your opinion, how has Hawai'i changed over the years?

There's a lot of people now. The explosion of people and increase in population has taxing demands on the environment and land resources, which is very significant. I hope that we can protect our environment and our neighbor islands.

What are some changes in the local legal system that you would like to see?

More women judges, as we're still not at 50 percent at the circuit level.

What can we do to make that happen?

The court, the judicial system, governor, and the judiciary are working very hard to do that. There are, right now, six openings, so we do have an opportunity to enhance that.

We should always be picking the best candidate, but if there is an opportunity to appoint a woman who is qualified and up to par, they should.

What are your hopes and aspirations for Hawai'i?

I hope that we can continue to find the balance between our economy, our resources, and the beauty of the islands, so everyone can have a good life.

What do you do to relax?

I enjoy crafts. I sew, cook, and bake. I enjoy these things.

What pisses you off?

Injustice.

What is your guilty pleasure?

A glass of wine. *(laughter)*

- Who would you like to have a sit-down with?

    My late maternal-grandmother.

- Who are your role models?

    My dad and my late maternal-grandmother, who lived to 100.

- What would you say when you meet God?

    Thank you.

- Ruth Bader Ginsburg is …

    A hero.

- Trump is …

    Not somebody I want to think about.

- Who gets your vote for 2020?

    A moderate Democrat, who can pull away the Republicans that don't support Trump.

- Your life philosophy on a bumper sticker …

    Be a giver.

- If you're writing a memoir, the title would be …

    She Managed Well.

- How do you want to be remembered?

    As someone who gave back, both in practice and to the community.

THE RENAISSANCE WOMAN

Ligaya Stice

I feel so gratified being able to mentor these young women in their formative years. Many of them are so caught up in a buzz— doing things to please their parents or live up to societal pressure that they fail to pause to listen to their heart and find out just what makes them tick. I identify with them. I took a while to find my own voice and know that what they are doing is a recipe for disaster, so I wish to empower them toward living their dreams and their own passions.

Ligaya Stice is a practicing pediatric anesthesiologist at the Kapiʻolani Medical Center for Women and Children and an assistant clinical Professor in the Department of Surgery at the University of Hawaiʻi John A. Burns School of Medicine. A proud graduate of Castle High School and UH Mānoa, she attended medical school at Boston University, and completed post-graduate training at Cornell University and The Children's Hospital in Denver, CO. A former Miss Hawaiʻi, Miss Oʻahu and Miss Hawaiʻi Filipina, she has extensive training in jazz and ballet and was also a professional cheerleader for the New England Patriots. Ligaya is the executive director and one of the founding members of I'm A Bright Kid Foundation. She has also served on the boards of the Honolulu Theatre for Youth, the Hawaiʻi Theatre Center and the Distinguished Young Women of Hawaiʻi Scholarship Program.

You are very much the multi-hyphenate. You are not just a doctor, but a yoga teacher, thespian, active fund-raiser, and youth mentor, amongst others. Share with us more about who you are and what you do.

Yes, I guess you can call me a multi-hyphenate, as I do find defining myself a rather difficult task. Labels are futile as, first and foremost, I do feel that we as human beings are so much more than just our occupations. Secondly, if we do find ourselves in a stressful job, that it is so important to find that mind-body balance and to indulge in activities that are relaxing and joyful, which probably explains my interest in gymnastics, dancing, acting, and yoga.

Share with us about your family background.

My father moved here from California to study at the University of Hawaiʻl, but my mother was born here. Her family left the Philippines for Lānaʻi to work in the plantations during the 1940s.[1] My maternal-grandfather first came on his own and worked in the sugar mills in Kahuku. He later moved to Maui to work in the plantations there, before finally moving to Lānaʻi, where

---

[1] Poor economic conditions and a string of natural disasters in the Philippines motivated workers to migrate to Hawaiʻi. The first wave of immigrants were mostly Ilocano from the northern regions of Luzon, while the rest were Visayan and Tagalog from the central islands of Cebu, Leyte, Siquijor and southern Luzon. Many Filipinos were sold on a glamorized version of plantation life, but the reality was harsh ten-hour days in sugarcane fields or twelve-hour days in the mill for six days a week. In 1934, immigration from the Philippines was limited to fifty persons per year, but in 1946, a new recruitment drive brought seven-thousand workers to Hawaiʻl, including Ligaya's maternal-grandfather.

my mother and her sisters were raised. My mother was definitely the first in her generation to go to college.

What is interesting about living on Lānaʻi was that there was a close-knitted Filipino community, and as a result, my grandparents never found a need to learn or speak English, and spoke only in Ilocano, a dialect from the north. They also always thought they would return to the Philippines, but once their daughters got married and the grandchildren came, they knew Hawaiʻi was going to be home, even though that was never the intention.

I was born and raised in Kāneʻohe on the Windward Side. I recall growing up in the 1970s in Kāneʻohe and it was a very quiet town then. It is very different now, but I still find a great amount of comfort being there. When I first returned to Hawaiʻi, I lived in town but I couldn't get used to it, so I knew I had to return to the lush, green, quiet side of the Oʻahu.

I left the islands after graduating from UH Mānoa and went to read medicine at Boston University, and later completed my residency in anesthesiology at Cornell Medical Center. I went for additional specialty training at Denver Children's Hospital and met my husband there. I returned home to Hawaiʻi a decade ago, but am now orchestrating my move to Colorado, where my husband's family is based. The ideal is was for us to shuttle between Hawaiʻi during the summer and Colorado over the winter. I know most people do it in the reverse, but we love the snow, and I am very involved with the I'm a Bright Kid Foundation, which is very busy over the summer.

> **You are very accomplished. Do you think your humble beginnings instilled in you a sense of strive and laid the foundations for your strong sense of work ethics? How did the beauty pageantry come into play?**

Yes, that is certainly part of it. My parents were very driven and it is not an understatement to say that they had high expectations of me.

As for the beauty pageant how came into picture, you must first have an understanding of pageants here in Hawaiʻi. It is less seen as a beauty pageant, but more of a celebration of diversity as the island has many ethnicities. These ethnic pageants, such as the Narcissus Queen, the Cherry Blossom Festival Queen, Miss Oʻahu Filipina and Miss Latina Hawaiʻi, stem more from a need for ethnic communities to perpetuate their culture, stay connected to their roots, and yet demonstrate their Americanism. First generation immigrants tend to want to assimilate into the migrant culture, whereas second generation immigrants, like me, feel quite removed from our ethnic roots. I did not grow up speaking Ilocano or eating Filipino food. So you can say that I was driven by my need to know my own roots and culture, as I was so alienated from that, except during family gatherings.

My pageant years also coincided with that age where one is seeking for an identity, so it seemed like a good fit. Besides, I was very interested in performing, and these ethnic pageants functioned as a bridge to suture our American citizenry and our ethnic histories, while giving us the platform to get involved in modeling and become a spokesperson for various causes—all of which interested me greatly as a young person. It also helps that these pageants come with a scholarship component as well.

Anyway, I took part and won the Miss Oʻahu Filipina, then Miss Hawaiʻi immediately after I graduated from UH. I honestly had no idea or vision what the future holds, but all I could think about was that I won and I now have a job! I later went on to represent the state in the Miss America pageant in Atlantic City.

> You seem to be a Renaissance woman—well versed in both the arts and the science. Have you always been that way?

I have always been good in math and science, and was a chemistry major. But if you look at my transcripts, you could see how I could also have been a theater and dance major, as I would take classes in the performing arts every semester and was even one of the New England Patriots Cheerleaders! I feel fortunate to have studied acting under such wonderful teachers—Ron Bright at Castle High School, and later Terence Knapp and Glenn Cannon at UH—which is part of the reason I run the I'm a Bright Kid Foundation now, as I wish to continue the important, life-changing work that Mr. Bright did.

But my choice to go to med school was not clear at the onset, but came about later as an afterthought while I was an undergraduate. What I thought I was really interested in was research in genetic diseases, which was why I applied to MD PhD programs. But I soon realized that I did not have the personality for it, as it was very lonely and I was better and happier when I got to interact with people.

In fact, I left my work at the lab for a stint in New York, where my sister was based at the time. I took the year off to work way-off Broadway and live the life of a working actor. I pounded the pavement; went to auditions, and boy was it was tough, and I was out of practice! But the practical side of me knew that I needed to get it out of my system. Being successful was not the objective for me as much as it was to try and gain the experience. Suffice to say, I had a wonderful year and was ready to head back to med school. But I enjoyed my time in New York so much that I decided to apply for my residency at Cornell, and spent four more years there!

What brought you back to Hawaiʻi then?

By the time I was done with my fellowship training in pediatric anesthesia at The Children's Hospital in Denver, Colorado, I was already on the Mainland for more than fifteen years. I was in my late thirties and felt that I was ready to come home in 2005. I have to say that I did think about settling in Colorado, even before I met my husband, but I knew that there was a need here for what I was doing. Besides, my sisters, who were all based on the Mainland, also decided to return to Hawaiʻi to raise their kids, so I wanted to be a part of that.

I found my way back into the community very quickly by being part of programs that were deeply meaningful to me, such as the Distinguished Young Women Program.[2] I am the executive vice president and chairperson for the program, where we provide scholarships, and recognize the accomplishments of high school senior girls and provide them with skills to succeed. I feel so gratified being able to mentor these young women in their formative years. Many of them are so caught up in a buzz—doing things to please their parents or live up to societal pressure that they fail to pause to listen to their heart and find out just what makes them tick. I identify with them. I took a while to find my own voice and know that what they are doing is a recipe for disaster, so I wish to empower them toward living their dreams and their own passions. I have met incredible young women and mentors through this work, which gives me so much joy.

This is a perfect segue to ask you what piece of advice would you give to a young person reading this book?

Regardless whether they are in Hawaiʻi or not, I think it is a global phenomenon that many feel that they have been thrust in situations where they don't have a choice, when in reality, I think there is a choice. It saddens me when people make decisions that do not bring them joy. I have certainly made those missteps, such as going into medical school because of societal pressure, though I have learned to embrace it now and genuinely love what I do today.

In fact, it took me a long time to recognize that my job is not my identity and that I do not need to prove or justify anything to anyone. When I decided to pride quality of life over strategic career moves, I have had people tell me

---
2 Formerly known as the Hawaii Junior Miss Program

that my choices were a waste. It is so typical, especially in physician communities for doctors to suffer stress, burnout, and intense pressure in silence. Now that I am fifty, I know that I need only do what makes me truly happy.

So what makes you happy?

Just being quiet and in the outdoors. That is why Colorado is attractive, as there are opportunities for me to break away from routine, stress, and people. It is like being in Hawaiʻi, where I can be in awe of nature, stand at the top of a mountain, and watch the waves. I find joy and beauty in the little things, and the icing on the cake is being able to share the moments with someone you love.

What do you love about Hawaiʻi?

This is home, so what can feel better than home? But what I love about it is that I can live out my life the way I want it. There is instant access to nature—I look out my window and I see the Koʻolau mountains as I sip coffee with my husband. It also gives me access to the people that I love.

What changes have you seen in Hawaiʻi over the years?

Kids don't speak pidgin anymore! The things that immediately pop to the surface are the superficial, palpable things—it has become more crowded, my favorite local hangout is replaced by a Starbucks. But, on a subtle level, what has changed is the sense of community. Our communities are a little more disjointed and less connected than how it was when I was growing up. My cousin, who lives on Lānaʻi, was on a flight to Honolulu and he said that he did not recognize anyone on the plane and this was telling, as back in the day, everyone knew everybody.

When I was a child and my mother needed childcare on Lānaʻi as she was headed to work on island, she could literally take me to the departure gate at Hawaiian Airlines and leave me with literally anybody there to take me to my grandmother, who would be waiting on the other end on Lānaʻi! It is nostalgic, but it was this sense of community that is really hard to find anywhere else.

I also noticed there is more widespread homelessness, and this is certainly not something I saw growing up. It makes me sad when I see people suffer in this beautiful place grappling with homelessness, the lack of opportunity, or education. I know there are no easy solutions, as we are not a homogeneous population that can be fixed with a boiler plate, one-size-fix-all solution.

It is an extremely complex situation that has to do with legislation, housing rules, investment laws, and people are so divided on how best to fix it. It isn't simply about just finding a place to house them, but how we can best bring comfort to them and alleviate it at the source.

: Speaking of comfort, what would you say when you meet God?

I am not religious and do not believe in a deity. I believe that god is love, so the question I might ask would be, how can we bring ourselves closer to the source of love and bring more comfort to those in need.

: How would you like to be remembered?

This is easy, as this goes to the root of my name? Ligaya is Tagalog for joy, so I do aspire to that and I am finally at a point in my life where I can be joyful and not have to find an excuse for that or justify my happiness.

I find a tremendous amount of joy working with the Distinguished Young Women Program and now the I'm a Bright Kids Foundation,[3] because I want to pay it forward and know how joyful that type of work can be. Launching the I'm a Bright Kids foundation has made my whole world pivot, as I know that I am doing something important, meaningful, and above all, it makes me feel at home and happy.

: Finally, what are your hopes and aspirations for Hawai'i?

I would like Hawai'i to be a place where we can all enjoy and appreciate it equally. It has become somewhat divided into two, with one-half living in paradise, while the other is unable keep up with the new pace and standard of living. We seem to have lost the middle class, which is the core of any community and that can be detrimental for any society, not just Hawai'i or the USA. My aspiration for Hawai'i is to see the disparity be evened out, with more opportunities for education, community outreach, individual support that can better enable us to all be part of this wonderful island state I call home.

---

3 Affectionately known as "Mr. B.," Ronald E. Bright has inspired thousands of people with his passion for the arts by continually encouraging his students to reach beyond their capabilities. In 1992, in commemoration of Ron's years of educational excellence at Castle High School, the theater was renamed the Ronald E. Bright Performing Arts Center.

THE KISMET CHEF
Lee Anne Wong

Allow yourself the ability to change and go with the flow. Be like water. Don't give up. Be kind to yourself and others around you. Respect is earned not given. When I give advice to my team, I remind them, "It's not about my ego but it's about you, the customer, the food service industry."

The Kismet Chef

Since she traded her burgeoning fashion career for the culinary world, Chef Lee Anne Wong has been bringing her modern-global fusion cuisine to the people. Born and raised in Troy, New York, Lee Anne, a second-generation Chinese American, was not drawn to the kitchen but sports. However, her passion for cuisine ignited during her first year studying fashion design at FIT, when she started cooking for friends in the privacy of her own home. Were it not for her friends encouraging her to enroll in culinary school, we may never have been able to taste the genius of her artistry and fiery passion. After graduating from The French Culinary Institute (FCI), Lee Anne jumped into the restaurant world and worked for several years at Marcus Samuelsson's Aquavit. She later served as an integral part of the opening staff at Jean Georges Vongrichten's Chinese venture, Restaurant 66. She has also cooked and staged in kitchens all over the world, including The French Laundry, Charlie Trotter's of Chicago, Nobu, The Four Seasons, Trio, Casa Oaxaca in Mexico, and Cap Jaluca in the British Virgin Islands.

Lee Anne's skills go beyond the stove when she returned to the FCI as the executive chef of event operations. There, she honed her event production and recipe development skills and, soon after, brought her culinary skills to an even wider audience when she appeared as a "cheftestant" on season one of Bravo's flagship series' Top Chef. The show's producers saw her innate talent and brought her on as the supervising culinary producer on Top Chef, and its spin-off Top Chef Masters. Working on seasons two through seven for Top Chef and season one for Top Chef Masters, she was integral in shaping the show into the powerhouse that it is today. She also worked as a culinary consultant on No Reservations, as well as PBS' Chef Story, and Bravo's . While developing a media presence, Lee Anne continues to cook, participating in countless events, competitions, and charitable causes, such as Women Chefs and Restaurateurs (WCR) and Project By Project, a volunteer-based organization that supports Asian American nonprofits.

A culinary polyglot, Lee Anne loves to travel and experience new cultures and flavors, and has a deep love for everything porcine—so much so that many of her recipes incorporate pork in its many incarnations. Lee Anne's role in the culinary industry continues to evolve and, in 2013, she made the giant move from New York City to Honolulu to open up Koko Head Cafe, an island-style brunch house in Kaimukī. In addition, in 2015 she joined Hawaiian Airlines' culinary team as part of its Featured Chef Series, becoming the carrier's executive chef in 2018.

When we met at Koko Head Cafe, Lee Anne was dressed in an austere all-black ensemble, looking very much like a martial arts instructor. I realized that I had unwittingly subscribed to the stereotype notion that all chefs wore white, and Lee Anne is certainly no cookie-cutter chef, pun intended.

We sit down for a chat and she tells me that her baby would be with her—she wasn't kidding. I had expected to see a two year old, or a bouncing six month old, but at time *of writing, Lee Anne's baby, Rye, was literally brand new—a five-week-old bundle of joy—and Lee Anne was already up and about, being every inch the #girlboss at her café.*

Share with us who you were before you became a celebrity chef.

I don't like the term celebrity chef because I still work for a living, but I was born and raised in New York City and also went to college there where I studied fashion design and minored in fine arts. But I fell out of love with that at twenty and decided that I wanted to try my hand at cooking, even though I never cooked all that much growing up. My mom was a great self-taught cook, but I grew up eating spaghetti, Domino's pizza, jalapeño peppers—the usual New York fast food fare—and I never had to teach myself to cook until I went to the French culinary school, which really changed my life. I always worked in the restaurant industry since I was fifteen.

How did you decide to make that switch from fashion and fine arts to culinary school?

You know, magically enough, I was living in a big apartment with my then boyfriend in a really rough neighborhood in Brooklyn, and we watched a lot of Food Network and I used to think, "Wow, what a cool job. They get to eat and talk about it all day on TV." Anyway, subsequently, we ended up moving into a tiny 250-square-foot apartment in Times Square and had a futon mattress, a thirteen-inch TV on the floor and cable hanging over the ceiling.

Unsurprisingly, we didn't get many TV channels, except channel two, four, ten and thirteen, but by some miracle, we had the Food Network! So I started dabbling in the kitchen and, back then, broccoli was my gateway food and Shake 'n' Bake was a big night for me! I started cooking for my friends, who urged me to attend culinary school. I was not ready to leave New York City, so I enrolled for evening classes at the French Culinary Institute (FCI). I ended up giving up my bartending job and started working at Aquavit with Marcus Samuelsson while I was still in school. That really was my first job and I stayed there for three years. It was a huge learning experience and a tremendous foundation for me. After that, I did a short stint as a private chef and hated it! I then went back to the FCI as their executive chef of event operations and handled all of their custom events, cooking for their continuing education classes, journalism classes, cheese courses, and customizing unique menus and events for the clients of the school's International Culinary Theater. I also coordinated the chef demonstration program, working alongside numerous culinary heavyweights. I had to see to everything, from getting them car service, recipes, food orders, tastings for the demonstrations, and the list goes on. I was essentially producing live food television and that was also when I was cast in the first season of *Top Chef* and did well on that.

It was that opportunity that opened more doors. Subsequently, the production company and Bravo hired me as the supervising culinary producer on *Top Chef* and its spin-off *Top Chef Masters*. So I ended up working on seasons two through seven, and one season of *Top Chef Masters*. At that time, there wasn't that type of "reality-show food television" that we are familiar with now. Most of it, then, was studio cooking, so they found my experience both as a contestant and what I did at FCI very useful, and it unwittingly helped shape the show into what it is today. I must say it was a huge learning curve and it took me a while to adapt, but it was great!

I ended up producing the show for four years and quit as soon as we won an Emmy! I felt that I have done what I had set out to do and wanted to feel grounded, as I had been traveling all over with the production team—over forty-five days at a stretch without a single day off, lugging food and equipment around every day and still working for the FCI! It was very hard job.

By 2009, I was definitely ready to pursue my own career, as I didn't get much of a chance to cook at all this whole time, but worked to produce television shows as an employee of Bravo. Ironically enough, I was invited back as a guest on *Top Chef* last spring of 2017, battling eliminated chefs and seasoned veterans to get on a spot on season fifteen. It certainly felt like déjà vu, though it made me realize that I didn't enjoy being the cheftestant anymore, as I am now forty-one, and have been on the other side of the camera for so long. They also take away your phone and internet, and you feel like sequestered cattle! But what I would always appreciate was being able to have been part of the program at its inception and see how it has grown and morphed into this pop cultural icon over the years. It certainly launched a sidebar career for me as a culinary producer, food stylist, and consultant, though what I really wanted was to get back to the kitchen.

What are your thoughts on the reality show phenomenon?

That they are not reality at all! I used to battle the producers of Bravo who would say it's a reality show and we would insist it's a cooking show! My job was really to help shape the crazy ideas that the creative directors had and set up the parameters for the challenge that made it look like a reality show when it was all shaped and constructed. Some ideas would not fly or look good on TV or we knew some contestants would resist or rebuke or there was certainly a lot of pre-planning before. What we really had to do was to find that balance between entertainment and finding better cooks every season. As the seasons wore on, we got some really established chefs and that is what makes great TV. It was great to be part of this whole machine.

What made you decide on Hawaiʻi?

I had been consulting and traveling all over the country with Food Network and my travels frequently took me LA. By that time, my mom had a divorce and also decided to move to LA. By kismet, I met a friend who is now more like a brother to me. I took up his offer to bunk in with him in Venice, California, whenever I was in town.

As luck would have it, a friend of his from Hawaiʻi, Mike, was in town and we became pals. He, too, offered to house me if and when I went to Hawaiʻi, so I did, as figured I have ʻohana on the island. So I started visiting Oʻahu more frequently. On my second or third trip, I was casually remarking to my friend that I needed a change, as I have become a little jaded and disenchanted with New York. I was about thirty-five years old at the time and most of my friends were getting hitched and having babies, and I just suddenly felt a little lonely in New York. Anyway, Mike convinced me to stay for longer on one of my visits. The next morning, I met an aspiring farmer whom I ended up dating long distance for the next one and half years before my eventual move here. During my travels then, I would always do a pop-up or a food event and started getting connected with the local food community here. They were very supportive and accepted me as part of the ʻohana.

I knew that I would need a job if I was to move here. By then, I had already met Kevin Hanney, who is now my business partner and owner of 12th Avenue Grill, at a mango contest at the Moana Surfrider hotel some years ago and had awarded the prize to Kevin's team for the best mango dish.

Anyhow, he was looking for someone to take over this current place that is now Koko Head Café, as he had moved to a bigger space down the street.

He had the idea to do a breakfast place and was by kismet, re-introduced to me by my cousin. So we talked and decided to work on a concept café that is what you see today. It was truly perfect timing, as I had half a dozen concepts and menus written up and just turned down a job as a banquet chef at a hotel when Kevin called an hour later! So I flew up here, looked at the space and he basically gave me the football and I ran with it.

When I first opened it, it was crazy, as I was here from 4 a.m. to 11 p.m. every day and worked for close to six months straight, before I took a day off. That really was a labor of love. Four years on, this is a well-oiled machine. We have received national and international acclaim and it is all due to the team that works here. Everyone does an incredible job. All I really had to do was build the structure, the framework, and empower them. The intention was never to have me stand in the kitchen for five days a week, but to train other people to do that so that I could go out to build and expand the brand. With this footing here in Koko Head Café, I was invited as a guest chef on Hawaiian Airlines on the inbound flights from Japan. That gig was great as that, in turn, attracted many Japanese and international visitors—in fact, some of my guests are very well known in Japan themselves!

What is in the works for you?

For me, I am looking to possibly move this brand to Maui and, perhaps, also create another restaurant there. I am also looking forward to raising a child and getting married to Lyle. We want to build a life together. We are watching Rye grow up every day.

How are you coping with motherhood?

How will I balance being a mother and being a lady-boss? I don't know but I will figure it out. But it comes down to parenthood. Fathers are equally involved and we are a team. The mother is the carrier and the source of food for the baby for the first year and a half, and it is time consuming. I can't just leave for the day and be as independent as I was. But even at five weeks old, Rye is a social baby as we take him with us almost everywhere we go. We didn't want him to stay snookered away but incorporated him into our daily lives.

I always dreamed of raising my kid in the restaurant and having him as a part of our lives. It helps that Lyle is a graphic designer, amazing artist and jack-of-all-trades, and is able to work from home—that is a huge thing for us. It is so amazing for me to see how Lyle is as a father and he is simply the best father I have ever seen. He took to fatherhood like a duck to water—and that came from my mom, which is huge. We know that not all parents have the luxury of having their child with them at work, and we don't want a stranger raising our child either, so we are working hard to create the lifestyle that we want for us and for Rye.

What would your advice be to a young chef who is torn between career and motherhood?

We are glad that we waited. I am forty-two and Lyle is forty-one. We have both sown our wild oats and we are ready to be parents. It can be hard as society pressures you to have a kid at twenty or get married at thirty, but you must only do it when you are ready. You give up a part of yourself to have a child that can consume you, as it is the most precious thing to you, so you must be ready.

I know many of my friends who have their kids early and there is some tinge of regret, as they had to give up a lot. Not for us. We are at a good place in our career—I have a great support network and staff at work, the timing is right, we don't party anymore, and are at a different stage of maturity. If this restaurant was in shambles and I didn't have good team, I would have a very stressful pregnancy and motherhood. So while I can't speak for everyone else, I can say wait till you are ready.

What would you say is your leadership style?

My staff is my 'ohana. They are my family and they do a great job. Part of that is giving them the opportunity to realize that they get to create and what I do is advise. We do a dozen specials a day—they text me and I send them recipes or ideas and we do events together. I encourage them to give me their creativity and I help shape them. I always want to make them feel capable and confident to do it on their own.

I have to say that my style of leadership comes from my first job at Aquavit. As a second-year line cook, I was given the opportunity to move to the café, and the team gave me homework to come up with menu ideas. I was allowed to write the specials for the day, even though I was not a sous chef. They saw that I had the drive and confidence. The type of guidance I got really made an impression on me.

While I was at the FCI, I got to work with the deans and worked side-by-side with Jacques Pepin, Andre Soltner, Ferran Adria, Tyler Florence, and

Martin Yan. Andre Soltner is my other mentor and inspiration, as he was a legend. In his seventies, he was the oldest of the deans and always did his own food prep, whereas I had to do the prep for the rest. I would be doing my prep next to him as he prepared for his demo the following day. I would ask him questions to pick on his brains, such as, "What would you do for beef bourguignon?" He used to share with me stories on how he used to be an apprentice back in the 1930s and 1940s before there was technology, so they would stick a towel in the oven to regulate the heat as there was no temperature gauges! I would bear in mind all his anecdotes as stuff will break down in the kitchen and you have to not cry and think on your feet.

I am reminded that people have been cooking for centuries without technology, so whenever I face a crisis, I would ask myself, "What would Andre do?" He reminds me of what is at the core of cooking that is in total contrast to, and yet works in tandem with the TV shows I do which aim to put out all the bells and whistles like cooking on a moving bus or in the desert in the sandstorm,. But they all ask the fundamental question, "Who are you as a person? What are your core values as a chef and technician and how do you handle stress?"

Would you say these experiences have shaped you as a person and how you dealt with the failure of your restaurant Hale Ohuna?

Yes, definitely. It was a lesson in humility. That was hard and it took me a solid year to get over it. It was a decision of my business partner at the time, while I believed that we would have done really well had we stayed open. We opened at the wrong time of the year in Honolulu, over budget and it was the perfect storm of bad conditions. It took us three months to work out the kinks, and we needed to find our footing. Sadly, business was picking up and we were gaining recognition just as we were closing. That I was actually the last to know about the impending closure really stings and made it altogether a very tough experience for me. It was a bitter pill to swallow, but I am tougher for it and know what mistakes to avoid.

Having said that, even though it is all done and dusted, it still feels good when people come up to ask me about Hale Ohuna. We had a crowd of regulars who loved it and ask when it may re-open and I tell them, "Look out for us on Maui."

With the benefit of hindsight, share with our readers what lessons you learned from the experience.

Communication is key. I was very busy at the time and doing work for Hawaiian Airlines, going to Japan a lot and my cooks were stressed without me around. I learned that I am only as good as the people I have working with me, so I took it upon myself to see that it was my failure as a leader at the time to have not been there for them. In the next business I do, I know now that I have to build that brigade, the infrastructure, and cultivate strong people to help me run the business—and being on the same page with your business partner for starters!

As a New Yorker, what were some the things you had to get accustomed to in Hawai'i?

I am still a New Yorker a heart and I was a screamer when I first started this restaurant. I have had to evolve and slow down, though I still get road rage and curse a lot in the car, loudly, to myself. I am used to being go, go, go, and I was pretty intense when I first got here, especially when I first set up Koko Head Café and people were saying that I was "so New York" and I'll say, "You bet your ass I am so New York and I am never gonna lose that!" I have an easy-going way about me but they know when I mean business. The New Yorker in me is what made me but I have chosen to stay here.

Which begs the question, why Hawai'i?

Double rainbows every day! The older I get, the more I can't stand the cold and I have built my own 'ohana out here now, whereas I lived alone in New York for twenty years. I think being involved in the food industry, where everyone is chasing the fame makes it all too intense in New York. I did the backwards way, I did TV first on both sides, the festivals, and now I finally own a restaurant so that is my focus.

If people want me for food TV, they will call and I no longer have a fear of missing out anymore. I have had such a rewarding and eclectic career that has taken me all over the world, worked with so many different chefs, met great industry professionals and I no longer have envy. I am at that age where I am able to choose and envision the life I want, so Hawai'i is perfect as it gives me the space to care for what I love and the people I care for. Besides, Honolulu is blowing up and we have so many talented chefs and Michelin-star worthy restaurants here, so it's a great place to be at now.

What advice would you give to a young chef?

Allow yourself the ability to change and go with the flow. Be like water. Don't give up. Be kind to yourself and others around you. Respect is earned not given. When I give advice to my team, I remind them, "It's not about my ego but it's about you, the customer, the food service industry." It's a reality check.

Cooking is not about scoring a date or being on the cover of a magazine, but it is about customer service, as we are in the service and hospitality industry and it is a business after all. I remind them that we only have one chance, as people remember the service they receive. If the food is great but they receive bad service, they will never come again. If the food is mediocre and the service is excellent, the customer is inclined to give us a second chance. Koko Head Café is built upon great service and we have become like a community diner.

Who would you want to have a sit-down dinner with and what would you cook?

I would really love to sit down with Andre again. He loves Chinese food and asked me once to teach him how to make him fried rice, but I would make him really great French food, as I don't get a chance to do it very much anymore.

I would also want to sit with Gandhi, and I'll make him a great bowl of South Indian vegetarian curry.

And I would love to cook for Julia Child and I'll make her pot roast or a French classic, like roast chicken.

What is your favorite food?

I spent a lot of time in Japan in my thirties, so my favorite food, in terms of presentation and philosophy, is definitely Japanese. I could eat Japanese food all day. I traveled to Mexico a lot in my twenties, so I have a soft spot for Mexican food. But, where I differ as a chef, is my international exposure and I am a bit of a culinary polyglot, so I will try anything new three times.

What is the craziest thing you have eaten?

I have eaten loads of offal cooking, lots of bugs. Nothing is particular crazy to me, but the one thing that I could not eat again was stinky tofu. Unlike bleu cheese, this was so fermented, it looked like it was covered in fur! I imagine this is what dog poo tastes like. It was so rank and funky, like the durian, I had to spit it out!

Favorite spot in Hawaiʻi?

The Kula farmers' market on Maui is an incredible source of inspiration. I could spend all day there. Upcountry is also very beautiful.

Kauaʻi is also a favorite as it's where I met Lyle. He took me to Polihale, which is a remote beach on the western coast. We camped on the beach and barbecued. It feels as if you are at the edge of the universe with the oceans roaring and the sky as an open amphitheater. The natural beauty in Hawaiʻi is just amazing.

My life philosophy on a bumper sticker would be …

Eat Dumplings, Live Longer.

If you had a memoir, the title would be…

Something to do with Wong … *Eat Dumplings, Live Longer* or *Eat Dumplings All Day Wong*!

What would your epitaph say?

I haven't thought that far ahead yet!

THE GAME CHANGER

Kim Coco Iwamoto

I am known for speaking the truth and letting the emperor know that he or she is not wearing any clothes. Often, our leaders are kept in the ivory towers and siloed off. People are afraid to tell the truth, getting pushback or rocking the boat. I have not been able to afford to live in that kind of fear or make decisions based on fear, or based on what people tell me I can or cannot do. I will not do the work of the oppressor, nor will I silence myself.

Kim Coco Iwamoto is a Japanese American, Hawai'i politician. Born on Kaua'i, she received an associate of arts in merchandising from the Fashion Institute of Technology (FIT), a bachelor of arts in creative writing from San Francisco State University, and her Juris Doctor from the University of New Mexico School of Law. Shortly after her undergraduate degree, Kim Coco moved back to New York City, where she attended FIT and became more aware of social injustice.

Using her own life experience as a transgender woman, Iwamoto spent time volunteering at a local community center, helping youth develop leadership skills. It was here that her passions for helping houseless LGBTQIA youth were fostered and became her motivation for attending law school.

When Kim Coco returned to Hawai'i, she became a licensed therapeutic foster parent and served as a commissioner on the Hawai'i Civil Rights Commission. She was previously elected to serve two terms on the Hawai'i Board of Education. Her election as a trans woman in 2006 made her, at that time, the highest-ranking, openly transgender elected official in the United States and the first openly transgender official to win statewide office. She was subsequently re-elected in 2010 with 25 percent more votes than in 2006 and recognized as a Champion of Change by President Barack Obama in 2013. In 2018, she ran for lieutenant governor of Hawai'i, but lost to Josh Green. That same year, Newsweek listed her as one of fifty need-to-know pioneers for LGBTQ rights.

She remains firmly committed to social justice, denounces doing "the work of the oppressor," and works to combat homelessness. In the sanctuary of her home, she oozes joy and radiates maternal bliss in her role as mother to her daughter, Rory.

Share with us who you are before you became the public figure, Kim Coco Iwamoto.

Obviously, our family background and our childhood shapes who we are. My family taught me that hard work is rewarded, so even though we grew up in a fairly affluent neighborhood, my parents instilled in us a strong work ethic. I was barely ten years old when I started to deliver the afternoon newspaper, pedaling my bicycle up and down the mountain. I also worked for the family company: washed cars; and took rental car, catamaran, and tour reservations. I also worked on the boat at night. So I grew up working very hard. I think this is typical of family businesses—everyone in the family pitches in.

My father would recall stories of how he used to miss the high school football games, as he would be washing the cars of our uncles and aunties that were borrowed to use as rental cars on Kaua'i. My mother made sacrifices, too. Her family moved from Japan to central California. They were cantaloupe farmers, so everyone worked on the farm. But my mother realized that she was great with numbers and could do bookkeeping, so she stayed indoors.

You shared that your mother had gone through the Japanese internment and that really shaped your cultural imaginary subsequently.

(nods) When she was younger, my mother's family was sent to internment camps. Mom was five years old when she was imprisoned by the U.S. government, simply for being who she was: a person of Japanese ancestry living in California.

When I was growing up, mom would share her stories about the internment, and what it was like after she came out as an eight year old. Mom had eight siblings, and they finally returned to their two-bedroom farmhouse in the middle of Central Valley when the internment ended, only to find a family living in it. My mother remembers camping outside her own home, as the family that was squatting in their home wasn't ready to leave.

When I was younger, I didn't understand the shame and indignation of what they went through and didn't really have an awareness of these deeper injustices till I was twenty-three years old.

What happened then?

I was working in the fashion industry in New York City, when my employer basically told me that her largest corporate account was not comfortable working with me because I was trans. I was shocked, found myself out of a job, and I had to deal with the social injustice and the economic impact it had on me. My job paid my rent and put food on the table. That really hit me hard, because I had no idea this could happen.

Growing up in Hawai'i and working for my father's company, I was unaware of the social injustices prevailed, as we had trans people working at the company, so it was never a big deal. Being trans wasn't anything noteworthy. So yes, I became woke when I had that experience. I, then, sought the help of a free legal clinic at the local community center.

This happened in the early '90s. I found out that the law protected employers and their right to discriminate against trans people. I also realized in that moment that I needed to go to law school to better understand the law, and then change the law, because what was happening was simply not acceptable. It was as if I found a utility pole had fallen and was now blocking my path; and yes, while I may personally have the resilience to jump over that pole, I felt I needed to remove that obstacle for others walking on the path, too. And so, I changed my career course and thought this is what I needed to do.

That was your aha and coming to consciousness moment …

(nods) At that same time, I also saw that transgendered people were being murdered and left to die because the governments weren't responding to the violence targeting us.

There was the case of Tyra Hunter[1] in Washington D.C. She was in a car accident and lay injured in a crosswalk. The paramedics came and realized in treating her that she was trans and backed away from her body. She bled out and died. Witnesses heard them exclaim, "That's a man," as they stopped saving her life.

This really angered me, as it showed that her life didn't matter to the paramedics because she was trans. We protested in the streets in front of the mayor's office and we wanted to make sure that the mayor knew that trans' lives mattered. We also went to the trial of the murderers of Brandon Teena.[2] We flew to Nebraska and we picketed in the street in front of the court house to make sure the media knew that Brandon's life mattered.

That was how my grassroots activism started. Eventually, I made it to law school and graduated, but I returned home to care for my mother in Hawaiʻi, as she had a stroke, and I wanted to be close to her. I thought I'll take the bar in Hawaiʻi, which I did and passed, and thus started working with local activists to change the state's civil rights laws.

---

1 Tyra Hunter (1970–August 7, 1995) was an African American transgender woman, who died after being injured as a passenger in a car accident and was refused emergency medical care. Emergency medical technicians at the scene of the accident uttered derogatory epithets and withdrew medical care, after cutting open Tyra's pants and discovering that she had a penis.

2 Brandon Teena (born Teena Renae Brandon; December 12, 1972–December 31, 1993) was an American trans man, who was raped and murdered in Humboldt, Nebraska. His life and death were the subject of the Academy Award-winning 1999 film Boys Don't Cry, which was partially based on the 1998 documentary film The Brandon Teena Story. Both films also illustrated that legal and medical discrimination contributed to Teena's violent death. Teena's murder, along with that of Matthew Shepard, led to increased lobbying for hate crime laws in the United States.

> Being "woke" and seeing all the energy and transformation in New York City must have really inspired you.

Yes. We formed and built that community of people, who are willing to protest in the streets. That gave me strength to show that our lives mattered and that we need to do something about it. Working with local activists to change the laws is a start, and we wanted to ensure that sexual orientation was accepted along with gender identity and expression. We worked on all of these laws and, eventually, my first career job as an attorney was doing legal clinics in homeless shelters.

> Did you know this would lead to a career in politics?

No. I was really just working in the community, but I understood the importance and value of educating people about their rights. So I did that and I volunteered for the Legal Aid Society of Hawaiʻi. Eventually, I became a certified licensed therapeutic foster parent. I foster-parented five teens who identified as gay, bi, and/or trans, some of whom I pulled out of the youth correctional facility.

What I really wanted to do was advocate for them, their educational needs, and prevent them from being bullied and harassed in schools. That's actually what led me to run for the Hawaiʻi State Board of Education (BOE). I would go to the board meetings and try to get the BOE to hear the complaints of the students, try to get the principal and administration to do something when my kids were being bullied. I just wanted to make sure they were being responsive to the needs of these students. What I got were just blank stares and there was no indication or affirmation that these LGBTQIA students would be treated fairly. There was no accountability and I knew this was wrong.

This was around 2005, so I decided I had to run for the BOE and launched a campaign. I was running against fifteen other candidates for one of the top three seats, including some career politicians. We had very little money but we ran an amazing campaign. My family supported me with contributions back then, as I had no idea what fundraising was.

Anyway, we made it through the top five in the primaries, then top three in the general elections. I won a seat on the BOE and people were simply blown away that someone could launch a first-time grassroots campaign and succeed! It was clear to local politicians and the media that I'm open and out as a trans person. Being trans and winning an election in Hawaiʻi was such a non-issue. I had invited all the local media to my election-night headquarters party, but nobody came. Not even a phone interview.

It wasn't until the national media picked up the story about a trans person who was elected to a statewide office—apparently I became the highest ranking, openly trans official in the nation—that the national networks were asking their Hawai'i affiliates for footage and sound bites. Suddenly, the local media went crazy. I went from having zero media interest to being hounded on the streets. It was a media circus all the way up to the swearing-in ceremony. And then it was back to normal, and not one media outlet mentioned my trans status for the rest of my time on the BOE.

That election was a watershed in many ways …

It was important, as it signaled a change that trans people not only mattered, but we wanted to make a positive difference in our communities. Though, it also underscored the beauty of Hawai'i, as being trans was a non-issue to begin with and that is ideally what we want to achieve nationally.

In recent years, we have seen so many trans people being elected into office and I made sure I was able to support all of them early on with large contributions. When the tide comes in, all boats rise, so I think it's important to help each other reach their dreams and, in turn, become role models for the community.

Can you share with us your transition or journey as a trans person?

I've always been me and I've always been Kim Coco. I was born as Kim Coco Iwamoto. My mother went into labor at the Coco Palms Hotel and that is how I got my name. There's a childhood photo of me and my brothers in football jerseys with our names on them: Scott, Troy, Mark, Chad, and Kim Coco. Growing up, I was clearly different than all my brothers, but I did not feel singled-out. It was just who I was.

But when I was twelve, I was enrolled in an all-boys high school and the gender disparities were undeniable. The school knew I was different, but everyone was cool with it, and I was even elected class president in my sophomore and junior years. I have always been very open about who I am, even when I did not have the exact language—I got my point across. I just told people that I was going to be a nun, "I'm going to marry Jesus!" So while this idea of transition is true for many trans people, for me, it felt like an evolution, or a natural maturation.

I've always been me and there has never been a "before" or an "after" that wasn't equally as awkward as any cis teenagers' transition to their adult maleness or femaleness. I never had to come out of the closet, as I was never in one. I recall being in the department store in my high school uniform and the sales associates would ask me if I was wearing my boyfriend's uniform! *(laughter)*

How do you think people viewed you?

I don't know. At that age, I didn't have the vocabulary to unpack gender. Today, I understand the concept of a social agreement within a social construct. I feel as if two different people can experience the same individual at the same time as two different genders, depending on how they code gender—it may have nothing to do with the individual's identity.

People seem to find it more comforting when others have clearly identified gender markers. I think at this point, I am beyond gender. I think my brand transcends gender. I suspect, when most people want to point me out in a crowd, they no longer say "That's a guy or that's a mahu." More likely, they say, "That's Kim Coco."

So do you identify with being both male and female?

I identify as a trans woman and I know my strength comes from a feminist perspective. I claim space at the table as a minority (trans, female, and bisexual) and as an act of resistance against the patriarchy.

I also make space for other minorities. Where I have privileges as a person of Japanese ancestry—part of the settler-class used by colonizers to occupy Hawai'i and displace kanaka maoli—I consciously restore opportunities for kanaka maoli leadership. Where I have privileges of wealth, I remove economic barriers to diversify leadership, etc.

You ran for lieutenant governor in 2018. What were the major issues you saw as relevant and wanted to take on?

I wanted to turn the lieutenant governor's office into the people's office and had hoped to create a physical space where community organizers and activists alike can come together to work on anything from the homeless issue to environmental matters. I wanted the office to be their space.

I have always believed in collaborative problem-solving, instead of having activists knocking on the doors of legislators and begging for scraps. I wanted to bring all these groups together to the table and make them part of the solution. I think this is a game changer. That was why I ran for lieutenant governor, as there are many resources allocated to the lieutenant governor's office, which has thus far been underutilized. What I truly wanted to do was to improve the quality of life in Hawaiʻi. We know the people of Hawaiʻi deserve better.

How do you deal with a crisis of leadership?

Good question. I want to talk in general terms as opposed to just speaking politically.

I am known for speaking the truth and letting the emperor know that he or she is not wearing any clothes. Often, our leaders are kept in the ivory towers and siloed off. People are afraid to tell the truth, getting pushback or rocking the boat.

I have not been able to afford to live in that kind of fear or make decisions based on fear, or based on what people tell me I can or cannot do. I will not do the work of the oppressor, nor will I silence myself. I take it as a sign of respect and a gift when I offer up truths to someone and tell them that they can do better. This means that I respect you enough to see your potential—that is why I am sharing this with you and will continue to do so.

I cannot control how people wish to receive my advice, but I can certainly control the sincerity and respect I offer up to them.

Where does your courage or fearlessness come from?

I think from hearing my mother's stories of internment. We live in a representative democracy, so when I heard my mother was imprisoned at age five, that was a wakeup call.

The deep sense of shame felt by them lingered. I started to question, "We are Americans, so why is America coming against us and why is everyone silent to that?" It's a silent complicity, because no one wanted to stand up.

What we are learning today, seeing the Trump resistance movement is that people are feeling the need and desire to call out complicity and vocalize. I feel as if I have been doing the work for decades and others are catching up, and there, finally, is a name for it now. And that is resistance. It is speaking out against what is wrong, and, somehow, I've never been afraid of doing that. Perhaps, when you're viewed as an outlier, people don't expect much from you, so you don't have formal power. By that same token, you don't wait around for somebody to give you permission to speak out. So what I feel is not courage per se, but that I have a sense of responsibility to speak up and speak out.

Does having a supportive family help fuel that sense of responsibility and voice?

Yes. I definitely think from an early age they affirmed who I was. They didn't always agree, but I was visible and valued at my core. This is a message that all parents need to really hold in their heart—that no matter who your child is, you should make them feel loved, as that will see them through a lot of hardship and struggle. And if they know they are loved and lovable, they see their own potential and can better give to their community.

What are some of the biggest obstacles you faced?

Some of the most difficult challenges I feel is being a parent. Being a parent to teenagers was really hard and, at that time, it was the hardest thing I've ever done. I was a foster parent to young teens, who had very amazing survival skills which were not necessarily conducive to being parented.

They were used to living on the streets on their own, so who am I to tell them what time to come home and that they need to go to school? These teens are adults now and they're still in my orbit. I still love them and I find opportunities for them to be part of my life. Some of them have mental health or substance-abuse challenges, but every single one of them have reached back to me as an adult supporter.

And you are a mother again?

Yes, I adopted a two-year old from China three years ago—she is six now.

How has motherhood changed you?

This feels a lot different than fostering, as those teens had parents so I never really had an opportunity to be a mother to them. What I could do and did was to support them. But being a mother to Rory is different—it's just her and I. I'm all she has, so it's a different relationship.

My daughter is so full of love and she will tell me she needs "a thousand-and-one loves." Motherhood has really grounded me and kept things in perspective. Things that used to bother me before, don't anymore, as my priorities have changed. I am such a heady person, but I get home. She gets into my heart-space right away.

She is growing up, very expressive, a lot of fun, and super smart. In fact, some of the parents of the other kids would tell me that their child came home saying how hysterically funny Rory is. She has this innate sense of physical comedy.

> Now that you are mother and career woman, do you think a woman can have it all? Sheryl Sandberg garnered so many brickbats when she said women can have it all.

I don't see the impossibility of anything. I just don't listen to, or do the work of, the oppressor.

And frankly, why should anybody do the work of the oppressor? Why should any one of us internalize any of these messages that create double standards or any kind of limitations or expectations on ourselves?

I have to say that I've always found the greatest success where there have been forces that underestimate me, so I welcome it and use it to my advantage. For example, if there are people who think that I shouldn't access space or opportunities as a trans person, I make them expose the true face of their sexism, racism, and all the isms they embody.

I choose to refuse to read the subtext, so if they want to communicate their hateful message, they had better do it really loud, as I don't want these horrible people to get away with veiled, bigoted improprieties.

> What advice would you give to an aspiring politician?

I think anyone who aspires to be a politician, shouldn't be one. I think that ideal needs to be more organic. I ran for office for the Board of Education because it sprung from a very particular need which needed a very specific resistance. I was really going in to be an advocate for the students.

I'm not a career politician and I've partnered with different organizations since I served on the Board of Education. But I see what I do as service to the community and not part of my need to be a politician for formal leadership.

Yes, being a politician does allow access to influence policy, resources, and capability, but that shouldn't be the raison d'etre. So when I see people who study to run for office like some kind of game, I often feel that's a mistake. So maybe my advice would be to get in the trenches and serve the community, and if you see a need to rise up, then elevate the conversation.

Even for my last campaign, it wasn't just about winning. I'm trying to elevate and build a movement. So the language of my campaign was about empowering voters to join our movement, even through single-dollar donations, as this helped us record them as a supporter. Other campaigns try to build up huge war chests to aid in media buys to access voters, but I'd rather go directly to the people and invest resources to nurture the relationships with the voters instead of going through the middleman media. I wanted to create a direct link and make them feel like they are a part of this democracy. I wanted to be the candidate who is accessible, like Obama and Sanders.

In short, it's really about democratizing a campaign. In fact, I noticed that the language from my campaign literature has already been adopted by the masses. And that feels great. And yes, even if I didn't win, I felt like I've been heard and I am immensely thankful.

So what are your thoughts on social media?

That's another axis to connect with people and it can be a very powerful medium, especially for voters who are looking to connect with authentic candidates. It's one thing to have a conversation face-to-face and some people of a certain age group value that.

But a growing demographic find face-to-face communication too confrontational and sales-pitchy, and would rather use social media as a form of information. They want to process the information on their own from the periphery, so it is challenging to manage all these varied demographics, communication channels, and diverse expectations.

During my campaign, I worked with my campaign manager, who is in his thirties and a millennial. He was amazing and brought great energy to the campaign and the community.

I've always been in a position of empowering and uplifting new leadership, and have even advocated for a high school person at our boards that tend to be full of adults. I have always valued young leadership and diversity.

In hindsight, how do you feel now that the elections are over?

I did not earn the Democratic nomination for lieutenant governor. Although I lost the primary election, I do not feel our campaign was a loss. The work continues, as it did before and during the campaign: building our collaborations to coalesce our power to reclaim our democracy.

It would have been great to have the prime real estate of the lieutenant governor's office to continue that work, but the campaign itself has brought so much attention to the issues raised in our platform around our underfunded public schools, lack of affordable housing and resources to support our homeless, and the need to invest in preserving and protecting our natural resources.

What are your fondest memories growing up on the island?

I was born on Kauaʻi. Although I was raised in the urban core of Oʻahu, we always spent our weekends and holidays back on Kauaʻi, where we were surrounded by nature. I loved camping on the beach, fishing, hiking in the mountains. I love all those memories just being with family and having adventures.

What has changed then?

As a child, I would have never been attuned to the cost of living, so that wouldn't have come on my radar. But now, as an adult looking at how life was before, I see how the cost of living is crazy here. It has definitely gone up and it is definitely challenging for a lot of people. We have the highest rates of personal credit card debt in the nation per capita, while also having the highest number of people living paycheck-to-paycheck on the verge of homelessness. We have the worst homeless crisis in the whole nation.

The commodification, buying and selling of land ensures that prices keep going up. I own an apartment building and, within the first year, I was offered double the amount to sell it.

Instead, I fixed it up and rented it to my tenants at an affordable rate. My company is called Affordable Quality Apartment Rentals (AQuA), where 50 percent of my apartments provide housing to low-income or previously homeless families. Now, I could choose to sell it and make more money but then I would be part of the problem, so I would rather be part of the solution to preserve the urban core and provide working families an affordable place to live. It is still a sound investment and yet it is a win-win formula.

The key is to not be greedy and capitalize on short-term gains. At some point you have to ask what is enough; be responsible and stay connected to your community. I can only say that it starts with me, so I'm doing what I can do.

What changes would you like to see in the near future?

The homeless issue is key for me. The huge income gap and foreign investments coming in are key drivers of the homeless issue.

London is going through similar issues, as too many homes are investment properties with no one living in them, so money isn't circulating into the economy and dwellings are taken out of circulation. It doesn't help that the rise of Airbnb rentals have seen homes, such as on the North Shore, being rented out at high prices, which the locals can't afford, and so the houses remain vacant even as there is a homeless crisis.

There used to be 4,100 long-term rentals that were made available to Hawai'i residents, who could not afford to live in the urban center, but now, they are all part of the Airbnb stock, so that compounds the problem. One solution is to reach out to owners and get them to understand the repercussions of their actions.

Another suggestion is to institute a different tax rate. If you own property in Hawai'i and if you do not have an identifiable Hawai'i resident connected to that property, then maybe your property tax rate should be higher. But if you had a state resident living in the property, you get a different exemption, so, this way, we encourage people to rent to the local residents. We need to have more carrots dangling in front and sticks tapping in the rear.

Same goes for building affordable housing options. Developers are building luxury, as that is where the profits are compared to affordable housing, where everything is calculated to pennies so one can't pay competitive wages for the manpower. So we do need to dangle carrots to encourage supply of affordable housing, and people need to recognize that there are impacts and social costs of constantly catering only to the super rich.

You have so much going on. What do you do to relax?

I play tennis and I run.

These days, I love taking my daughter to the beach and taking her to new experiences. The first six months when Rory came home was like a vacation for me, as I took her to the beach, zoo, and had tons of activities for her to explore and get acclimatized to Hawai'i. I love spending time with her. I also took her to the Big Island, showed her the volcanoes, and she's been learning about Pele. I love that her learning and childhood is not just about Disneyland, but the natural environment and running through the rain forests of Hilo.

Who would like to have a sit-down dinner with?

I've met so many amazing people and had amazing conversations with people who aren't known or famous. Yet, I've been totally transformed just by hearing their stories.

But if I had to pick, I will say the former President Barack Obama. I think he's lived an amazing life. And, Michelle Obama. I think having them over for a quiet dinner would be great. It is great to meet people who are creative, analytical, and so integrated with their mind, heart, and soul.

What would you say if you met God?

It is less what I would say than what I feel. I feel as if I experienced God all the time when I meet people, and we connect through our bodies, hearts, and minds, and through our shared intuition, vulnerability, and compassion for others, and with the natural environment. These are all God's connections and I honor that.

What is your life philosophy on a bumper sticker?

Do not do the work of the oppressor.

What would the title of your memoir be?

I don't know that one. I think it's premature to come up with a title, as I feel I haven't lived enough to justify a memoir yet.

How would you like to be remembered?

She was always right! (*laughter*) One of the first phrases I taught my daughter in English was "Mama knows."

One night, we were having dinner with some friends and she overheard me speaking in an authoritative way and she looked up and said, "Mama knows." Everyone burst out laughing—so, yes, Mama knows, and maybe that's a good title for my memoir, too. (*laughter*)

THE AMERICAN DREAMER
Christine Camp

It comes down to knowing what you are worth. Never doubt what you're worth, and ask for what you need. However, remember that it goes both ways. In asking for what you need, you must give your client, your boss, or your investors what they need—performance, commitment, and loyalty.

Christine Camp

Christine Camp is the president & CEO of Avalon Group, a real estate development and brokerage services firm she founded in 1999. Avalon has since acquired 177 acres of industrial land in Kapolei for development and is currently developing a $165 million apartment complex in Hawai'i Kai. With over twenty-five years of industry experience and leadership, Christine has gained recognition as an expert in real estate and finance issues. Her insights are frequently solicited by local and national publications and she has been a speaker at various media and industry groups. She was vice president of development and acquisition for A&B Properties (NYSE: ALEX) and senior project coordinator for the planning and engineering division of Castle & Cooke.

Christine is highly visible and active in the community. She previously served as chairwoman of the Honolulu Chamber of Commerce, chair of the Honolulu Police Commission, and president of the Hawai'i Developers Council. She is currently on the board of Central Pacific Bank and its parent company Central Pacific Financial, the Diamond Head Theatre and Blue Planet Foundation. Her many accomplishments include being named a YMCA Women Leader, 40 Under 40 Community Leader of the Year, and Building Industry's Developer of the Year.

Christine received a degree in finance and business administration from Hawai'i Pacific University, is a licensed real estate broker and is a Certified Commercial Investment Manager (CCIM). But her proudest achievement to date is being a mom to her eleven-year-old son, Ethan.

Poised, articulate and warm, her petite frame belies the gargantuan stresses and responsibilities she has had to shoulder in an erstwhile male dominated field of development and real estate. She shares candidly about her desire to fit in as a young Korean immigrant, her entrepreneurial spirit, and her fervent pursuit of the American dream.

Share a little bit about yourself, your background, and how you got here.

It's a fairly simple immigrant family story. I came from very humble beginnings, and that allowed me to learn lessons much earlier and faster than anyone else. I started my own business when I was twelve and had my first subcontractor when I was twelve with a babysitting business. You know, I'm in an industry dominated by men, so I couldn't have done this without all of the experiences and hardships I endured in my youth.

What would make a twelve year old start a business?

I lost my father within the first year of our arrival here, so my mother had to work. There were five kids and I'm number four. That is probably why I was focused on finances and what puts food on the table from a young age. When I was twelve, I noticed there were little postcards at a laundromat with people's numbers offering their home-based services. I thought I could do that, too, so I practiced my handwriting to make sure that it was legible and put little index cards at the supermarket, at the laundromat, and around the neighborhood where we lived.

After that, the phones never stopped ringing. I was so busy that I was making more than minimum wage. When it got really busy, I hired my sister and later my best friend. So they were my employee number one and number two. That enterprise allowed me to save money so that I could do things that other kids could do, like buy athletic shoes so that I could play basketball. I didn't have to ask my mother for lunch money and could also save money to do extracurricular activities, such as etiquette class, where I learned how to use forks and knives in a proper setting and learned how to dress. There was never a question that I wouldn't help my family. I saw how hard it was for my mom to raise us in America, and it made me try harder and work harder at an earlier age than most.

What did you do then as the "breakout" child?

I wanted to be American so badly, but my mom kept reminding me who I was. I wanted to escape from home as I felt that I was smart, hardworking, and an active participant in school. I was a cheerleader and was president of my class. But my mom never recognized any of that. All she wanted was obedience. She wanted me to study, do the chores, work hard, and not be distracted by friends. I just felt that it was unfair so I ran away from home, but I quickly learned my lessons in life between the ages of fifteen and sixteen. I soon decided to return home, as I realized that home was really better after all.

Do you think that leadership is intrinsic or do you think that you were extrinsically motivated?

There lies the perennial nature versus nurture debate. I think that nature has quite a bit to do with it but nurture is key, as my attitude was honed out of necessity. My strength came because I was willing to try. I don't know if leadership is predicated on nature or nurture, but I saw my mother taking charge of her life and her family without fear. She did so because she had no choice and had to put food on the table and afford the mortgage.

I saw her try everything. She tried different businesses and worked three part-time jobs as a waitress. She did everything and, yet, all of her businesses failed as she knew nothing about doing business in this country. She spoke very little English, she got conned, and she did not know how to file her taxes, yet this never stopped her from waking up the next day and trying again. Watching her try, and try again ingrained in my siblings and that failure was not the end. If one door closes, there will be another door. I don't know if I was born to be a leader or if growing up observing my mother normalized for me the concept that nothing comes easily and everything was a result of hard work and perseverance. All of her five kids tried their hand at having their own businesses, and two are still at it. I think not being fearful of failure gives you the courage to get up and do it again.

Tell me about the Miss Korea Hawaiʻi pageant and what did that do for you?

When I was around twenty years old, my grandmother came to visit and she read the local Korean newspaper and saw that they were recruiting Miss Korea Hawaiʻi contestants. She insisted that I take part.

The decision to enter the pageant was one of the most cathartic events in my life. The process taught me what it was like to be a Korean, which was the identity I sought to run away from in my bid to assimilate and become an American. Miss Korea instilled a sense of pride in my culture and I began to study Korean culture—history, clothing, food, and took interest in all the things I took for granted. This cultural immersion became so important to me as I knew I had to represent my culture if I won.

I was not the tallest, most beautiful, nor was I very talented, but I knew who I was as I had been studying my culture. I am certain it was my cultural poise and confidence that won the judges over. I spent my teenage years running away from my identity only to rediscover myself in my twenties as a proud Korean American. Through the process, I found my voice and a sense of who I was.

> Given today's tense climate on immigration and the Dreamers in the current administration, share with us a little more on your struggle with identity and how you coped personally.

Up till the pageant, I downplayed who I was, as I wanted to be like everybody else. I didn't want to be that immigrant. I wanted to be seen as local like everybody else.

But the pageant taught me so much about my heritage, history, the fights of our people when they first arrived, the struggles they had, the kinds of food they ate, and how we came to be. What most moved me was their spirit of perseverance against all odds that made me swell with pride. It made me feel proud that this is me. This is who I am.

> Let's switch tracks now and talk more on entrepreneurship. You are exceedingly enterprising. What can we do to encourage enterprise in Hawai'i?

Because we live in Hawai'i, people want to protect what is precious here including the way we do business. As a result, I think our laws are so protective that it hurts the economy and business landscape. For example, getting our permits and the processes to get people licensed and to start a business are real tough. Not everyone is as tenacious as I am.

While I understand the need to protect the consumers and the safety of the public, it can make it hard for an entrepreneur to break into the business or industry. As mentioned, the licensing laws, paper work, and process can be very intimidating. There are numerous different and often confusing steps to get to the starting point.

To be honest, I don't pose to know how to fix this problem. But what I can do on my side is look at things that truly need fixing one thing at a time. We can encourage more enterprise in Hawai'i by simplifying the steps and processes with our government. We have to care enough to speak out and be heard, to make a difference to ease burdens for our businesses one step at time.

> What have you learned about leadership over the years?

The year 2019 marks Avalon's twentieth anniversary. If I have any regrets, it would be that I wish I had the courage to jump off five or ten years earlier. Still, here I am and I'm glad to admit that my leadership style has changed over the years. I think I am a better leader now than before. Back then, I was so worried about being liked by others. I felt that if people who worked for me liked me, then they will follow. I have learned that is not true leadership because it takes a lot of courage to step up and make hard decisions.

Today, I focus on doing the right things for the right reasons to move us forward, even when it means I may not make the most popular decisions. Sometimes, it is lonely at the top.

There is always a tipping point or aha moment for any successful leader. What was yours?

It would be eleven years ago in 2008. I became a mom that year and Avalon had the worst struggle during the start of the great recession.

It was a year that I thought was going to be triumphant. I felt comfortable enough to be pregnant and was about to give birth when the great recession started and the whole economy started to crumble. I realized that my company was in trouble and I had to come back to work.

Three weeks after I gave birth to my son—that was the earliest I could get clearance from the doctor to go back to work—I came back to fix things so that I could save our company and employees' jobs. I felt responsible for my staff's livelihood, as they have mortgages, kids in college, private schools, etc. I was in debt, borrowing money to continue paying for people's salaries I could not afford, and spent a year depleting my savings and all my resources before I started laying people off.

Nothing can be as bad as when I had to lay off half our staff and walk away from millions of dollars of investments into projects. The loss took me the next ten years to pay back, but the aha, or cathartic, moment came when I realized we almost failed but we didn't. We became stronger.

The team I led stepped up and helped me save the company. We expanded our services and we have since re-hired most of the staff. Our team became more adept at changes and that made us more nimble. We built a cash-flowing business in addition to the investment and development business. We became smarter and more profitable. Now we are five times the size that we were ten years ago, and we are ready for the next ten years. We endured, and we are better for the experience of knowing we survived.

What was it like being a single mom and a career woman?

I knew that I was ready to raise my son on my own. I am not that religious, but I do believe that God guides me in everything, and everything that happened was meant to happen. The near business failure, divorce, and becoming a single mom was all part of the evolution of who I am now.

I can tell you that being a mom made me a different person. It was the best decision I could have made because decisions were easier to make. I knew from the moment that I became a single mom that I can't give up. I had a little boy who depended on me. I was the sole provider and it was wholly my decision to bring him into this world, so this recognition made me get up every morning, and prevented me from going into a depression when I was going through the toughest time of my life.

He gave me joy every day in the most fundamental way. If you are a woman leader and are a mom, I think you're blessed because you'll experience something men won't get a chance to. Motherhood is so instinctive and fundamental in the way that I can't even explain.

I wake up every morning feeling hopeful for his future. He is hope to me. Looking back, I think that's how my mom survived. I see it now. I think God gave me what I needed just at the right time because, when everything fell apart, if I didn't have my son, I might have fallen apart. But instead, I have a child who gave me every reason to move forward every day.

> **What would you say to a woman who was in your shoes, deciding between family and career?**

I would not have made the decision to become a mom had I not looked around and seen what support system I had. Of course, I had the luxury of having three sisters and a mother who lived in the same city who had the ability and desire to help me. So my advice to any woman who is a professional, who wants a career and having it all is to look around to see what support system she has.

I didn't have a husband then, but I had a support system. And when my family wasn't around, I hired the best nanny I could.

So if I were to give advice to anyone who wants to be a mom and a professional, I'll say you can't have it all unless you plan for it. And the way to plan is to support yourself and have a village of supporters. When Hillary Clinton said it takes a village, it absolutely takes a village to raise a child.

In fact, when my son is on spring break, I have other moms in the office bring their kids to the office too. I'll let them play amongst themselves and they are running around a lot. But yet, we can work. We're here, the kids are here, and we're supporting each other by having all the working moms take turns to watch the kids.

What can a working mother do to achieve greater equity?

A woman professional must not be afraid to ask for some accommodation. "Can I bring my child" or "Can I work from home while my kid is on vacation?" It comes down to knowing what you are worth. Never doubt what you're worth, and ask for what you need. However, remember that it goes both ways. In asking for what you need, you must give your client, your boss, or your investors what they need—performance, commitment, and loyalty.

I give everybody the flexibility that they need at Avalon. We have flex-time and paid time off for staff to take care of their parents, children, and other life matters. For me as an employer and a mom, I do the best I can to lead by example. I also ensure my staff that I am flexible. I ask them to give me your loyalty and commitment to the success of this company, and I'll give you what you need. That's our philosophy here.

From what you have shared, you seem to be a transformative, not transactional, leader, so how do you deal with people who abuse your system which works on reciprocity? By extension, how do you deal with negativity or disloyal staff?

It's really about performance. Loyalty is a great marker, but that may cost companies to invest a great deal of time and energy. But what we ask for is performance. When people don't perform, we will take the time to review them at least once a year and more if required. For the staff who are struggling, we review them twice to four times a year. Sometimes, we may not be the right fit for them. We believe that we are not doing favors for non-performers if we don't let them know how they are doing, nor do we want top performers buried or sidelined.

This goes back to what we spoke about earlier that leadership is having the courage to tell a staff member that he or she is not pulling their weight and may have to go. That kind of conversation is not fun and is negative. But I also do not wish to be untruthful as it is a social contract we have when the staff joins us. The staff has an obligation to perform and meet the expectations here.

We are pretty clear about communicating our expectations, though we don't stipulate it in a job description. We tell people that if they need a job description, then this is not the company for them. There are companies that require strict job descriptions where everyone is siloed into their specific duties, but here, we want utility players who are able to do various functions with a slight advantage of some specific subject matter. Everyone is focused on each team member's success because their success becomes the company's success.

What would you say is the secret to your success?

The secret of our success is our people and our ability to be nimble, which can only happens if you let people pitch in wherever and whenever way they can. So as much as I like to say I'm the greatest person, I can't. It really is about the people who can follow your vision and execute the vision and principles.

You just got married. How did you find time to find romance?

I don't know! *(laughter)* I've been so busy running my business and being a mom. So yes, there was no time for dating. But my now husband was and still is my tax attorney, advisor, and his firm does our taxes! *(laughter)*

We have known each other for over ten years. One day, he worked on a tax issue that saved us over a half million dollars just by him writing a letter for us! I wanted to thank him and celebrate and even that took four months to plan. *(laughter)* Anyway, we went to our celebration dinner and, here we are, happily married.

What are your thoughts on Hawaiʻi? What changes have you seen?

Forty years is a long time! Our skylines have certainly changed. There is definitely more traffic now! But the people have not changed and that is why I still love it and it is home. When I first came, there were far fewer people and it felt like a small island.

For a few years, I opened a satellite office in Los Angeles and was commuting back and forth between California and Hawaiʻi on a weekly basis for several years, but I felt that I could never really leave Hawaiʻi. I just love this island so I decided that I would commit fully to Hawaiʻi only. Hawaiʻi has been and still is a very generous, kind community and I want my son to grow up here.

Everything that I do today is for my son and the future he will inherit. I'm on the board environmental foundation. I support clean energy. People ask why a developer would support the environment and I say that it is because I am a mom. I want my son to have a future where he and his children's children can experience clean water, air, and environment.

What specific plans do you have to achieve that?

As a developer, I am focused on creating sustainable communities. You can't just have housing without places of work. You can't just have a rail to bring everybody to town but you need to create places where people can work and live.

For example, in Kapolei, I see people driving for hours just to get to work, which is why I am building two business parks to create jobs as well as help establish communities. We have been developing in Kapolei for the past ten years and will be continuing to do so for the next ten years. Our business park is 178 acres.

We also just built the only rental housing with 269 units in Hawaiʻi Kai and will be building 800 more units at Kapiʻolani. We are in the middle of planning and permitting. I hope that we will be able to build more homes and make meaningful contributions in this community.

What are some of the obstacles you face as a developer?

Length of permitting, exactions that push the community's costs on to new developments, and fundraising are the biggest obstacles I have.

Many aren't keen on Hawaiʻi as there is high risk of government intervention. Potential investors may also hear horror stories of permits being stopped by the government, or taking twenty years instead of the expected one to two years for permitting. For example, the Hawaiʻi Superferry was granted its permits and production was underway when the government stopped the operation. Same goes for the Thirty Meter Telescope. It does not help that we are so far away. Investors tend to think of Hawaiʻi as an international location and not part of the United States, so much so that they term us under the Pacific Rim-International Fund. (*laughter*)

As a result, we tend to be considered tertiary and not a primary or secondary market. So I will say, Hawaiʻi itself is a challenge.

Many people may say that gender is an issue in my industry but I can honestly say, it is less about gender than about Hawaiʻi being a difficult place to develop and Hawaiʻi's distance from everything else. Its geography makes it difficult to do business.

Speaking of the next ten years, aside from your succession planning, what else can we expect from you?

We have been doing mostly commercial projects, business parks, and shopping centers, but you will see us doing a lot more housing projects. We entered the housing market in a most definitive way with the completion of the $170 million project in Hawaiʻi Kai. We are now embarking on our largest housing project, the $450 million Sky at Ala Moana project, so the next five years will be spent doing that. The five years after will be focused on looking at existing areas for redevelopment rather than greenfield projects. We want to increase density and build more affordable housing. I think approachable, accessible housing is a good vision.

It sounds as if Avalon's vision is very Hawai'i centric and has no intentions of expansion to the Mainland or overseas.

Yes, Avalon has always been a Hawai'i-only company. We tried for a few years to make it happen in California where I had residence. What I found was that, as a developer, I want to build communities for people who live and work there and I could only be a good developer if I was part of the fabric of the community. I live here and so, I decided, the buck stops here.

How do you want Hawai'i to be remembered?

As it is—safe, peaceful, beautiful, and a part of the United States.

You're so incredibly busy. What do you do to relax?

I go skiing twice a year. We are a family of skiers. My son is also my biggest hobby as he just brings so much joy. He's into baseball and basketball. I can't attend all of his practices, but I attend all his games including travels to the Mainland to compete. We spend time planning his trainings and his goals. That's my hobby. My son brings me down to earth and keeps me grounded.

Who would you love to have a sit down dinner with?

President Obama. You know why? Because he was a black child, raised by a single mom and his grandparents. He did not let his circumstances get to him and rose to become the president of the United States of America. He was elected not once but twice. He had so many things stacked against him and yet he achieved the American dream. Regardless where one's politics lie, it is admirable that Obama never looks back and is always forward thinking. He truly is a role model.

And this is also why I love the United States of America. It is the land of opportunities and possibilities.

My son was just three months old on the day President Obama was elected in 2008. When they announced the election results, I realized tears were rolling down my face. I remembered feeling that my son, too, can one day be president. That American dream is possible. Anything is possible.

As an immigrant, what are your thoughts on the forty-fifth president?

Don't let Trump get to you. He is just a blip in history. Most of us in the U.S. still believe in goodness and that the country was built by immigrants and their descendants.

How do you want to be remembered?

As a Korean American, who loved her adopted home, who made a difference in her community, and who left the place better for the future generations.

What would you say when you meet God?

Thank you. You were there whether I asked for it or not and you gave me exactly what I needed at the exact moment of need. I was truly blessed by you.

What is your own life philosophy on a bumper sticker?

Be fearless and give it all you've got.

Suppose you are writing your memoir. What would the title be?

I don't know. Success is what you make it out to be. *American Dream Actualized*?

I was born hungry and poor. I am an immigrant. I am a teenage runaway. I am a college graduate. I am a businesswoman. I am a mom. I am a community leader. I am the American dream actualized.

THE ISLAND SERENADER
Raiatea Helm

Technology has allowed more to gain access to our Hawaiʻi traditions, language, and history, which is all good. But the thing that I question is, "Can one really live and feel it?" Take me, for example. I am this girl from Molokaʻi, but when I sing, there is this connection and vibration with the past…my passion is derived from the richness of my genealogy, my lineage.

In 2006, Raiatea Mokihana Maile Helm made history as Hawai'i's first solo female vocalist ever to receive a Grammy nomination for her sophomore CD Sweet and Lovely. Then twenty-one years old, she was one of the youngest performers to attend the Grammy Awards in Los Angeles, California. The New York Times wrote that Raiatea "sings in the high-voiced throwback leo ki'eki'e style without a hint of kitsch … is poised and utterly elegant." She has gone on to win numerous awards, including female vocalist of the year, the coveted favorite entertainer of the year award, as well as multiple Nā Hōkū Hanohano Awards. Few performers can match that achievement.

Raiatea Helm has also proven herself to be as versatile as she is talented, and has ventured into jazz, receiving rave reviews. Her virtuoso recordings and performances have already launched her onto the international music scene with extensive concert appearances throughout the Mainland, as well as in Asia. Today, Raiatea has firmly established her reputation as Hawai'i's premier chanteuse and is a formidable part of the national as well as international music scene.

Her newfound voice in activism and pride in her Hawaiian ancestry is evident in our second interview. She shares fresh new insights into her lineage and provides a startling new revisionist narrative as a stark counterpoint to the current published accounts of Hawaiian history, which certainly leaves much food for thought, fodder for investigative journalism, and certainly inspiration to Raiatea's musical oeuvre.

Share with us who you were before you became this vocal virtuoso and Hawaiian star.

I was born on O'ahu in 1984 and raised on Moloka'i. I had a wonderful upbringing in a very small community, where everyone knows everybody. I was always surrounded by family and was raised by my maternal grandmother though my paternal grandmother would also watch us from time to time when Mom and Dad were working. I think those ties laid my foundation to the past. I never knew my paternal-grandfather, as he passed away before I was born, and I was too young to remember my maternal-grandfather, who also passed away in my childhood. But I was very close to both my grandmothers, who were both born in the 1920s, and their values were different from ours today.

My tūtū grew up in Hanapēpē, Kaua'i, in an era where the men worked and the women raised the family, so that's how tūtū grew up, raising her siblings. Tūtū Olga did in fact work. She had a significant role with legal aid on Kauaʻi, which led to assisting many families from the private Island of Niʻihau. As she came of age and became a young mother, she had lot of responsibility as she had eight children, one of whom was my mother. I was very close to tūtū ,and she was the one who taught me my very first song that is about the seashells—*Pūpū Hinuhinu*. Tūtū didn't have much to say, but I knew it was all up here in her head. It helped that I was a good listener, even when I was a little rascal. I always made time to listen to my grandparents as a form of respect. Unconsciously, a lot of what I know today is passed down through talk story and my keen listening—culture, history, spirituality—a lot of knowledge was passed down.

Was the performing arts part of the family tradition?

Communicating and academic study did not come easy to me. I had a hard time reading but I had no problems listening and remembering stories told to me. It helped that we had great storytellers on Molokaʻi who would share the legends and folklore of the islands. I still remember all of that today. I guess I learn best through memory and memorization.

Anyway, dancing hula was a part of growing up in Molokaʻi; I started at three years old. Back then, I didn't really like it as I wanted to be athletic, like my two brothers. I felt that I was always trying to impress my dad in sports, but I could never get into it no matter how hard I tried. I also remembered feeling I wasn't pretty. I had low self-esteem, was a tomboy, and didn't understand makeup and dressing up. I just never felt as if I was really good at anything. I was the funny girl, the class clown, and was very friendly but I didn't realize that my gifts and talents were different.

Anyhow, I did compete in the prestigious Merrie Monarch Festival three times, representing Molokaʻi. I was never competitive and always danced in the back, so the Merrie Monarch was a really big deal for us. The hula industry has changed since fifteen years ago.

What are some of the biggest changes you see?

Hula has modernized, and many things, like music and artists, too, have become commodified. Don't get me wrong. I know it is a necessary progress with time but, for me, I always felt like I had to find my own journey. So take the simple idea of packaging or imaging, I never understood the importance of looking good or dressing up as we didn't have to on Molokaʻi, but one of the things I later learned from being in the industry was that I had to dress the part.

These days, I also realize that some people may not have the aloha spirit anymore but I tell myself not to judge, as I do not know how their day went. I remind myself to try to make others happy every day, even if someone else was not very kind to me. We need to bring back aloha spirit.

I can tell you are a simple girl at heart, so how did being in the music and entertainment industry make you feel?

Yes it wasn't easy at the start. It was a tussle. I started singing at the age of sixteen and had no idea what I was getting myself into. All I knew was I finally found something I was good at even though I had no formal training at all. When I sang, it was as if a voice from the past was coming out of this sixteen-year-old girl from Molokaʻi. People began to take notice of me when I sang and I started to think, "OK, this is cool." It was only then that I realized maybe I did serve a purpose—to act as a bridge between the past and the present. But more on that later.

How were you discovered? What was your big break?

It was my parents who noticed that I had a voice. You see, both my brothers were smart, athletic, and they went to Kamehameha Schools. I was inspired by "watching" the Kamehameha Schools song contest. Anyway, in 1999, the theme for the contest was *Hawaiʻi Calls,* inspired by a popular radio show from the late 1940s and 1950s. The event honored the music of one of the most well-loved soprano mezzo singers Nina Kealiʻiwahamana, who is still alive today, as well as Jeffrey Apaka, who is the son of Alfred Apaka—a singer so highly-respected back in the day that people called him "Frank Sinatra." In fact, Frank Sinatra, himself, came to watch Alfred Apaka!

Back then, I never heard of these guys as I was on Molokaʻi and was not exposed to Hawaiian music. I didn't even grow up in a house that spoke Hawaiian. But once I heard Nina sing, I was hooked. All I wanted to do was to keep listening and I would rewind the tape to listen again and again. I recall asking my dad to teach me the chords to Nina's song. And that was when it all started. I would stay in my room playing and mimicking Nina. The inspiration was seeded and all I could think about was music.

When I went to high school, I was pretty much the only kid who wanted to pursue Hawaiian music. And that, in turn, became an even bigger source of inspiration to me, as I realized not too many in my generation wanted to study Hawaiian music. What was considered cool, then, was reggae and hip hop. I found that pushed me to want to learn and do more.

Hawaiian music spoke to your soul.

Yes it did. I realized so profoundly it was the music of my grandparents, my ancestors, and that it was already in my DNA. The seed was there and now all I had to do was water it.

So you inadvertently became part of a Hawaiian cultural renaissance?

Yes, today, the technology has allowed more to gain access to our Hawaiʻi traditions, language, and history, which is all good. But the thing that I question is, "Can one really live and feel it?" Take me, for example. I am this girl from Molokaʻi, but when I sing, there is this connection and vibration with the past.

I think we are living in an interesting era, where we are all discovering who we are because so much has been taken away from us. I, too, am not 100 percent Hawaiian, as I have a little bit of German, Welsh, Scottish, and Tahitian, so there is so much more to being Hawaiian. But my passion is derived from the richness of my genealogy, my lineage. I guess I have always been inspired and attracted to the past and loved to delve through old photos, newspaper articles, and old music, which is also why the songs that I sing are songs that were written a long time ago. What I did whenever I sang a song would be to consciously imagine how it would be if I was living in the past. I would place myself in the shoes of these old singers and imagine their life, culture, and politics then. The environment has changed drastically, but the identity struggles were similar and still very real.

Today, the industry is a lot more competitive, which is one of the things I don't really enjoy and find a challenge.

Share with us more about that.

I was in a relationship with my then manager and we broke up. He was the one who was seminal to and managed my entire career. I was the artist and didn't get a chance to really learn the business. Even though I was a millennial, I functioned differently and was an old soul but I also wondered if I should try to fit in and be more visible on social media to get more likes. Yet, that's not me so I struggled. Over time, I have learned to become more observant, patient, and kind of standoffish.

You see, when I was at the peak of my career and won numerous Nā Hōkū Hanohano awards and received Grammy nominations, Tower Records was still around and there was no social media to take advantage of. So back then, I had to decide if I wanted to stick to my roots or become a commercial singer—work with big production companies, present a lūʻau with fake orchid leis, and partake in the commodification of culture. But I felt a voice in me who wanted to stand up against this cultural appropriation. I wanted to create music that was of the highest standard and that I would be proud of in the long run.

Even today, it is still a dilemma for me—should I start a YouTube channel and invest more in social media or Facebook ads? I still question it, though I am definitely better now at creating networks and being social with others. I also decided to go back to school and am currently in the music department. It was a challenge but it's OK, as it is my dream to go back to school and embark on a process of self-discovery, as my late Auntie calls it.

How was this process of self-discovery and how has school been?

It has been good, you know. I recently watched Lionel Richie on CNBC and he said something that resonated with me, "It's not how you start, it's how you finish." It really got me thinking about how all of us can bring all our diverse talents together for a common good. I really hope that our society can put aside differences and work together. I am really hoping that this book can shed light on this need for diversity and harmony.

That is exactly my intention. So let's go back to how you manage that sweet spot, navigating between what modernity demands and your old soul.

I manage this through prayer. That's the key to patience and understanding. The generation now demands everything right away and I'm like, "Whoa. Wait a minute." I am not afraid to take my time to think about it first. That's really what I learned during my break from singing. My late godmother, who's my mom's older sister, had a cancer battle that made me pensive, and I started to recollect about my past and started to feel that we really do need to slow down and embrace what we see around us in our very hectic lives.

Do you have any regrets?

There have been so many lessons and so many things I could have done differently, such as not allowing someone else to manage my career and control my life. I am thirty-five now. Most of my friends have a job, are married, and have children. I still feel as if I have not yet lived my life and am still trying to figure things out but it's OK, it's all good.

What are some of your biggest challenges and how did you cope with that?

I would say, when my relationship ended, that also signaled an abrupt end to my career. My ex did everything in my earlier albums. I worked prolifically and it was great for me career-wise, but the relationship wasn't. I was drained and was so depressed the whole time. I was so unhappy and knew that I had to stop working at this pace or I would really hurt myself. I had to learn that I didn't need to rely on someone else to make me happy and that I can rely on myself, but I was so young then and was so lost. I didn't know where my career was headed at all. Outwardly, I was doing so well but deep inside, I felt as if I was stuck in a huge hole that I could not get out of. I ended the relationship eight years ago in 2011 and had to really face the consequences. I have never really shared this but I trust you, and I know this story has to be told and shared.

After the dust settled, I went back to school, as I always wanted to go back to school, but I held out because of my career. All those years, I had to tell myself that I cannot regret my decision as it was my choice. Now that I am more mature and back in school, I feel like a different person. I am learning new things to better my music abilities and my craft.

In my first semester alone, my mind was blown away by the sheer diversity of musical genres and musicians! We had students from marching band, rock singers, musical performers … it was just so exciting. I am learning so much and feel that there is more to come.

Knowing what you know now, what advice would you give to a budding artist?

I don't know if I am in a position to give any advice. Yes, I managed to make a name for myself, though I sometimes still cannot believe how many people I have touched with my music. Perhaps this has to do with my low self-esteem. But when I'm singing, I'm transformed and I feel good. Though, of late, many artists take advantage of the power of social media. But for me, I think being genuine is the most important. Don't rush into anything. Meditate on it and don't rush into projects.

Have you tried to reinvent yourself?

Yes and no. The majority of my audiences tend to be older people, though I have millennials coming up to me to say they heard my music when they were in elementary school and I feel good about it. (*laughter*) I definitely feel more comfortable in my own skin than I did ten years ago. Because I know for sure that I always do the best I can and there's no one else that does that kind of music that I do.

But like you, I have a vision and now know that I have control over my music. I have the confidence and ability now to go out and find the right people that can help and support me in my future creations that would see me exploring new sounds and styles.

The year 2018 has been a year of self-discovery. I stopped drinking two years ago and it has given me so much clarity. I realized that I have been distracted all these years and now need to clean up my ways, learn to love and appreciate myself so that I can do the work I am meant to do.

Much has happened and I want to share about my Auntie Wilma, who is my mother's oldest sister. They were many years apart and Auntie took care of my mother as a baby. Auntie also raised me as she didn't have children and was never married. She was a person of her own and education was key for her. She was very well-educated and served on numerous nonprofits that support Native Hawaiians. She also took on the kuleana, or a responsibility, to bring back the remains of our ancestors who have been placed in museums all across the world. She is spiritually, mentally, and physically strong, and an inspiring woman.

Her death has clearly had a profound impact on you ...

Yes. After Auntie Wilma died in January 2018, we witnessed the Big Island volcano eruption and many storms. In Hawaiian culture, we believe in kino lau[1] and I find myself embracing my spiritual side. As Hawaiians, we believe

---

[1] Kino lau literally translates into "many bodies" or the myriad of the 400,000 gods that make up the Hawaiian pantheon. Every plant and animal is an embodiment of a god, and so are clouds, rain, the movement of lava, the currents of ocean and air. Hōkūlani Holt, a Hawaiian cultural expert and revered kumu hula (teacher of hula) explains that there is some connection between the characteristics of the god

that after our kupuna leaves, we still need to carry on their work. I strongly feel that I am now continuing my Auntie Wilma's lifelong efforts and feel that I am here to continue the work of my generations' past.

Please share with us this discovery.

In order to do so, I wish to share a sacred story that we have kept in our family that goes back almost two hundred years to a moment in our Hawaiian monarchy where there is a missing link. All of us know of Kamehameha the Great who united the islands and his dynasty extended to Kamehameha V. After that, there were claims that Kamehameha V did not have children, so the throne went over to his cousin Lunalilo, who didn't last long. The crown then went to King Kalākaua, and eventually to Queen Lili'uokalani, who was the last reigning queen of the Hawaiian monarchy. But here is the missing link. We apparently have a direct tie to Lot Kapuāiwa, or Kamehameha V, who was rumored to not have any children.

Lot had attended Royal School that was put together by his uncle Kamehameha III to teach young ali'i on governance and world affairs. There, he met another princess, Abigail Maheha who comes from a strong line from Maui, which is the Kamehameha Nui line. In Hawai'i, you have to understand that it is the women who hold the bloodline, which is why Kamehameha the Great had so many wives, as he wanted to ensure he expanded his bloodline to strong families. Anyway, Lot and his siblings come from a strong bloodline and were considered the highest ranking ali'i, which is why, when Lot did not leave an heir, there was a scramble to find the next in line for the throne.

Is this where the plot thickens?

Yes. Lot apparently did leave an heir, as he impregnated Abigail Maheha while they were in Royal School. Lot was about sixteen, while Abigail was about fourteen, so to cover up the scandal, Abigail gets sent away to the island of Kaua'i and marries the gardener of her aunt who was the Governor of Kaua'i, a powerful woman. The low-ranking gardener was to assume the role of the father of the child, a daughter called Keanolani, who went on to marry three times. Her last husband was Olopua Kamali, also known as Uurupua Tamarii, and they had three children. I am currently learning more of him

---

and the kino lau and offers the example of Kāne, who, along with Kū, Kanaloa and Lono, is one of the four main Hawaiian gods. As Kāne's realm includes flowing and upwelling water, "many of his kino lau are either water bearers or plants that need lots of water: taro, bamboo, 'awa ... " says Holt. (https://www.mauimagazine.net/kino-lau/)

and have found new discoveries that he himself, although from Polynesia, is of the Kamehameha line. Two children died except for one daughter Hyacinth Keōpūolani Kamali, who was the only surviving offspring who went on to have children. She had two sons, one of whom she named Alexander Liholiho Kali, who later changed his name to Albert. His daughter's name is Olga Pualani Kali, who is my tūtū. Albert is my great-grandfather.

I learned all this from my Auntie Wilma. My mother wanted to start life anew with my father and leave behind her past, as she grew up knowing how much her family had to endure, and hiding their identity all through history. But now, the plot thickens further. You see, although King Kamehameha V died without naming a successor, he did state in his constitution of 1864, Article 22 that the crown should belong to a progeny "of my body ... lawfully begotten." So the big question is? What does this mean, as he did have a secret life with Abigail and he did leave a daughter, Keanolani. In fact, Abigail died in the site where the current ʻIolani Palace is and, just in 2018, I receive this invite to perform in the ʻIolani Palace, so it really is all very poignant.

When I was singing at ʻIolani Palace, it struck me that I was a direct descendant of the Kamehameha line. The Kalākaua line only ascended to the royal throne when the males of the House of Kamehameha were presumed to have died out. I feel that is the truth that people need to know and understand.

I can foresee that there may be controversies unleashed when this story is shared with the public.

Yes, as what will unfold is a story of the clash between Hawaiian traditions, American ways, as well as political intrigues. When America came to our lands, some of the Hawaiians, like Kamehameha V, were loyal to his people, but some wanted to curry favor with them. Above all, it is a story about crown lands that were wrongfully taken away from Keanolani by her supposed aunt, Princess Ruth Keʻelikōlani, who became the landholder of what would become the Bernice Pauahi Bishop Estate.

Apparently, there are records that Keanolani actually spent time in ʻIolani Palace and attended Queen Liliʻuokalani's birthday in 1903. She was recorded to have died in 1902 as a result of a seizure outside the water feature on the estate. All this happened while she was supposed to be under the protection of Queen Dowager Kapiʻolani's two nephews, Prince David and Prince Kūhiō.[2]

---

[2] Jonah Kūhiō Kalanianaʻole (March 26, 1871–January 7, 1922) was a prince of the Kingdom of Hawaiʻi until it was overthrown by a coalition of American and European businessmen in 1893. He later went on to become a representative in the Territory of Hawaiʻi as delegate to the United States Congress, and was the only person ever elected to that body who had been born into royalty.

Kūhiō's legacy is now in the hands of Abigail Kawānanakoa, who is embroiled in controversy of her own.

Keanolani is buried in an unmarked grave at Kawaiaha'o Church,[3] surrounded by a beautiful cast-iron fence, which would have cost a lot of money back then. If she was a commoner, she would not have had such an elaborate grave. Why wasn't she buried with her father at Mauna 'Ala, the Hawaiian mausoleum in Nu'uanu, when she was the guardian there? Does that mean she had very strong ties to the ali'i? Clearly, many things do not connect in the published accounts today, and there are many missing pieces.

I also have another aunt who still lives on Kaua'i, and she has the gift of memory and is able to recall all the names and dates, so I am documenting everything I can from her.

What have you decided to do with this new discovery?

I would like to take on the rewriting of history, by telling Keanolani's story, maybe through my music and, possibly, a book.

As this revelation is potentially controversial, what will you do if it does turn ugly?

Like my father, I want to make sure that things are done in a pono way without any fighting and violence. I am aware this road is hard as I only have a limited number of people on my side, but I do wish to right the wrongs done.

I hear you. And I truly cannot wait for what the future will bring given your coming of consciousness and newfound identity. Now, for some trivia. Who are your biggest musical influences?

I grew up listening to Celine Dion, Anita Baker, and R&B vocalists. I listened to Michael Jackson and a lot of Hawaiian music. The Hawaiian female vocalists inspire me, and I also listened to a lot of my uncle, a known activist, George Helm—he had an amazing voice. He had an ability to bring people to-

---

3 Kawaiaha'o Church is considered the Westminster Abbey of Hawai'i and is the national church of the Hawaiian Kingdom and chapel of the royal family. Turmoil erupted when a massive pit with over 600 iwi unearthed and forty-four bone fragments were exposed during recent erosion. The project to build a multi-purpose center has since been mired in protests, lawsuits and government bureaucracy. As of November 2018, the idea has been dropped.

gether because of his voice. And I realize I have this gift, too, so I do tell myself that I have the best job in the world.

I also had many mentors including my late aunt. She was always a reader and an educator, and always told us that reading and education were important, even for a musician.

Who would you like to have us sit-down dinner with?

Oprah and Martha Stewart.

What would you sing for them?

I would have a five-piece string orchestra or a quartet. Or I'll have a harp and sing old, classic Hawaiian songs. Many don't really know what classical Hawaiian music sounds like, as what they hear tends to be commercial "touristy" sounds, made popular by Hollywood movies and even Elvis Presley.

Recently, what's been trending is the slack-key guitar that was heard in the soundtrack of George Clooney's *The Descendants*, so many from the Mainland would relate to that. But I want to bring back the old sounds of the steel guitar from the 1920s.

What do you think best represents Hawaiian music?

Going back to school has reignited a passion in me to learn new and different sounds. We had a discussion on which instrument represents Hawaiian. Some said the 'ukulele, others said the steel guitar, and some said it would be the voice itself. It was exhilarating.

What is your take?

The voice, because when you listen to Hawaiian singers, the most unique part of that music is the voice.

Reality shows like *The Voice* and *American Idol* —yay or nay?

Well, it is definitely yay for them!

Musician or entertainer?

I'll say it depends on one's goals. If the aim is cultural preservation as a musician, then make sure you do your homework. In most cases, it takes years to master a musical genre.

What would you say when you meet God?

I pray every day and I tell him that I leave it in his hands. And that I will work hard and take it one day at a time.

How do you want to be remembered?

I want to be able to help others, especially as a woman and a Hawaiian. I want to empower other women and I wish to be able to share that guidance and inspiration.

What song sums up your life?

Oletta Adam's *Get Here*.

Define music.

Music is a tool that has the ability to unite people and to experience love on a different level.

What more can we expect from you in the near future?

That I will make smarter decisions, have more balance in my life, and create new music and sounds that people don't typically associate with me. I intend to record a new album in the next couple of years that I composed and arranged. I will be that artist that I always knew I would be—more empowered, confident, and knowing that whatever I choose to do will be really great. And, you know what? I know I'm almost there.

THE DYNAMIC DEVELOPER

Kathryn Whang Inouye

There is a deep sense of satisfaction in helping others…while we may not be able to independently change the world, we should each work to do what we can, even if it means helping one person at a time.

The Dynamic Developer

Kathy has recently taken the role of senior advisor at Kobayashi Group. She previously held the position of chief operating officer and oversaw its development activities. With over forty years of real estate development, her experience includes managing the development of various affordable housing residential projects on Lānaʻi, Molokaʻi, Maui, and Oʻahu; and the design and development of master-planned residential communities, as well as managing the planning, entitlement, and construction of condominiums, hotel-condominiums, schools, hospital facilities, the University of Hawaiʻi Cancer Center, shopping centers, and office buildings. She is also actively involved in all areas of the development process and is currently overseeing the 902 Alder Street project.

She received her bachelor's degree in secondary business education from the University of Hawaiʻi and has served on numerous professional and nonprofit boards, commissions, and fundraising committees. She currently serves on the board of directors for Child & Family Service and Hawaiʻi Pacific Healthcare, and was previously appointed by the former Governor Benjamin Cayetano to serve two four-year terms on the Board of Land and Natural Resources, as well as two terms as a board member on the Stadium Authority, appointed by former Governor Linda Lingle. She has also served as a board member for Mālama Learning Center, Girl Scouts of Hawaiʻi, Blood Bank of Hawaiʻi, Chaminade University's board of governors, the Korean American Foundation of Hawaiʻi and others, as well as director positions with industry-related organizations.

She has been honored with numerous professional and leadership awards over the years, most recently as an honoree of the 2015 Oʻahu YWCA 38th Annual Leader Luncheon Awards and was Pacific Business News' Businesswoman of the Year in 2010. She is being designated as an outstanding alumnus in 2019 by the Public Schools of Hawaiʻi Foundation.

Despite her decorated career and larger-than-life persona, Kathy exudes a genuine affection for everyone she meets. I first became acquainted with her as a mentor at the inaugural Girls Got Grit leadership program at Sacred Hearts Academy and was impressed by her humility and generosity during her time with the students. She mentored without being cloying and inspired the students to greater heights without being draconian. My mother always reminded me that the mark of a person's character was not who they are when in the company of greatness, but who they are amongst ordinary people. Kathy inordinately passes my mother's character-smell test—plus, the doorway to her well-appointed office has kiddy scribbles on it. It's a small detail, but one that makes her all the more human, authentic, and real. I guess one can say, with Kathy Inouye, the writing is on the wall, literally, and I mean that only in the best possible way.

Tell us about your family and growing in Hawai'i.

I grew up as one of four girls and the daughter of a country physician in Wahiawā. There were six of us in a two-bedroom, one-bath house. My father worked hard, but was not well compensated and often accepted trades or produce for his services. We may have been poor, but we were not deprived, and as children we were very happy.

When I was about eight, our financial situation improved when my father became a partner in a medical clinic and they were able to purchase their first home in Wahiawā. This is also when my older sister left for college, and I took on the role of the older sibling. Reflecting back, I can see that my personality traits manifested around this time, such as feeling the need to care for, protect, and entertain my younger sisters. For some odd reason, I anointed myself this role for the neighborhood and became the organizer of neighborhood events! I'd gather a group of kids, and we'd head to Lake Wilson to fish and build huts out of sticks and branches. The fire department was called on us more than once when we built bonfires while attempting to cook what we'd caught. Pushing the envelope with a kolohe streak became another personality trait, often upsetting my parents, while I sometimes inadvertently ran afoul of the law. But my sisters and the neighborhood kids loved it!

In elementary school, I worked hard to be a model student. Self-motivation has always been a part of me.

So you are actually of Korean descent?

Both my parents are of Korean descent but were raised to speak only English. My mom and dad each came from a family of six children and they both went to college. This was rare for children of immigrants at that time. Their story to Hawai'i would be familiar to many local families. My father's mother came here as a picture bride and spoke no English. Growing up, we were told the story of how she traveled here on a boat with no possessions and got seasick from the difficult journey. She told the story about landing here in Hawai'i and holding a picture of a tall, very handsome young man to whom she was to be married. Instead, a short Korean gentleman in a suit came up to her and simply said, "You're my bride." My grandmother was tall and insisted, "No, I'm looking for *this* man," and gestured to the photo she held. The man told her, "No, we all paid him to use his photo." Without further argument, they were married.

Despite her very limited English language skills, she started to amass a real estate portfolio that she personally managed. I guess you would say she was the first in our family to be in the Hawaiʻi real estate business! Back then, immigrants had no access to credit for bank loans, so she managed a "tanomoshi,"[1] where several individuals pool their money and bid on an interest rate. My paternal grandmother was the "bank." She would then purchase rental properties, followed by modest apartment buildings, and finally vacant land. She was exceptionally enterprising, and none of us realized how much property she had owned until she passed away.

What was interesting, but unfortunate, is that neither of my parents learned to speak Korean or learned much about Korean culture. They were both born and raised in Hawaiʻi and their parents felt that they should only speak standard English and learn to adopt the American culture in order to be successful. Both my parents were educated on the Mainland at some time during their high school and college years. Therefore, growing up, we also never learned to speak Korean. Other than Korean food, we knew extremely little about the culture. My first exposure to the culture was when my mother and grandmother entered me in the Miss Koreana pageant when I was a senior in college. This was not something I aspired to do and I had absolutely *no* time nor desire to devote preparing for it. I protested and said I have absolutely no talent and refuse to parade around in a bathing suit in front of hundreds of people. My mom must have known I'd protest because she said she had already asked and neither of those categories were part of the pageant. She convinced me to do it, saying it would make my harlmonie[2] proud. Because I loved my harlmonie dearly, I acquiesced. Unlike the other contestants, I didn't get my hair or makeup done professionally, didn't have time to get a proper gown, and didn't prepare responses to a list of possible questions during the interview segment. That day, I pulled a long dress out of my closet and just drove down to the Korean Consulate where the pageant was being held. Indeed, my harlmonie showed up on a bus with a dozen of her friends from the senior center. I'll never forget the glow on her face when I was crowned.

With the exception of a few people, this achievement is something I've never discussed until now, as I felt it would hinder rather than help me in my career.

---

1 Tanomoshi refers to a locally organized social finance scheme that had existed in Japan at least since the middle Kamakura Period, ie. 1185–1333. The principle was that each member would contribute a sum at regular intervals and would receive a single payment when their turn came round. This scheme required mutual trust among those involved. The institution facilitated personal savings, investment in property and enterprise, insurance, personal loans, and assistance of poorer people. By the Tokugawa period, between 1603–1868, tanomoshi was widespread, and by the nineteenth century, most tanomoshis, were incorporated into mutually financed mujin companies. The system also operated among Japanese immigrants to the United States and Brazil, helping them in establishing new businesses there. While the system diminished in Japan, it remained of great importance to overseas Japanese communities.

2 Grandmother in Korean is 할머니 pronounced Halmeoni. It tends to get romanized to "harlmonie."

Tell us a little more about your childhood.

Since my father was a doctor in Wahiawā, I grew up near the Schofield Army and Wheeler Air Force Bases and spent most of my elementary school years at Wheeler Elementary. I was one of very few local kids in my class and most of my friends were transient military kids who would move when their fathers were re-stationed elsewhere. It was always difficult to lose newly made friends every year, but I learned to accept transient friendships as a part of my childhood. When I finally went to intermediate and high school off-base, I was able to develop long-term and even lifetime friendships. A lot of those people are friends of mine to this day, and even though we've taken different paths, we regularly get together. I know that my beginnings in Wahiawā have had a major impact on the person that I've become.

That must have honed your sense of humility?

Yes, as well as one of my first jobs. When I was a sophomore in high school, I told my parents I was going to spend that summer working in the pineapple fields. They tried to discourage me and suggested that I could do a number of other things. But I told them that being from Wahiawā, I wanted to have this experience. It was important for me to prove to myself that I could do the physically demanding work. So off I went to the fields that summer, and I certainly learned to appreciate the value of every dollar I earned, one pineapple and blister at a time.

The experience also exposed me to a different community. Although I was working with some of my girlfriends from high school, I also worked alongside Filipino immigrants and boys from a juvenile detention home in Nānākuli. It quickly helped me realize that despite our differences ethnically, culturally, and socially, each person wants and needs to be respected, regardless of their background or economic status. This is where I learned I could find something in common with almost anyone.

How did you choose your path after high school?

I didn't want to immediately go to college, but the concept of a gap year didn't exist back then, so I told my parents I was going to join the service, see the world, and then go to college on the G.I. Bill. My dad knew I was a bit of a contrarian and nonconformist, so instead of saying I had to go to college, he said, "Well, you probably think you don't want to go to college because you'd like to do other things, but going to college is a wonderful life experience and it's part of growing up. You should go now with people your age and see the world later. Go to college now and have fun." I'm sure he knew that this tactic would be far more successful with me rather than his insisting I go to college.

With this encouragement from my dad and the revelation that if I enlisted it would be for at least four years, this nonconformist decided I'd better go to college instead after all. At least I'd pursue a degree in business and increase my chances of employment upon graduating. However, due to my procrastination, my college options were limited. I attended the University of Hawai'i as a secondary business education major in order to get my business courses, since the deadline to apply to the College of Business had passed.

Although my parents could now afford to pay for my college education, I wanted to prove my independence and was determined to support myself through college, which included sometimes working two jobs. During my senior year in college, my advisor recommended me for an instructor position at Kapi'olani Community College.

I taught community college for three semesters while I was studying for my master's degree in education. I also taught adult night school courses and would survive on fifteen to twenty minute naps between my day job and my master's classes, before teaching night school. After my night classes, I'd correct papers, prepare lesson plans, and do work related to my own classes. It was a difficult time and I was a sleep-deprived during much of that period.

My future husband, Myles, was doing the same thing alongside me.

And you liked that about him?

Yes, that's one of the many things I liked and respected about him. He was going to school full time and was also working long hours. We shared a lot of the same values, but one of the things that impressed me about him was that he respected me and my ambitions. Very early on in our relationship, without prompting, he said he felt I had a promising career and he would be supportive of whatever I chose to do. This was even before the pinnacle of the women's rights movement, so I was impressed by how forward-thinking he was.

He has continued to be supportive of me and my career. I feel he has made sacrifices in his own career in order to support me and our kids. I'm often asked how I was able to balance my career with the long work hours and raising two kids, and it's because I had an extremely supportive spouse. I also had my parents, my husband's parents, our kids' sitter and her family, and our entire extended family as our support group. They took turns cooking for our family and watching our kids when I had to travel for work, or had to work late many evenings. We owe much to our own personal "village of supporters" for their love. We speak to our children often about this to make sure they understand and appreciate all that others have done for us.

What is your philosophy as a parent?

As a parent, you hope that you've raised your children to be loving, caring adults who find work that is financially, but more importantly, personally rewarding. We have taught them to give back to society. If they don't yet have the financial means, we encourage them to give their time to social causes that are important to them. From the time they were seven and five years old, we had them involved in community service.

I remember a story. It took place just before Halloween when my kids were quite young. We were out delivering goody bags to homeless kids. It was getting late and it started raining. They hadn't eaten dinner yet, but we had one last donation to make at a homeless shelter. The kids were fussing and they were hungry and cold. I comforted them by reassuring them this was our last stop, but I also took the time to explain to them that what they were feeling was what these homeless kids experience almost every night. They understood this concept even at this young age and agreed to go on.

As we started to unload the goody bags from the car, one of the women in the shelter asked if we would like to come in for a visit. She explained how the families lived in this tent city and how the kids spent their days and evenings. This experience was the formal start to my children's exposure to homeless communities. Since then, they have continued to volunteer to help the less fortunate, both here in Hawai'i and abroad.

One Easter, we went back to that homeless tent shelter and found that the tents had been dismantled. Upon inquiring with several social service agencies, I discovered that some of the families had been moved to a shelter on the Leeward side of O'ahu, but we were not allowed access due to privacy and security issues. We were asked to drop off our donations at the Child & Family Service office on Vineyard St. I persisted and shared that my children have always made donations directly to children, because it's important that they see their faces in order to understand and appreciate their plight. I eventually managed to get us clearance, and we arrived that weekend to find a very small, hot, crowded house with no air conditioning. There were probably eighteen mothers and children, who had sought temporary shelter there due to abusive home environments. I recalled seeing two mothers trying to help their children with homework on one kitchen table—trying to create a sense of normalcy in a difficult situation. As I sat there, the critical need of an appropriate facility became immediately apparent. I knew this wouldn't occur quickly if I were to seek and apply for state or city funding. So instead, when I went to work the following Monday, I called a friend who is an architect and asked him to help design a study room for the shelter. I reiterated that everything had to be manuahi.[3] I then called subcontractors—carpenters, masons, electricians, painters, and roofers—and shared my story. They were all willing to donate their services and materials for this modest project. The generosity from these companies on such short notice was amazing, and many of them brought their office staff to personally do the work.

I spent many hours there, while the project was being constructed, and got to know some of the women who sought refuge in the shelter. Two women, in particular, would sit down with me in the afternoons and weekends when I was there coordinating the construction. They shared that they do not receive emotional support or sympathy from their families regarding their domestic abuse situations. Domestic violence was somewhat normalized and accepted in their families, and they were often told they must have done something wrong to make their husband or boyfriend so angry. There is nothing normal about domestic violence, and I insisted that they break the cycle for the sake of their children. I asked if they wanted to do something to better their situation permanently, and they both agreed. We spoke about the importance of getting an education so that they could seek meaningful employment, and I suggested they first obtain their GED.[4] They both did and went on to Leeward Community College. It was no easy feat. They had to take the bus to and from campus, and had no convenient childcare support. They had to work late into the night in a computer lab on campus to complete their course work, then get back on the bus to pick up their kids before heading home to Waiʻanae. I gave them my cell number in case they ever needed to hear a word of encouragement. At the end of the first semester, they both shared with me that they earned straight As! We got together to celebrate this amazing achievement in the face of their many obstacles.

Each woman eventually moved out of the shelter and permanently away from their abusive environments, and we maintained contact for a long time to come.

---

3 Hawaiian for "free."

4 GED, or General Educational Diploma, is for those without a high school diploma. The study and subsequent tests are meant to certify one's aptitude, knowledge, and skills. It is designed for those that did not complete high school and can be taken at a local test center to certify that the North American test taker has met high-school level academic skills.

You have a deep sense of empathy. What propels you to do what you do?

There is a deep sense of satisfaction in helping others. I hope by sharing some of these stories, it inspires people to either reach out to help others or to seek help. There are so many stories I could share as I've done this for so many years. Some of the young girls I've met were severely abused by relatives who suffered from drug addiction problems. One girl told me that her father would lock her in the bathroom with him since she was six years old, give her crack, and sexually abuse her. Another showed me the scars all over her arms from years of self-mutilation. I mention these two young girls, in particular, because after shadowing me at work one day, I brought them with me to observe a Child & Family Service board meeting. I told them they could see the people that were behind the organization that supports their program, but they wouldn't have to say anything. However, once the girls were there, they asked if they could share their personal stories with the board. By the time they were done speaking, many in the room were crying—even some of the men.

We've told our kids that while we may not be able to independently change the world, we should each work to do what we can, even if it means helping one person at a time.

Your children are a reflection of you, no doubt. So let's get back to how you started in real estate?

After college, I taught for three semesters at Kapiʻolani Community College and realized that I wasn't going to make enough money to support myself. So I went to work for an employment agency, which I figured was the best way to discover what jobs were out there. I subsequently became a recruiter, as well as the company's manager. One day, a businessman from Japan walked into the office. He looked as if he had slept in his suit on the plane. He said they were starting a real estate development company in Hawaiʻi and needed to hire accountants, project managers, administrative assistants, and several other positions. Interestingly, he emphasized that none of the hires should be able to speak Japanese. I proceeded to write up thirteen job descriptions and started to recruit people to fully staff this company.

One day while I was placing the weekly ads for my company with the local newspaper, I was told that our company's checks had bounced. I called the banks and learned that the owner of the company had withdrawn all the funds and was nowhere to be found. I had to break the news to my staff and asked them to call all our clients to inform them of the immediate closure of the business. The Japanese developer I spoke of earlier asked me to come to meet the executives at their office and they created a job for me. That company is now known as Haseko.

So I started out in real estate development in 1979 as an administrative assistant. Half of the employees were from Japan and spoke very little English with no practical U.S. business experience. The other half (as per the recruitment request) could not speak any Japanese because the company felt this would force their Japanese employees to learn English. This resulted in a bit of a communication gap within the organization. Since I spoke English, I would get calls from the architects or contractors asking me to convey messages regarding various issues they were having. I found it easier to just do the research to find answers to their questions or to find solutions to problems rather than trying to explain it to a Japanese counterpart, who spoke very little English. I started by routing plans through the building department for permits. I would read everything, take copious notes, and asked a lot of questions. This is when I started learning real estate development. It was on the job, task by task, and by taking on responsibilities.

That is an amazing story! Do you think your career has been a function of luck, fate, serendipity, or function of choice and will?

I can't say I attribute a lot of a person's career successes to luck, but I do believe if you work hard, you'll be recognized. We all have the power to create and maximize opportunities for ourselves. Once I had a job in a real estate development company, I seized every opportunity to learn about development. I wanted to learn as much as I could about the design, construction, legal, and political aspects. I enjoyed the creative process, the problem solving, and the myriad of seemingly endless challenges. I realized I also enjoyed bringing different groups together to reach a common objective. It was an exciting and interesting time for a twenty-nine-year-old female, working for a Japanese developer at the height of the Japanese real estate boom. I ended up working there for five years, until the Japanese bubble burst. It was time for me to move on.

When I tendered my resignation, Haseko asked me to stay and offered me a position in either their New York or Los Angeles office. After some reflection, I felt I needed to take on a new challenge and wanted to build affordable housing for Hawai'i residents. Before I started a job search or even applied anywhere, I received a call from the State of Hawai'i Housing Authority (or HHA, as it was known at that time). The state was just beginning to create large master-planned communities on three major islands—the Big Island, Maui, and Oʻahu. The "Second City" of Kapolei on Oʻahu was the first of these communities to be developed. I was excited to become involved in what I felt would make a significant impact on housing for local residents. When I started, I helped work on legislation for affordable housing and worked on some unique projects and programs. But it was a challenge to fit in. I was one of the first two females in the project management section, and naive to the political climate.

What was it like working in a male-dominant environment?

I was advised by someone that used to work in the government, "Don't work too hard, don't be too aggressive, and keep your head down." I thought I understood his advice but didn't fully realize the impact of what he was saying. I wanted to just do the best job possible and stay under the radar, but my pace and work style was just different in this environment. The department head assigned me to a few projects the agency considered significant and that they wanted expedited. I thrived on the challenge. However, in doing so, others felt threatened, and I was ostracized and harassed by some of my male peers.

I became pregnant shortly after being hired, and there were a few physical challenges working throughout the pregnancy. I remember sitting on the floor reviewing plans, because we only had work cubicles with very little space. Because the women in the secretarial pool sympathized with my condition, one day they found me an unused table in a back storage room and carried it to my work area! That day, one of the guys noticed it and insisted it was his table. I explained that the secretaries found it in a back room and brought it to me so I could read plans on it. Fortunately, one guy in the group stood up for me and told him to leave me alone since I was hapai.[5]

And this was in the 1980s?

It was 1984. Sexism was still rampant and, remember, I was a young and female in a political, bureaucratic work environment and was not a political appointee. Things were different back then, and I felt like an intruder in an old-boy network. The good thing is, the department head that hired me was very progressive. He would invite me into brainstorming and planning meetings. Both he and the executive director were extremely supportive and rewarded me based on the results of my work.

---

5 Hawaiian for pregnant.

Before I left for maternity leave, I was given a promotion and a raise, even though I had only been in the job for a few months. This was not accepted well by my immediate supervisor. He told me the promotion was "not his idea" and that, before I receive another raise, I would have to work twice as hard as any of the guys there. Back then, I didn't see this as a sexist statement, and felt that he was offended because he wasn't consulted. When I returned from maternity leave, I had the opportunity to work on some wonderful affordable housing projects. I enjoyed what I was doing, but could see that I couldn't thrive in this environment in the long run.

Around the time I was contemplating my options, I received a call from someone at Castle & Cooke. David Murdock had just purchased the majority of the island of Lānaʻi and slated it for some major development. By this time, I had a young toddler *and* a baby ... and here I was headed into a challenging, corporate environment. I took a job overseeing the development of housing on Lānaʻi. I was commuting to and from Honolulu to Lānaʻi and Maui. I'd often get up at 3:30 am to catch the first flight out to Lānaʻi or Maui, and wouldn't get back until late in the afternoon. I often had to grab a quick nap in my car in the airport parking lot just so that I would be awake enough to drive home.

That job is really where I started to learn more about construction in the field and what it was like to be a woman in a predominantly male environment. Despite what one might expect, I developed a great working relationships with the construction guys on our Lānaʻi job sites. I'd walk the site with them and ask them how we could more efficiently design the homes for better constructability. They appreciated that I wanted to hear their ideas and learn what they did, and they were generous with their feedback. I'd then take their comments to the architects, and we'd incorporate many of the recommendations into the plans. This did not sit well with the construction superintendent, who claimed I was just creating more paperwork for him.

One day when he came to Lānaʻi for the weekly job site meeting, he yelled that I stay off his job site and not talk to his men. He, then, proceeded to kick dirt on my construction boots. I somehow managed to maintain my composure. This confrontation took place in front of several of the guys in the field, who later told me how much they respected me for not buckling. The situation was brought to a head when the CEO of our company told him he technically worked for me.

After a few years of this difficult commute, and having a family with two young children, I asked to be reassigned to Oʻahu to work on the new Mililani Mauka master plan project. By that time, some companies, including Castle & Cooke, were much more sensitive to sexism in the workplace. While I was there, I hired and promoted both men and women in project managerial positions with full support from the executive team. I remained at Castle & Cooke until 1995 when I joined Kobayashi Group.

How did that happen?

Throughout my time at Castle & Cooke, I was often contacted by recruiters but I usually turned down interviews. However, by 1995, I felt it was time to move on in my career and wanted a more entrepreneurial environment. I received a call one day from an attorney, who stated his firm was representing the Association of Apartment Owners on a project against a developer. The attorney asked if I would be an expert witness for the plaintiff. I asked whether they had first attempted to resolve their concerns with the developer. They had not. After listening to their list of complaints, I told them, except for a few items, I felt they had bought into a project with quality that was consistent with what they had paid. I further suggested that they speak to the developer and provide him the opportunity to address their concerns. I then contacted that developer so that he'd be prepared with appropriate responses. Later that afternoon, I received a call from the attorney, who said they spoke to the developer, and their concerns would be addressed.

The same attorney then said he had also been in a conversation with Bert Kobayashi and that Bert wanted me to call him. I did so, and Bert and I arranged to meet after work that day. He told me he had just sold his construction company via an ESOP,[6] and wanted to focus on a real estate development company. He offered me the position of partner and chief operating officer. He said his kids had just graduated from college and didn't yet know the business. All he asked that I do is commit three years to his company and then I could move on. That was almost twenty-two years ago, and I'm still with Kobayashi Group.

---

6 One of the most difficult problems for owners of closely held businesses is finding a way to turn their equity in a business into cash for retirement or other purposes. The decision to sell can be more than an economic one as an owner develops strong feelings of identity with the company over time. In addition, the owner often has a sense of loyalty to the employees and would like to see them have a continuing role in the company. For some business owners, the answer to these problems will be to turn over the company to an heir or sell to a competitor. But many owners do not have heirs interested in the business, and outside buyers are not easy to find. Even if they can be found, they may want to buy the company for its customer lists, technology, or facilities, or may just want to put a competitor out of business. As such, ESOPs (employee stock ownership plans) can be a very attractive and tax-favored alternative.

> What a story. You have both been denigrated and exonerated as a woman. Given what you have witnessed and experienced, would you say you have created policies that have enabled women to excel?

I don't think I've done nearly enough to benefit women with the creation of any policies or legislation. But I hope that I've been a good role model and that I've paved the way for more women to hold leadership positions in the industry. Unlike when I started, the industry is now very accepting of women serving in the lead roles for architectural, engineering, project management, and construction management companies. So much so that I have seen female-dominant management teams on projects. I recall an incident a few years ago. I walked into a meeting and it was an almost all-female leadership team—a female project manager, female engineer, female inspector, and female architect.

It's been exciting to see the transformation. We have come so far that a woman is hired because of her ability, and gender is no longer an issue. There is much more respect for women in the industry today, and it's less of an anomaly to see women in construction or design leadership roles.

> What would you say is your biggest failure?

They're related to hard lessons learned from trying to manage or mediate difficult relationships in the work environment. I would also say that I regret the stance I took in my first major negotiation at the beginning of my career. I took an all-or-nothing approach, and although I achieved the intended outcome for my company, it was rigid and unnecessary and left the other side feeling wholly defeated.

> What would you say to a young woman who is torn between her career and her family?

I tell young women (and men!) to always carve out special time with your family. In mentoring young leaders, the men will ask me almost as often as the women, "How do I achieve a work-life balance?" The men do want to be present fathers. This generation as a whole strives for a more balanced lifestyle. However, when you're starting on the leadership track, it's difficult not to put in the long hours. Realistically, you'll sometimes have to make sacrifices.

Many times, work-life balance feels elusive and sleep deprivation is common. Oftentimes you'll feel maxed out between the demands of work and family commitments. I tell them I have taken off from work and worked late into the night just to be at birthday parties, baseball games, ballet recitals, dance competitions, and May Day programs. My schedule was crazy while my kids were growing up, but I've never regretted it. Your kids will fondly remember special times you spent with them, so, as a parent, it's important to be there for them whenever you can. And unplug when you're with them! Listen to them. Take the time to have real conversations about issues important to them. My kids still talk about special things we did together while they were young. We laugh about some of the silly things we did when we thought no one was looking and the many gatherings I'd put together with extended family.

What do you appreciate about growing up in Hawaiʻi?

I appreciate the ethnic and cultural diversity in Hawaiʻi. I think this exposure makes us more accepting of others and more willing to try new and exciting things. I also appreciate that we are an embracing culture and are maybe quicker to make friends and introduce them to our social, family, and business networks. I also know that if I'm ever in a bind, I'd have at least a dozen people willing to help. And they know I'd be there for them as well.

As a real estate developer, do you believe in "keeping the country country" or "selling a slice of paradise?"

This could amount to an entire chapter of its own! Just the other day, there were several of us in a taskforce session at city hall, where we were discussing the extreme demand for affordable housing in Hawaiʻi and what sort of legislation was needed to support its development. Our cost of construction and land prices are very high—among the highest in the world. We need to focus on building affordable rental housing targeted at those making 30 to 60 percent of area median income. We need to provide housing security. Importantly, zoning regulations need to be moderated so that developers can actually make a dent in providing affordable housing. We need to incentivize the development of tens of thousands of truly affordable homes. Ask anyone in this industry—if we are given the right tools, we all want to do something to help and strengthen our community through affordable housing.

So if you could wave a magic wand, the first thing you would do is:

Revamp our public education system. A good education is a social and economic equalizer and a good public education system is critical to our community. Major changes need to occur in order to make this possible.

How do you want Hawai'i to be remembered?

I think you'll hear from almost everyone that we want to be remembered for our culture of tolerance and acceptance. We're proud of our diverse traditions, different cultures, environment, and a wide array of delicious foods. I want us to be remembered for being so embracing. Many of my guests say they don't experience this warmth and diversity in any other part of the United States.

How do you want to be remembered?

It may sound trite, but first and foremost, as a good wife, mother, and friend. When I mentor young people, I always share this, "What will make you happy is to earn enough money to live comfortably, but what will really make you happy money can't buy. It's also important to give back to your community. You'll need to make the time to do this!" As a family, we talk a lot about effectuating social change. My son is a huge proponent, and I need to reel him in sometimes! He will say, "If you don't think big, nothing will happen," and I'll say, "Yes, but if you don't compromise, nothing will either."

What do you do to relax?

I love to travel, spend time with family and, at the end of the day, sit down with my husband over a glass of wine.

You speak so fondly of your husband. There is a saying that behind every successful man is a successful woman. In your case, it is more "behind a successful woman is a very supportive man."

Oh absolutely! I can't imagine being able to raise our kids the way we have, being able to establish my career, and having such a happy marriage without the husband I have.

Who would you like to have a sit-down dinner with?

It would not be someone famous. I love sitting down to dinner with a small group of men or women, who I like and respect, to openly discuss a range of topics without fear of negatively impacting our relationships. The topics would range from the cerebral, to what we're going to do to create positive change in our community, to making fun of each other! Our sit-downs often go for four hours!

Which begs the question, what inspires you?

My children! My husband and I were just talking about how we wanted to raise kids who would be better than us. And I think we did. Our children have become very inspirational to us.

What is your favorite development?

The most recently completed project is always my favorite. So I would have to say Park Lane, as it's a beautiful project and one of the most challenging projects in which I've been involved. But I am also pleased to have been part of the development of the University of Hawai'i Cancer Research Center, as it focuses on the research of cancers that impact our diverse ethnic community.

Favorite architecture?

The Taj Mahal, not only because of its timeless beauty, but because it represents undying love; and Sagrada Familia by Antonio Gaudi, because of its extreme uniqueness.

What would you say if you met God?

Thank you for the blessings in my life.

What's your life philosophy on a bumper sticker?

Live life with no regrets!

THE IRREPRESSIBLE ENTREPRENEUR

Isabella Ellaheh Hughes

Don't play by the rules. There is no one-size-fits-all way to do things. The rules set by academia in the arts or museum culture can be quite daunting to the emerging artist, but please do not be afraid of your own vision. Building a team is the next key component [and] be open to sharing your vision and not hold on to too much ego and ownership.

Born and raised in Honolulu, Isabella Ellaheh "Bella" Hughes is a graduate of Punahou School and earned a BA in art history from Boston University and an MA in museum studies from Johns Hopkins University. She is best known as an arts and culture leader, entrepreneur, and sustainable agriculture advocate.

Currently, she is the president and co-founder of Shaka Tea, as well as director emeritus and co-founder of the Honolulu Biennial Foundation. A member of the 2018 Pacific Business News' 40 Under 40, Hughes was appointed by Governor David Ige to serve on the Hawai'i Technology Development Corporation Board (HTDC), in addition to serving on the board of Honolulu Biennial Foundation. And in 2019, she was appointed by Mayor Harry Kim to the Merit of Appeals Board serving Hawai'i County.

Bella is also a frequent public speaker and moderator on the arts, culture, entrepreneurship, and agriculture around the world. As an independent curator and writer, she has worked both locally and internationally for more than a decade, running Isabella Arts Advisory. Focusing on contemporary art from the Middle East, Asia, and the Pacific, Bella has been a nominator for the Smithsonian Artist Research Fellowship Program, the Jameel Prize, and Abraaj Capital Art Prize. She also has served as a juror for the YICCA International Contest of Contemporary Art, Art Omi International, and the annual Hawai'i Craftsmen show, amongst others. As a curator, she has curated exhibitions globally for the Smithsonian National Museum of the American Indian, U.S. Embassy in Abu Dhabi, Art Dubai, Maraya Art Center, and Ayyam Gallery.

She was also a winning "Trailblazer" for Food Vision USA 2016; a finalist at New Beverage Showdown 12, presented by Bevnet; a finalist for Coca-Cola's Venturing & Emerging Brands (VEB) in 2016; a two-time finalist for the Hawai'i Venture Capital Association Awards (2017 and 2018); and most recently, won a spot in the Burt's Bees Natural Launchpad, which focused on woman-led, natural consumer packaged goods businesses. Most recently she won the Judges' Choice CPG Award at Foodbytes! presented by Rabobank in San Francisco in March, 2019.

Share with us about your family, background, and who you were before you became the co-founder of the Honolulu Biennial and Shaka Tea?

I was born and raised in Hawai'i and am fourth generation kama'āina on my dad's side, and my mother is a first-generation immigrant from Iran. I was fortunate to attend Punahou, which gave me a great educational foundation. Culturally, like many kamaʻāina deeply appreciative of our host culture, I always felt very connected to Hawaiʻi and Hawaiian culture, in particular through dancing in a hālau when I was growing up, being surrounded by Hawaiian family friends, my dad passing on a deep love of Hawaiian history, and being immersed in Hawaiian culture growing up here.

Being multicultural and with a flight-attendant mom, we traveled a bit growing up to visit my mom's family on the continent, who she got green cards for when they left Iran after the revolution, and we went to Japan and Europe during my formative years.

I've always been interested in the arts and spent a lot of my childhood at the Honolulu Academy of Arts and The Contemporary Museum, which merged and now are known as the Honolulu Museum of Art. I was also fond of the Bishop Museum and would go often with my dad. Some of my earliest and favorite memories were in art and cultural exhibitions. I remember being fascinated with the artists' narratives and our local history and culture, especially at the Bishop Museum. Even as a nine year old, I remember planning our travel itinerary when we went to Chicago, which would include trips to the museums.

Later on, I was also very taken with contemporary artists and their engagement with current social issues. In retrospect, I realized that my efforts in co-founding clubs to help organize political rallies in high school were all very entrepreneurial.

So how and when did you decide to co-found the Honolulu Biennial?

I am a firm believer in doing what one is innately good at and has a passion for, rather than go on an uphill battle against one's natural abilities and inclinations. As shared, I was always interested in museums and art. I guess you can say it started in high school when I did an internship at the Honolulu Academy of Arts. I took AP Art History at Punahou and realized there were tangible ways to be in the arts and not become an artist but as a curator or museum director. This led me to study art history while I was an undergraduate at Boston University. I later did my masters in museum studies at Johns Hopkins and was always interning, working, and volunteering for cultural organizations and museums. I started my formal career as an independent curator, cultural projects consultant, journalist, and author for all six years that I was living off island. But Hawaiʻi, my home, was always close to my heart.

One of my biggest frustrations as a young arts professional working globally was recognizing that there was a dire lack of representation of our kānaka maoli, kamaʻāina, and Hawaiʻi-based artists in museums, art fairs, and galleries, which is how I curated the first exhibition on contemporary kānaka maoli artists when I was twenty-two years old. It was called *This IS Hawai'i* and came out of a project proposal for a graduate course I was doing in curating.

I ended up reaching out to Transformer, a two-hundred-square-foot, storefront-like gallery space and proposed to their executive director, Victoria Reis, that we stage this exhibit as a two-site, collaborative project with the Smithsonian National Museum of the American Indian, featuring the work of Solomon Enos, Puni Freitas (now Jackson), Carl FK Pao, and Maika'i Tubbs. The exhibit was small, but powerful, and by the time it opened, I was twenty-four. The experience taught me the importance of being proactive, and to have grit and focus.

Usually in the arts, especially when I was starting out, the art world was quite rigid and academic. You couldn't curate exhibits, especially without a PhD, so you have a culture of folks interning often into their early thirties as they complete their PhD. Envisioning, curating, and collaborating with an array of partners to make *This IS Hawai'i* happen made me realize that there are ways around strict confines and constraints of any established system.

This IS Hawai'i was a thematic, mini-intro to contemporary indigenous Hawaiian art and challenged the voyeurism and the hyper-marketed pastiche of what the world thinks Hawai'i is. There was a lack of knowledge of our insanely talented, contemporary indigenous Hawaiian artists. I was, then, actually living abroad in the UAE, but flew back for the opening. I spent time in the galleries, anonymously listening to conversations amongst the visitors, and one of their first questions would invariably be, "Where *is* the Hawaiian art?" As this was the first exhibition on contemporary kānaka maoli art in DC, I realized folks were expecting art depicting tourist scenes, beaches, and maybe hula dancers.

So the idea was really born out of your observations and passion to share Hawaiian art with the world?

Yeah. All these observations really fueled my desire and impetus to work to position and highlight the talents of artists of Hawai'i and important stories their work often shares. It is quite content-rich, as a way to more meaningfully and authentically reflect our island, our history, and our culture. We wanted to use contemporary art as a vehicle to challenge what Hollywood and the tourism industry had been selling for the past sixty or seventy years.

Through synchronicity, Honolulu Biennial Foundation (HBF) was co-founded by myself and Dr. KJ Baysa, another kama'āina arts curator and physician, who I had met when I was an intern at the Vera List Center for Art and Politics in 2007. We stayed in touch and he came down to see the opening of *This is Hawaiʻi*, where the initial conversations for HBF began.

By 2014, we became formally incorporated and our co-founder, Katherine Ann Leilani Tuider, who is from here, joined us via a chance posting I had put online on Idealist.org looking for someone to lead our development and fundraising. She joined remotely when she was finishing grad school in Paris to turn what was only an idea into reality. She is actually part kānaka maoli and, after completing her MBA in arts management, she moved home and became the first one on the ground, after being away for many years.

We received our 501(c)(3) status in 2015, debuting officially in 2017 with the inaugural Honolulu Biennial, curated by Fumio Nanjo of Tokyo's Mori Art Museum and Ngahiraka Mason, who was a curator at the Auckland Art Gallery for many years. We presented many pre-Biennial projects ahead of time to build up audience and credibility, which was critical for fundraising, starting with *Chain of Fire* in 2014 that I co-curated with Dr. Baysa, and then bringing Yayoi Kusama, which I curated, to Hawaiʻi in 2016.

How was it like starting out with limited resources?

Katherine and I worked on fundraising and built a strong board. I moved home in 2016 to focus on HBF and Shaka Tea. For nearly the first three years, Katherine and I were volunteer directors, hustling numerous other jobs so it took a lot of grit, focus, and tremendous support of our community.

In the early stages, Maile Meyer of Nā Mea Hawaiʻi, Nick Vanderboom, who formerly was at The Howard Hughes Corporation, Carol Khewok, who at the time was at Shangri La, our board, and more than sixty partners actually helped to make Honolulu Biennial happen. Even though Katherine and I are both from here, we both don't come from established families with a long history in the business or philanthropic community. We, along with Dr. Baysa, worked from scratch to build up enough support and a network to raise $2.7 million to make HBF happen. It was a beast and probably the hardest thing I have ever done, but also the most rewarding and beautiful.

What have you learned from this experience?

The kindness and aloha shared between all the artists who were part of this, our curators, our army of 110 volunteers, and every single partner gives me chicken skin every time I think about what we did, and how two under-thirty-year-old women could so earnestly focus to live and breathe the Biennial like it was our religion. This really is the kind of focus you need to make something like this happen out of what originally was just an idea that grew out of that small exhibit I curated in DC!

> You have managed to build a brand in a short span of time! What do you think is the secret to your success?

We made our debut in 2017 and were able to position Hawai'i on the global arts scene. It was truly an incredible response from our community and also the art world beyond these shores. We had 97,000 visits, $4.1 million of public relations value and we were even recognized by media outlets like *Vanity Fair* and *The Today Show* as a top art event to attend in 2017.

Our board is dynamite and very active. Some of the members, especially our executive committee were in the trenches with our incredible exhibit designer Scott Lawrimore, our project manager Yoko Ott, Katherine, and I till late at night. I have this one photo of board members and our co-VPs, Kristen Chan and Gloria Lau, on an inflatable mattress, reviewing budgets at 11 p.m. a few days before the Biennial opened! Taiji Terasaki and his wife, Naoko, tirelessly hosted artists in their own home and organized so many incredible dinners and events for us.

The only way we, as an organization, were able to achieve success was via the multiple threads of collaboration and the generosity from our community and board. It truly is a team effort to make something this large and complex happen from nothing. This approach is also what I apply to Shaka Tea and growing the māmaki industry.

> Which is the perfect segue to ask how Shaka Tea came about?

My husband and I met in college and graduated during the height of the recession and ended up moving to Dubai together, where for a brief period of a few months, we actually worked together for the first time. I managed an art gallery and he managed the boutique hotel, connected to the art gallery. I, then, left to work for TDIC, for about six months, as they were building Saadiyat Island, and the Louvre, Guggenheim Projects in Abu Dhabi, before working as an independent curator and editor for ArtAsiaPacific for about four years. Harrison, my husband, worked in communications for Edelman and then joined the sovereign wealth fund of Abu Dhabi, Mubadala.

During our time abroad and, even before that, I had always been fascinated by "signs of Hawaiian life" abroad. There is a column in the *Honolulu*

Star-Advertiser, where readers send in photos of themselves anywhere in the world with something that references Hawaiʻi. Growing up, I used to enjoy that section of the local news.

For about a decade, I became obsessed with finding products that represented home, no matter where I was in the world. The interesting thing is that 95 percent of the time, especially in consumer packaged goods, the product is only using Hawaiʻi in the marketing or branding, but it is otherwise fake. No ingredients are actually from here or authentically reflect Hawaiʻi, and that bothered me. So anyway, we decided that we had to start a business and, if we did, I knew that it had to be reflective of my passion and interest in Hawaiian culture, as I concluded that there was a lack of authentic Hawaiian products.

As with the Biennial, you seem to be fueled by a disdain at the lack of authenticity in Hawaiian representation …

Seeing the bastardization of the Hawaiian brand was frustrating, especially since my background was in indigenous, postcolonial critique, art and culture. I wanted to see how we could take this academic ethos from my life in arts and culture and apply it to something that is healthy, authentic, and also profitable, even though that is secondary to our company values and vision. But, like any startup, the first three to five years are always financially challenging.

We decided on creating a product based around māmaki, as it's an endemic plant, traditionally used in lāʻau lapaʻau and has a number of health benefits. What is really exciting is the supply chain system we are building where a hui of farmers can practice regenerative agriculture, as planting māmaki is an act of conservation and, in turn, cultivate a relatively easy-to-grow, high-value cash crop. This embodies our ethos as a business: What's good for our ʻāina, our bodies, and our economy? It all came back to planting māmaki.

How was it like working with your husband?

My husband, who is from Seattle, is also enterprising like me. We had earlier met as undergraduates at Boston University and had always wanted to create something together. Our relationship finds great connection and satisfaction in working and creating together.

After we had our kids, Koa and Roya, both who were born in Dubai, I became very focused on getting our ʻohana back to Hawaiʻi. Harrison always knew that we had to move to my home because raising our kids with our values here was fundamentally important. We always wanted to be entrepreneurs and, during my second pregnancy, I was drinking a lot of māmaki, as it is an herbal, caffeine-free tea and I would add fresh fruits for sweetness. At that time, I was still working thirty hours a week on my passion project, the Honolulu Biennial, from remote. One day, as we were ruminating on how to come home, we decided to do a ready-to-drink māmaki tea with no sugar, because it hit all goals—a way to move home, create authentic products that honored Hawaiʻi, and fulfilled the "what's good for the ʻāina is good for the economy" model of business.

How was it going from being paid staff to self-made entrepreneur?

Most people who are self-made would think we are nuts to leave our very well-paying job. At that time, Harrison was working for Mubadala and even had sixty paid vacation days per year that complimented my independent work in the arts! Regardless, we put our life savings of $60,000 into 18,000 bottles of tea with not a single account signed and moved home! We had also just gotten our feet wet with food and beverage entrepreneurship via co-founding Lezzetli, a Turkish ice cream company with Roberto and Barbara Escobar in New York.

Anyhow, by this time, I was a co-director with Katherine for HBF with two startups and was unpaid. I quickly began consulting in PR for Piia Aarma, who runs Pineapple Tweed, and we also used Airbnb to rent out our master bedroom for a year. The years 2016 and 2017 were the hardest, most stressful periods of our lives but we were creating and turning ideas that we hoped would support our community in art and agriculture into reality. That is the best feeling in the world, amidst all the stress and challenges.

What were some of the biggest challenges starting out on your own?

It was really scary to have only six months of savings, two unpaid jobs, 18,000 bottles of tea and nowhere to sell it. One of the first people that said yes to us was Ed Kenney's[1] restaurant, The Kaimukī Superette and his new, Mahina & Sun's that opened up in The Surfjack Hotel.

I met with Natalie Aczon, who now runs Mahina & Sun's, one early afternoon with my then three-year-old, Koa, who handed her the info sheet.

---

1 Ed Kenney attended the Culinary Institute of the Pacific and trained in Honolulu's top restaurants. With a strong commitment to farm-to-table cooking, he opened his first restaurant, Town, in 2005 to rave reviews. Today, his four restaurants—Town, Kaimukī Superette, Mud Hen Water, and the newly opened Mahina & Sun's—are lively gathering places guided by the mantra "local first, organic whenever possible, with aloha always."

I was trying to emotionally blackmail her into buying my tea by pulling the "you have to buy this tea, I have a kid!" vibe! (*laughter*) Actually, she had already intended to order, as she was familiar with māmaki tea. They were our first account and opened so many doors, because Ed is an influential chef and change-maker. It then got easier to pitch to people. Prior to that, we would be driving around the island with the bottles of tea, and a one and three year old in the back of our car, worrying at night how we were going to pay our bills. Given how much was at stake, I just had to be gritty and went out to close accounts for Shaka, write proposals with Katherine, and raise two kids!

In fact, during that time, Katherine and I were working on bringing Yayoi Kusama to Honolulu on our pre-Biennial, which was our biggest project back then! We were collaborating with Howard Hughes' Ward Village and had to train the tour guides and create keiki educational programs all in the same month between March to April 2016 as Shaka Tea was just beginning to roll out. When I think back now, it was just pure insanity.

> Which begs the question, how do you manage your time as an entrepreneur, a co-founder of the Biennial, and motherhood?

Things have come full circle and I am now both an entrepreneur, president of Shaka Tea and, most recently, have taken a step back from HBF, moving into an ideation and strategic role, rather than day-to-day, as innovation director, since my bandwidth is extremely limited with Shaka Tea.

I recently had to refocus on the pace and priorities of my life, as I really want more balance and ensure I am a present mother. With Shaka Tea rolling out nationally with over 3,000 accounts across the U.S. in all fifty states, much of my focus now is on supporting new farmers, economy development, and promoting sustainable agriculture to grow the māmaki industry. People often ask me when I started my entrepreneur journey, when, in fact, I was always enterprising to begin with. The beverage business just came later.

Whether it was a curating project, editing a book, or now a business, it always starts with an idea, a pitch and then I work to manifest it through collaboration.

> The secret sauce it seems is collaboration?

Creative people are entrepreneurs, as it is the same skill set, but what it boils down to is indeed collaboration. That really is the key to how I am able to multitask. I recognize my strengths, which are creative ideation and strategizing, getting buy-in, building audience awareness, PR and marketing, but I am not strong in operations nor am I detail-oriented, so the best way for me is to collaborate with people who can fill the pukas. I am a firm believer in finding co-founders to balance you. I am also very thankful that I have a lot of support from my family. My parents live here and my dad moved in with us, which has been such a great help and a wonderful presence for the children.

The openness and family-friendliness of both my co-founders in the Biennial and Shaka Tea also helps greatly, especially with Shaka Tea. Many of my meetings are with farmers and it is usually such an incredibly family-friendly atmosphere. It also helps that my own internal body clock seems to flow with what I do. I wake up around 3 to 4 a.m. and bash through most of the hard work that I need to get done by 8 a.m. I tend to the mindless e-mails and endless meetings till 3 p.m. when my son gets out of school, and then dedicate the rest of the evening to family and domestic life. I am embracing my flow and appreciate being in control of my time and schedule.

In your career, have you experienced any #MeToo moments that you can share with us?

I've always been very good at moving a hand that went too high on my thigh or an uncomfortably close hug and directly saying, "That's not professional," even when I was in my early twenties and starting out in the arts. There were quite a few older artists and collectors whose behavior was borderline inappropriate. Once this became apparent, I would choose not to write about them, as I was heading the Dubai desk for ArtAsiaPacific at the time, which meant I had many one-on-one profile pieces and interviews. I would stay away from these collectors at all the parties—not because I was afraid, but more because their advances annoyed me. I was young, ambitious, focused, and there solely for work.

The more challenging moments I have had or my real #MeToo moments are not that of an overtly flirtatious or sexual nature. Rather, they have been direct assaults on my capacity as a leader and person in charge. I am thirty-two, and these incidents happened both in my capacity as a co-founder and director of HBF from 2014 to 2018, and also as the co-founder and president of Shaka Tea. As mentioned prior, I co-founded HBF in 2014, with the goal of launching an international arts festival, Honolulu Biennial, to raise the profile of artists from Hawai'i on an international platform. I also wanted to simultaneously support discourse, accessibility, and educational programs through contemporary art from the Pacific, coupled with creating an economic impact by attracting arts and culture tourists to our islands.

As we worked to raise $2.7 million for the first festival, I would meet with a number of key, highly respected, male business leaders, who would ask my colleague, another woman and I, "Where are the men? It can't just be two young girls." We would also go to meetings with local, elected officials and government leaders. Otherwise nice men, they would direct questions at the male board members we would bring with us. We recognized from repeated experiences that we were not taken seriously and referred to as the "girls."

Despite the sexism, I must also acknowledge that we have many men who are our top advocates—from early board members like Sonny Ganaden, Brett Zaccardi, and Bruce L'Orange who believed in our work to the key early donors from the private sector, with co-title sponsorship from Taiji Terasaki and his wife Naoko and Howard Hughes Corporation, which was championed by Nick Vanderboom and Steve Cornwell. We are grateful to all the men who got behind the "two girls" to launch Honolulu Biennial.

What advice would you give to a budding artist and entrepreneur?

Don't play by the rules. There is no one-size-fits-all way to do things. The rules set by academia in the arts or museum culture can be quite daunting to the emerging artist, but please do not be afraid of your own vision. Building a team is the next key component. My partners plugged the pukas of all the things that I don't know and enabled everything I have been able to do. Be open to sharing your vision and not hold on to too much ego and ownership. Create concepts that are big and visionary and collaborate to go after a win. You can actually make extraordinary things happen instead of going by the usual routes taught to us.

Let's turn our focus now on the island you hold so near and dear to your heart. Share with us your fondest memories growing up in Hawaiʻi?

Beyond museums, I remember being very involved in my hula hālau; keiki hula competitions, like Hula 'Oni E; going to Kaimana Beach with my mom and brother on early mornings; amazing dinner parties my mom would throw with Cesaria Evora or the Gipsy Kings playing; time spent with my parents' friends from so many different cultural backgrounds and orientations; reading Glen Grant's *Obake Tales* and *Chicken Skin* series; and having a lot of discussions with my dad about Hawaiian history, politics, and the environment. We also spent a lot of time going to different cultural festivals and events, whether it was a Filipino Cultural Festival at the Academy of Arts or a Tibetan exhibition and mandala demonstration by monks at the East-West Center.

I think my mom, who had traveled the world for Pan Am and lived in a half-dozen countries, really imbued in me a sense of interconnectedness, cultural vibrancy, and appreciation for other cultures. I also spent a lot of time with my younger brother and was also very involved in activism. In high school, I co-founded a club called Politically Active and Conscientious Teens (PACT) and we used it as a platform to be more aware as teenagers to know what is happening in the world around us, and also protested the second war on Iraq.

Those were all my fondest memories growing up here as a culturally aware and politically active teen holding up signs and speaking into microphones! I am thankful that my parents were always supportive, even when I asked to skip school to protest President Bush's Shock and Awe campaign. Clearly, I always held liberal views and the value of a Punahou education was such a blessing, as it taught us critical thinking skills and to always question the source of information or agenda a media outlet might have—that was pretty cool to be thinking that way at fifteen or sixteen.

What do you think has changed over the years?

There have been many positive changes in Hawai'i, but also some that are concerning. On the positive front, I do see that many kama'āina of my generation are motivated to return to Hawai'i to start their professional career. From business to art, Hawai'i has truly competitive and compelling talent, and when those talents come home, it gets me excited about the future. I was motivated by my peers Tyler Dos Santos Tam and Nicole Velasco, who are extremely intelligent, community-minded individuals who moved home before me.

Austin Kino, another entrepreneur with his Holokino business and apprentice navigator also inspires me with his involvement in business, civil service, nonprofits, and political activism. We know we may be making a lot less money or end up living with our parents, but we are all taking these chances because we believe in Hawai'i.

Was this different when you were growing up?

Back then, it was a common assumption that we had to head to the continent for college and work, then come home only to retire. It is different now. I am so inspired by everyone's commitment and vision.

What would you like to see changed or improved in the years ahead?

Some things that do alarm me are property prices! I am fortunate that I am a homeowner, as we lived overseas and managed to save up for a down payment. I don't see how the current market is sustainable in comparison to salaries not matching the rising costs of living.

I hate to give this advice to a younger person, but if you don't have family money to support and want to be a homeowner in your twenties here, your best bet is to do a few years in an emerging economy, save, then come home like we did, with a down payment. Homelessness, and how we are addressing it or lack thereof, is a great concern.

I would also like to see more honor from employers to pay and value their employees fairly and create jobs in high-growth industries that Hawai'i can be globally competitive in.

I also hope we won't use the bullshit paradise tax as an excuse to take advantage of people and pay unfair wages. It would be great if we could all work toward raising that standard. As a community and society, I hope we can remember where we came from. This is a culture of aloha, and thinking of the community first and foremost. We need to look out for one another and practice kindness.

What are your plans for Shaka Tea?

We just finished another angel round of investment, which means we have been able to bring on two, full-time employees and one part-time person. We are able to support our growth as we expand nationally to over one thousand stores and online on Amazon.

We also raised investment for Shaka Forest Farms, a 29-acre māmaki farm on the Big Island. We are championing preservation and forest farming, where we plant māmaki amidst old growth 'ōhia, koa and hāpu'u, preserving the native forest, which we will also use as a teaching farm since we are creating a hui of farmers to support our supply chain needs.

Māmaki is a burgeoning industry. It is a high-value, lightweight, exportable crop that supports sustainable agriculture. Our hope is to create a variety of māmaki huis on multiple islands. Eventually, we hope the Shaka Tea brand can branch into a variety of products, underpinned by an indigenous or an endemic plant as the core ingredient, thereby encouraging economic growth for our community through agriculture.

I am inspired by the ahupua'a system—how well managed and resourceful Hawai'i used to be pre-contact. Post-contact was ugly and exploitative with plantation workers being low paid and badly treated. Monocropping was not the best use of soil, and the use of pesticides is bad for the environment. The money really went to the plantation owners, not to the people.

What gets you excited?

Many things, but today in 2019, I get excited by the Guayaki model for its Yerba Mate beverage business from the Amazon, and Runa for its Guayusa leaf beverage. These companies have created a brand that supports our same value system—a "what is good for the ʻāina is good for their communities and their economies" business model. They are an off-loader, but they are also creating a demand for something that can be grown and honors their region in an authentic way.

You are certainly a multi-hyphenate, but would you say you are more creative or operational?

Creative definitely, even though my co-founders, Katherine and Harrison, are also both very creative in their own right.

Who would you like to have a sit-down dinner with?

That is a tough question as I am so assertive. When I want to know someone, I would just reach out. I also ask people that I admire to be my mentors, so I am hard-pressed to think of someone that I don't know that I haven't yet had access to …

Favorite artist?
I can't name just one, but the ones that I am interested in now are Bernice Akamine, The Propeller Group, Isabel and Alfredo Aquilizan, The GCC Collective, Brett Graham, Mata Aho, Taiji Terasaki, and Ruth Asawa.

If you had to create a tea for yourself, what flavor would it be?

Definitely the new flavor we are launching, Lilikoʻi Lemongrass—it's nice and tart, and my favorite flavor profile.

What would you say when you meet God?

I have a lot of gratitude and I would say, "Thank You." I remember a phrase taught to us when we were students of Punahou, "To whom much is given, much is expected." I have had the privilege to be well educated, be in good health, and live in Hawai'i, which presents amazing opportunities.

Write your life philosophy on a bumper sticker.

There are no noes. You can be told no, but you must figure out a way to turn that no into a yes. I had to work so hard to get trust from the community, donors, and eventually raise $2.7 million for the HBF.

Everything at the start, when I was about twenty-seven or twenty-eight years old was a no. We had no right to start a Biennial, raise funds, and create something that large with sixty-five partnerships. Even right now, people think we are insane to be able to turn māmaki into an industry that supports sustainable agriculture and community development, launched right out of Hawai'i. But I absolutely believe that we are launching the next big beverage brand and creating a global demand for endemic, Hawaiian māmaki.

There are no noes. You can turn no into a yes.

What would your epitaph say?

"She was someone who lived joyfully. Her greatest calling and commitment was Hawai'i."

I do believe in Hawai'i. Whether it is through art and culture, or a startup business in agriculture, everything I do is not about me but how I can leave an impact to help and benefit my community, the people of Hawai'i.

THE MULTI-HYPHENATE

Lauren Matsumoto

I've learned to throw my ego to the side. I'm not wedded to my name being attached to a bill, even though a common measure of being a successful politician is defined through the number of bills passed. I have chosen to define success differently. I believe that working together with all the stakeholders to craft effective policy is what makes a successful legislator.

The Multi-Hyphenate

Lauren Matsumoto is the sixth generation to be born and raised in the islands. Her great-grandfather started Peterson's Upland Farm in 1910 as a family-run business, supplying fresh eggs to the community. Her paternal grandfather, Douglas Cheape, worked at Waialua Sugar Company, while her maternal grandmother, Suzanne Peterson, was the first woman to serve on the Board of Agriculture and, later, became the director of agriculture under Governor Waiheʻe.

Lauren graduated from the University of Hawaiʻi with a BA degree in film production with the Academy for Creative Media, and minored in Business and Japanese. Her first experience with the legislature was with her documentary, Farm Grown, which helped pass the Feed Subsidy Bill. Lauren was a scholar-athlete at the University of Hawaiʻi as a water polo player. She was also a member of the student athlete advisory committee. Lauren won the title of Miss Hawaiʻi 2011 and represented the Aloha State in the Miss America pageant, where she won the talent portion of competition with a jump rope routine to the iconic Hawaiʻi Five-O theme song! To this day, Lauren continues to perform her jump rope routine, while speaking to children across the state and encouraging them to lead a healthy lifestyle and to volunteer in their community.

Lauren was elected to office in 2012, where she became the youngest Republican to have ever been elected to the Hawaiʻi State Legislature at the age of twenty-five. After serving for seven years in the legislature, she is still the youngest female. She has also been elected to sit on the national board of Women in Government, a nonprofit, nonpartisan organization of women state legislators across the country. In 2015, she earned an MBA from Hawaiʻi Pacific University, where she was a valedictorian and was selected as the commencement speaker. Despite her hectic schedule as a working mom and elected official, Lauren still found time to complete her doctorate in organizational leadership in 2019.

Outside of the legislature, Lauren enjoys spending time with her family and lifelong hobbies. She shares her love for dance as a professional hula dancer in Waikīkī. Lauren is an active member of her church, One Love, where she met her husband Scott Matsumoto, a firefighter with the Honolulu Fire Department. In August of 2017, they were blessed with the birth of their first child, Noah Matsumoto. And now they are anticipating their second child, expected to be a Christmas Day baby!

Share with us about your background.

My family arrived in Hawaiʻi in 1859 from New England and I'm the sixth generation to be born and raised in the islands. Our family home was right next to ʻIolani Palace, where the Hawaiʻi State Library is today. My grandfather still has the invitations inviting my family to balls and receptions at the palace, including the coronation of the king and queen. I also learned that my family brought the second sewing machine to Hawaiʻi, and sewed many of the gowns for the royal court. Presently, my family are egg farmers in Wahiawā on the land my great-grandfather began farming in 1910, and I am part of the fourth generation to be involved with the farm. I was born and raised in Mililani, attended Mililani public schools, and graduated from Mililani High School.

You were an athlete and involved in water polo and jump rope. What ignited your sporting proclivities?

When I was five years old, two things happened in my life and, to me, they were big. The first was my family's television stopped working. At the same time, our truck broke, and we didn't have enough money to replace them both. Obviously, my parents decided to fix the truck. In about six to eight months when they had saved up enough money to buy a new television, my mom noticed my brother and I were outside playing, doing puzzles together, and painting, so she decided she didn't want a TV. So for the next ten years, we were television free.

The second thing that happened to me of significance was when a jump rope team came to my school. I remember looking up at them and thinking, "Wow, they are so cool! They can do crisscrosses and double-unders!" I was a very determined kid so I went home and said, "Mom, I want to be a jump roper." There was a jump rope team in Mililani, where I lived, and I ended up joining and stayed on the team throughout my K–12 years. I was also able to perform at many different schools across the state to promote healthy living with the American Heart Association.

After I graduated from Mililani high school, I went to the University of Hawaiʻi and joined the water polo team, where I was the smallest girl. Many of my teammates were six foot, two-inches or six foot, three inches tall, and from countries like the Netherlands, New Zealand, and Australia. It was a tremendous opportunity for me. In my four years, I learned that I didn't have to be the star of the team to be a contributor. This was a hard lesson for me, because I was used to being the captain of the team and getting full playing time in high school.

How did you go from star athlete to pageant queen?

Ironically, for the girl who grew up with no television, I ended up majoring in film. In one of my classes, we had to make a documentary on Hawaiʻi.

At the time, my roommate was just giving up her Miss West Oʻahu crown, and I remember telling my teacher that I was going to do my documentary on the Miss Hawaiʻi pageant. I was joking, but my teacher looked at me and said, "Lauren, I love it. Do it."

The Miss Ala Moana pageant was in two weeks, but I decided to run so that I could make the documentary in a first-person perspective. When the pageant director asked me if I had a talent, I said, "jump rope" and, before I knew it, I was contestant number one. I had no idea what I was doing except I recall filming my documentary backstage, interviewing people, and getting great shots, so you can imagine my surprise when I was crowned Miss Ala Moana! Little did I realize that in two and a half months, I'd be competing in Miss Hawaiʻi. And what an amazing experience that was.

There, I got to learn about the program, and what I loved about Miss Hawaiʻi was the scholarship opportunity and the ability to make a difference in your community and be of service. So I went back the next year and I didn't win, but I got placed second runner-up. I was always told third time's a charm, so I went back my third year and still didn't win. I became very good at losing. But I learned so much each time that I participated and so, when I went back my fourth year, I won title of Miss Hawaiʻi. It was a blessing, as I turned twenty-four that year and could not compete again.

Being Miss Hawaiʻi truly is a job. I would be at events every single day. I remember, in one day, I was on three different islands for three different events! So I learned how to be very flexible. I learned how to present myself in a professional manner without knowing what was going to happen that day. I gained a lot of personal skills, including public speaking and media presentation, and these skills translated directly into a political career.

Which segues perfectly into our next question: how did you end up as a politician?

When I went to compete in Miss America in Las Vegas, I was the first contestant in ninety years to jump rope for my talent! I ended up winning talent at Miss America, in addition to being a finalist for the Quality of Life award. I also managed to raise the most money in the country for the Children's Miracle Network of hospitals.

On my flight home after the pageant wrapped, I reflected on the four years of my life as a pageant queen and realized that what I loved most about my job of being Miss Hawai'i was serving the community and advocating for issues I was passionate about. It occurred to me that running for office would be the next, natural progression.

While serving as Miss Hawai'i, I had already worked with several legislators to testify on bills at the capital. When I completed my year of Miss Hawai'i on June 9, I started my campaign for the Hawai'i State House of Representatives as a twenty-four year old Republican female in Hawai'i the very next day.

By the time I was sworn in, I was twenty-five years old and the youngest female in the legislature at the time. Once the legislative session started, I decided that I was going to make every decision I felt was best for my community and not factor in my re-election.

Contrary to public perception, your pageant experience actually aided in your political career. Any there any other misconceptions about pageants that you would like to debunk?

A lot of people don't see the amount of work, dedication, and willpower that goes into running for Miss Hawai'i or Miss America. It has made a huge difference in who I have become.

Unfortunately, all people see are women in their swimsuits for thirty seconds, or walking across the stage in their evening gown, or performing their talent for a minute and a half. What they don't see are who these women really are or hear the conversations that happen behind the scenes.

Many people also don't realize that Miss America is the largest scholarship provider to young women in the world, and that this has made a huge difference to me. My master's degree in business from Hawai'i Pacific University was completely paid for by the pageant, and so was my doctorate in organizational leadership.

Your grandmother was the first woman to serve on the State of Hawai'i Board of Agriculture and, later, became the director of agriculture under Governor Waihe'e. Do you think she influenced your political ambitions?

My grandmother is an amazing woman. She was raised by her grandmother in California and came to Hawai'i after high school on a one-way ticket. In order to earn a living and pay for school, she worked as a nanny and, during the summers, had a second job at the pineapple cannery. She later dropped out of college when she got married to have kids, as many women did back then. She had three kids, each a year apart. She was finally able to complete her college when my mother, who was her youngest child, went to college, and she received her bachelor's degree in psychology.

She became the first female on the Board of Agriculture under Governor Ariyoshi and the first female director of agriculture under Governor Waiheʻe. My grandfather would tell a funny story about the National Agricultural Conferences. Since my grandma was one of the only females nationally, my grandpa would be the only man with all the wives at these events.

She is a huge influence in my life because she told me that I could be whatever I wanted to be. When I first considered getting involved in government, I did think about following in her footsteps into the Department of Agriculture, but ended up running for state representative, as I wanted to influence policy in multiple areas. But I have no doubt, it was definitely my grandmother who set the example, not only for me but for many other women. Her life is an amazing story, as she was able to achieve so much from so little.

How is it like running as a Republican in a predominantly Democratic state?

There are challenges to being a super minority. Hawaiʻi is the most unbalanced state in the nation when it comes to our political party split. However, I always try to look for the silver lining and, for me, the personal growth as a result of being in the super minority has been a gift.

I've truly learned how to work with others, and I've learned how to build relationships in order to get things done, because you have to work much harder when you're in the minority. You also have to be very strategic in how you present things and how you decide to put ideas forward. Additionally, I've learned to throw my ego to the side. I'm not wedded to my name being attached to a bill, even though a common measure of being a successful politician is defined through the number of bills passed.

I have chosen to define success differently. I believe that working together with all the stakeholders to craft effective policy is what makes a successful legislator. I'm willing to share my ideas for bills with other legislators to have them introduce the legislation in order to have it have a better opportunity to pass. To me, it's about making sure we pass the best policy for the state and be able to work with others from differing perspectives.

What is the most challenging aspect about being in politics?

I think one of the most challenging aspects about being in politics is living a public life. Having everything that you do, and potentially your family, be subject to public scrutiny is really difficult. I don't necessarily care when I get criticized, as this is an expected by-product of being a public official. But I really struggle when people attack my family. Luckily in Hawaiʻi, that doesn't happen too often.

How is it like being a young mother in politics?

I end up having to put in much longer hours as there are so many different events I'm expected to attend. Being a mother to a young child adds extra challenges. My son is now eighteen months old, but I was pregnant and gave birth to him while in office. That was difficult. There's no maternity leave in the legislature — you can certainly choose to take time off but, depending on what's happening on the floor, you could potentially miss several hundred or even a thousand votes by just taking a week off. This could be used against you in the next election, so imagine taking two or three weeks off! Maintaining work-life balance as a young mother and a legislator is something I haven't really been able to achieve yet due to the legislative calendar and structure.

Another roadblock for me as a new mother is the difficulty I encountered in breastfeeding. On the legislative floor, sessions can range anywhere from four to up to thirteen hours. One time, I had to go into our caucus room to feed my son, but in order to be registered for a vote you have to physically be in your seat, and they came up to a vote much quicker than I was expecting. Luckily, they called a recess for me, but I still had to quickly zip up and run out onto the floor with my son. He ended up sitting with me through those votes as that was the only way to do it.

The institutional structure of the legislature is not built to accommodate young, working mothers. There are no designated breaks and how long you're on the floor depends on how many speeches people decide to give or how long the votes will take. It's challenging because it's just so unpredictable.

What campaign issues are most personal to you?

The two issues that come to mind are agriculture and cost of living. The district that I represent has some of the best, prime agricultural lands left on Oʻahu. Because I come from a farming family, these issues are extremely important to me. Supporting our local farmers and increasing local, agricultural production are policy areas that are key for me since I was elected, and is one of the reasons I ran for office. I remember talking with my grandpa after college about potentially working on the family farm with my mom and him, but he encouraged me to get a job in government to help farmers from a policy standpoint.

Most legislators have never worked on a farm so the policies passed at the legislature aren't necessarily the best for our farmers. Furthermore, as we rely on public testimonies and most farmers don't have the time to testify as they are busy with their day-to-day, I feel it's important for me to be a voice for the agricultural community.

The second issue that is important to me is the high cost of living in Hawaiʻi. I send out surveys annually to my district, and cost of living always ranks in the top three most important issues for the people in my area, and I can fully comprehend. Like many in my generation, my husband and I struggled to buy a home. After we were finally able to make the down payment, we needed a roommate for the first three years of our marriage in order to make our monthly mortgage payments.

Now that I have a child, I am also noticing that the cost of childcare is insane. It cost almost two-thousand dollars a month to send my son to preschool. That is the same cost as going to Punahou! Affording housing, food, and childcare are real struggles for many families in Hawaiʻi.

How do you deal with negative criticisms?

When I first got involved in politics, people would tell me, "Oh, you need to have really thick skin for this job." I remember thinking that I had already gone through this in my pageant years, as we were constantly judged on how physically fit, intelligent, eloquent, and talented we were.

I was criticized by people and definitely grew a really thick skin. The way I deal with negative criticism is to return to my core, and remind myself of who I am and my commitment to my duty. I also try to look any bad situation from a macro-perspective. Often, these negative criticisms are a single snapshot of my life, so remembering the big picture reminds me to not sweat the small things. Finally, I try to approach things from a glass-half-full perspective.

Has your gender been a boon or a bane in your career?

I consider myself very blessed because, when I first ran for office, I never even contemplated that being a female was a hindrance to being electable. I was more concerned about my age and running as a Republican in a predominantly Democrat district, but not about being a woman.

During my third year in office, I was nominated to be a member of the inaugural class of Women in Government. This is a national organization of twenty-five women from across the country selected from executive, state, and county levels of government, to come together to empower and mobilize women lawmakers to create sound policies on a state level.

At our first meeting, we went around the table and everybody shared how they got involved in government. Many of them told stories on how they had to overcome the challenges of being the first woman in their position. As the youngest in the group, I began to realize how lucky I was to have come on the coattails of these pioneering women.

Now that I have been in office for the past seven years, I recognize the subliminal biases against women. Not only are the legislatures set up in a hierarchical system that favors men's leadership styles, the power structure within the legislature makes it harder for women to break through. But, I'm hoping this paradigm will begin to change, as there's more awareness and more people are talking about the importance of women in elected office. I like to think there's hope for the future of women leadership.

Do you have a #MeToo encounter you can share and what did you learn from it?

I've been very lucky in that I have never had a #MeToo encounter in the form of overt sexual harassment, and have empathy and compassion for those who had to go through such a horrifyingly difficult situation.

The only experiences I've personally had were verbal slights with men saying, "You only got elected because you're a pretty face." On another occasion, one of my staff members came into my office and asked, "Representative, can I ask you a personal question?" to which I replied, "Sure." He responded, "You seem stressed." I responded, "Well that's not a question." He then proceeded to say, "I think you would be happier as a stay-at-home mom and open a yoga studio."

While there's nothing wrong being a stay-at-home mom or yoga studio owner, his comments implied I was incompetent at my job. It was extremely inappropriate, much less to your boss. These comments undermine my ability to lead and underscore that somehow I am less capable simply because I am a woman. I believe I am qualified in my position, because I add value, have a voice, and know it is important for me to be at the table. I have worked hard to get to where I am today and recognize that too many women receive inappropriate comments like these on a daily basis.

Many legislatures across the country were caught in the #MeToo firestorm, including Hawaiʻi. We had one of our own sitting legislators step down due to allegations. As one of the co-conveners of the Hawaiʻi Women's Legislative Caucus, we were in constant meetings to ensure that we addressed loopholes in our internal policies. While there are general procedures for staff, there were gray areas when it came to legislators, lobbyists, and the general public. There remains a lot of work that has to be done to update our policies and change mindsets in the capitol.

What do you think millennials can bring to the leadership table?

As a millennial, I think one of the things that we can bring to the leadership table is a greater demand for collaboration. In the past few decades, schools have placed more emphasis on teamwork.

Another thing we can bring to the table is our high valuation of happiness in our career, which is both a good and a bad thing. On the negative side, we are often seen as unreliable and disengaged as we job hop. But on the positive side, once we find our niche, we are extremely enthusiastic workers who are willing to work hard.

We are also digital natives and have a firm grasp on global connectivity and cultural sensitivities. With an increasing global economy, these skills are critical for leadership both in the public and private sector.

What advice would you give to younger woman in your shoes?

I feel like the advice that I would give is to get involved in things that you're passionate about—intern, volunteer, serve your community, and learn all you can in different areas. I always encourage younger women to really humble themselves. Don't feel as if you're too good to learn something new, as you never know when those skills will come in handy and may even translate into a job later.

When I talk to young people, I always tell them, if I can use jump rope to make a difference in people's lives, imagine what they can do with the skills they don't even think about! Each and every one of us has something special that we can bring to the table. That is a good reminder, as women often compare ourselves with others, and tend to focus on the negative instead of our innate skill and talents.

The other advice I would give to younger women is to not discredit yourself. We often think that we need to be perfect. Take running for office. I know many women who had to be asked several times before they would consider running. They would shrug off and say they don't have a political science background or a law degree. Women tend to think they need to have all their ducks in a row before they would commit. When I first ran for office, many people told me that I did not have the right background nor did I have what it takes.

But once I got into office, I sat on the education committee, as I went through the public school system and am a graduate of the University of Hawaiʻi. I also sat on the agriculture committee, as my family had a farm. While I didn't have the traditional background of a typical politician, I still had something I could bring to the table. So I would remind all young women that they can all contribute even if they don't know it yet. Don't be afraid to step out and step up. Be willing to try things you may not think you're quite ready for, as you can grow on the job.

You seem to excel in all you undertake. What do you think is the secret to your success?

I fail a lot and I think that's really important. As cliché as that sounds, I fail and I continue to try and try again. The biggest secret to my success isn't really a secret: I fully acknowledge and appreciate that I have amazing support from my parents, family, and entire extended family. I also now have the support of my incredible husband.

I honestly could not do anything I am doing now from politics to earning my MBA to finishing my doctorate without his support. Scott is an amazing partner. He went through three Miss Hawaiʻi's, one Miss America, and an election before he even proposed, so he knew exactly what he was getting himself into! He was there to bedazzle my jump ropes and shoes for Miss America and helped me build PVC frames for sign waving before my election. He helps me watch our son, Noah, so that I can attend conferences in Washington D.C. and write my papers. I could never pretend I did it all by myself.

This is important to underscore, because we often hear that women can do it all. I think that is not a helpful message. If you're trying to be a mom and have a career, or be a politician and go to school and sit on different boards, you need a great support system.

Conversely, what do you do if you are down?

I like to take a step back and think about the bigger picture, because I know I'm not going to win all the time. I believe that attitude comes from my sports background, as we don't win every game. So even though I'm down now, I know I can turn it around and win the next game. Having this mindset makes a big difference because I'm not focused on the failures of the now, I'm looking toward what I can do differently in the future.

Once again, this goes back to my support system. My family is there to remind me of the things that really matter. Just being able to come home, spend time with my son and husband allows me to re-center, gain perspective, and recognize there are many other things that are really more important to me than just the current situation I'm going through.

You have just completed your doctoral research on women in the state legislature entitled *The 28 Percent*[1] to reflect the percentage of women in the arena. Can you share with us some of your findings?

Deciding to run for elected office is not an easy decision. One has to weigh and recognize the amount of time, commitment, and personal sacrifice needed. Once elected, these challenges continue; this career is physically, emotionally, and mentally taxing, not just for the candidate or elected official but for their families as well. The gender gap between women and men in leadership affects all fields and, unfortunately, there are many barriers that still prevent women from ascending the ladder. This issue of under-representation of women is reflected in elected seats in government.

With women forming approximately half of the United States population, it should follow that representation at the government level would reflect this percentage. However, on a congressional level,[2] women comprise 23.7 percent of the 535 seats in congress. On a state executive level, there are nine governors and fifteen lieutenant governors in the United States, which is 24 percent of all executive office seats. According to the U.S. Conference of Mayors, for cities with populations of thirty-thousand and above, 21.8 percent of mayors are

---

1 For full disclosure, I was one of the supervising professors on Lauren's Doctoral Dissertation Committee, along with Dr. Cecile Morris at Argosy University in 2019.

2 According to the numbers published in *Women and the Presidency* by the Center for American Women and Politics, 2019.

women as of March 2018. At the state legislative level, women occupy between 20–30 percent of elected office at all levels of government.[3]

To date, there has not been a woman elected as president or vice president in the United States. These statistics demonstrate a far cry from achieving parity where half of the seats in government should be held by women.

> Based on your research, what can we do to encourage more women to lean in?

The participants in this research are all effective leaders and display a collaborative style of leadership. However, this style is typically considered weak because of erroneous, societal stereotypes about leadership. In order to combat these stereotypes, efforts first need to be made to normalize and emphasize the effectiveness of these collaborative leadership styles.

Additionally, one of the key recommendations for getting more women into office and helping to develop strong leadership is to engage them early. To do this, we need to create a legislative leadership pipeline. By creating a program in the elementary school system, young girls who are interested in student council or other leadership opportunities could be partnered with middle or high school students, who could act as mentors. State legislative women's caucuses could partner with these programs to provide internship and interaction opportunities for high school and college students. These interactions will also provide strong female role models for these girls and young women.

Another recommendation is to recognize that mentorships and networks are just as important for women even after being elected. Often, the only option to network is with the old boys' club. Women legislators need outlets, such as Women in Government and the National Foundation of Women Legislators, to encourage one another and build connections. However, these established organizations, while extremely helpful, are nationally based so we need to have more networks established within our communities and states.

Further, women need to repurpose their networks. Men tend to use networks to climb the leadership ladder, while women often use their networks for social support and relationship. While these groups are important, women need to be part of several different networks to include community service and professional ones as well. There are political advantages for those who are associated with multiple networks, as these groups can connect women together in order to move everyone forward.

---

[3] According to the numbers published in *Women in Elective Office* by the Center for American Women and Politics, 2019.

How do you manage to balance your career and motherhood?

To be honest, I'm still trying to figure this out *(laughter)*. I used to work twelve to fourteen hours a day, but once I had my son, I realized I had to change that or I would literally exhaust myself. I had to learn to prioritize and, initially, it was hard, as I loved everything that I did.

But, I had to take a step back, remove myself from some boards and service organizations, and focus on the ones I cared the most about. It sounds simple, but saying no wasn't really in my vocabulary. That's something I've had to learn and I'm still learning.

As a young mother and legislator, what changes would you like to see in the government?

I think the overall government infrastructure needs to shift to accommodate women legislators with children. Implementing a policy where new mothers, like Senator Duckworth, could vote via remote would encourage more women, especially younger women, to run for office. We should also have specific policies, such as substantial family leave policies, safe spaces for breastfeeding, and establishment of public preschools, to help with the cost of childcare.

How do you think motherhood has changed your style of leadership?

Motherhood has had an enormous impact on how I lead. Before I had my son, I was deeply involved in everything that went on in my office. I wanted to have a hand in all of the details, including the graphic designs, because I enjoyed it and liked being involved.

Now that I am a mother, I've quickly realized that my style of leadership was no longer realistic. I learned how to successfully delegate tasks to my staff. The current philosophy in my office is that I do the things that only I can do as a legislator, such as voting and attending various community events, and everything else falls to my staff. This was a monumental change for me.

What are your fondest memories growing up in Hawaiʻi?

I am very blessed because most of my family and extended family live here in Hawaiʻi. On top of that, almost all of my family live on the same street next to my family's egg farm in Wahiawā. I grew up seeing my relatives all the time. One of my favorite memories would be at Christmas. We would all walk over to my grandparents', great auntie's and uncle's house with a potluck dish and have a wonderful family celebration with up to fifty of my family members!

Now that I am older, I recognize how special that is. Not many people can say they are constantly surrounded by family, and maybe not everyone likes that (*laughter*), but, to me, it is the best way to spend my time.

What do you think has changed over the years and what changes would you like to see in the years ahead?

There have been so many changes to Hawai'i in the past thirty years. Traffic, demographic shifts, and a loss of agricultural lands, just to name a few.

In the years ahead, I would like to see the development of a robust technology industry here in Hawai'i. We have made a few steps in the right direction with regards to the tech sector.

However, I feel we can do much more. Hawai'i is the epicenter of the Pacific, between Asia and the continental United States. We are perfectly positioned geographically to become a leader in this field. Additionally, there is a great need for high paying jobs for local people. Given our lack of land availability in the islands, tech is an industry that is able to provide many jobs with a relatively small footprint. Partnered with an appropriate educational pipeline, this sector could be life-changing for my son's generation.

You are so incredibly busy. What is your idea of a great weekend?

Spending time at our family house on the North Shore with family and friends! I love being out in the water with everyone on anything and everything that can float! My dad may be on a stand-up paddleboard, my brother on a longboard, cousins on inner tubes, friends on kayaks, my mom treading water, and my husband and I going tandem on a soft-top. Just the laughter you hear from everybody, enjoying and cheering people on as they get on a wave is magical!

What would you say if you met God?

My Lord, thank you for your grace, love, and forgiveness.

Happiness is …

Family. It is the core of who I am and my foundation.

Who would you love to have a sit-down dinner with?

My paternal great-grandmother, Julia Gwin Ault. My nana lived with us until I was seven years old, when she passed away at the age of ninety-seven. From the stories my family tells, she led an amazing life. She was born in 1896 and became a single mother, when her husband tragically died in a car crash when she was nine-months pregnant. She worked hard to support herself and her daughter through jobs, like writing for *Silver Screen Magazine*, where she met many famous actors and, later, she opened her own travel agency, Ault Travel Bureau, on Kauaʻi. She always had the best sayings, for instance, if you were thinking and said, "Well …" she would quip, "That is a very deep subject for shallow minds." Even in her nineties, she had a quick wit. I would love the opportunity to talk with her and hear all of her incredible stories.

What is your life philosophy on a bumper sticker?

Have Faith. My faith is the central foundation of my life. I believe God has a perfect plan and purpose for my life. This core belief has led me to where I am now. Whether I am in a difficult spot, or enjoying success, having faith that God has a plan for me continues to be how I draw strength.

The title of your memoir would be …

Cheape Talk. (laughter) My maiden name is Cheape, as in inexpensive with a silent E at the end.

Growing up with a last name like Cheape, you have to have a sense of humor, be able to take everything that comes at you, and spin it to something positive. I would imagine my memoir would have stories of my life told with a humorous twist.

How would you want to be remembered?

I want to be remembered as somebody who served others, genuinely cared for others and made a positive difference in others' lives in a compassionate and kind way. Whether it was something as small as people remembering that I always gave them a smile in the hallways of the capitol, to passing policy that made a significant impact on the lives of people in Hawaiʻi.

THE WOMAN WARRIOR
Maxine Hong Kingston

Women have really special powers, distinct points of views, and perspectives. They are able to nourish and make lives and the world wonderful, so they have to really get to know and develop themselves.

Maxine Hong Kingston *is a writer, whose work is largely rooted in her experience as a first-generation Chinese American. Born as the eldest of six children to Chinese immigrant parents, Maxine attended the University of California, Berkeley on a scholarship and graduated in 1962. At Berkeley, she met aspiring actor Earll Kingston. They were married in November 1962 and had a son two years later. The couple taught at Sunset High School in California from 1966 to 1967 and then moved to Hawai'i, where Maxine taught for the next ten years.*

In 1976, Maxine published her first book, Woman Warrior: Memoirs of a Girlhood Among Ghosts, *combining myth, family history, folktales, and memories of the experience of growing up within two conflicting cultures. The book was an immediate critical success. Her second memoir,* China Men *(1980), tells the story of Chinese immigration through the experiences of the men in her family while,* Tripmaster Monkey: His Fake Book *(1989), combines Eastern and Western literary traditions while emphasizing the Americanness of its characters. In* To Be the Poet *(2002), written mainly in verse, Kingston presented a rumination on elements of her own past and the acts of reading and creating poetry.* The Fifth Book of Peace *(2003) combines elements of fiction and memoir in the manner of a Chinese talk-story, a tradition in which elements of both the real and imagined worlds become interpolated. Maxine has also published poems, short stories, and articles.*

In 1993, Kingston ran a series of writing and meditation workshops for veterans of various conflicts and their families. From these workshops came the material for Veterans of War, Veterans of Peace *(2006), a collection edited by Kingston, containing prose and verse on the experiences of war, domestic violence, drug abuse, and other traumatic experiences.*

We met at her son's home in Mānoa, where she relishes the role of eager grandmother to her baby granddaughter. We discuss issues of race, gender, and the future of publishing. Maxine also reminisces on her writing days of yore, expresses her disdain for Trump and his immigration policies, and lets known her lingering tinge of regret for not having been a "better mother, daughter, and teacher."

Whilst I may never gain any real justifications to her held sentiments, I know for a fact she inspired this young Asian girl growing up. I didn't have any other books to read with characters that looked and sounded like me, and so I let her know in no uncertain terms that she was my teenage book idol and that I was simply over the moon to finally meet with the Woman Warrior *herself.*

Share with us who you are, since, by your own admission, I know you despise what is written in Wikipedia. *(laughter)*

Yes. I looked at Wikipedia and cannot believe what they wrote. It is the worst! I think they used the word Chinese like four times in the first sentence—that I am a "Chinese American," who writes "Chinese books" for a "Chinese American" audience, and won several awards for her "Chinese books!" I have no idea what all that means!

But let me just say that describing myself in a sentence or a paragraph is hard, as I have taken six books to explore my own identity and I haven't finished yet. I even have trouble with the word "about" and don't know what it means or takes to write "about me."

It is the hardest thing to describe, as I have been everywhere and I like the idea of being a citizen of the world. I am so thrilled that my granddaughter has two passports. Why should we just lead one life?

I was especially thinking about this when Trump is trying to kick out immigrants. He even contemplated kicking out people like me, who were born here and attained our citizenship even though our parents were illegal.

Can you imagine what a huge ethnic cleansing that would be? I would have to be deported at seventy-eight years old!

I am a huge fan of your books. What prompted you to start writing?

I feel that I started writing at least three incarnations ago, because, as far as I can remember, I was always writing. My mother tells me I was just a few months old when I started to talk and I was already talking story. I even remember being a baby!

My mother used to tell me stories in Cantonese, as I didn't learn English until I was about five years old in school. So all my earliest memories of stories were all poems or myths in Cantonese.

When I first went to school, there was no such thing as ESL (English as a Second Language) and so the teachers thought I was dumb, as I could not speak English, so I flunked kindergarten. They gave me IQ tests and I got zero, so they put me in the corner with all the bad boys, which probably explains why I always felt an affinity and deep sense of empathy for the underdog.

I learned English very gradually. It was not until I was in second or third grade that I started to feel very good about speaking English. And then, there was the transition from just talking to writing.

Discovering the alphabet was a huge epiphany, as I realized you could write anything with the alphabet! Of course, at that time, I couldn't write just yet, but I remember making up poems and stories.

Once I discovered writing, I was hooked, as it allowed me to capture the rhythm of speech. When I first started to write, I would say everything aloud, either to myself or to other people, so that I can hear the rhythm.

How was that transition to English like given that your family spoke Cantonese at home?

My parents had told me stories of *Robinson Crusoe* in Cantonese, but I recall coming across a first-grade version of the story and things began to fall into place. But it was certainly gradual.

I had a sixth grade teacher and some high school teachers, in particular, my Latin and journalism teachers saw that I had talent. It was also around that time that I came across this notion of a "genius," and I remember telling myself that I want to be a genius! I figured if I worked really hard, I could be one, too!

To answer your prior question, I started to write stories in second or third grade, and by sixth grade, I was writing a lot of poems. My teacher would read them out in class and I would listen intently to the rhythm. I also recall that I would be writing poems in class, instead of doing my multiplication tables.

In one particular occasion, I recall that the poetry would just flow. It would keep coming and I just had to write it down. The poem which had to do with the light in the sky just came to me and it flowed with an ABAB rhyme.

Back then, I did not think of writing as a viable career, nor did I contemplate it as way of making a living, nor did I think about publishing. It was just my life—this constant outpouring of stories.

Do you think your gift of writing is nature or nurture?

It is probably both, as my parents are both very literate. In fact, my father was a Confucian scholar and had a good memory for classical Chinese poetry. My mother was a doctor. She loved to talk story to me about the history, myths, and ghost stories that abound in China. She was certainly very highly educated for her time. Her father had four daughters and he ensured that all of the girls were to be educated.

You see, back then, my grandmother had bound feet, so my parents ensured that they did not want to raise that next generation according to these feudal customs. My mother actually became a doctor while in America. She was already highly educated by the time my father was in America.

But before he sent for her, he wanted her to get even more education so that she could take care of herself and the family when she came to America. So my mother went to medical school in China. It was all very progressive as this must have been the 1930s.

How did you get your big break in writing?

I would say, it was just before *Woman Warrior* was published. I knew that it was different from what anyone else had done, as I was going out on an experimental limb. I played with many Chinese puns and did not think that I could get published. Anyhow, during that time, I also wrote an academic article and that got published in an English journal, which inspired me to then try to get *Woman Warrior* published, too. I thought my work was so different that I couldn't get published in America, so I decided to send my manuscript to England and Hong Kong. It was not till much later that I found out that they're much more conservative than Americans.

Anyway, I decide to locate an agent for *Woman Warrior* and, on my first try, I was rejected. In fact, it was less that I was rejected than the agent went out of business. But my manuscript was picked up by John Schaffner, who, in turn, sent it to three different publishing companies. One of them rejected the manuscript outright, and another called it "a pig in a poke." But the third one, Knopf, took it right away.

In comparison, to many writers, who have like fifty to one-hundred rejections, two is really not bad. In any case, I was not going to stop writing if I didn't get published. I figured I would keep copies around and, one day, somebody will find it. I even had ideas about how I could go door-to-door or sell it on the street.

What is your writing process like?

The process then is very different from what it is today. I would usually start writing in pencil, as it has so many dimensions. You could write with great intensity and make the font big or small. It was a very physical activity for me. I even made myself a quill pen when I was younger. I also used brush to write, because of my Chinese calligraphy background, just like my ancestors did that for thousands of years using only natural materials.

On that note, I also have a beautiful collection of fountain pens, including my father's, and have some precious ones with gold and platinum nips. Writing with pens makes you think and write slower.

Of course, these days, I use a word processor and my thoughts would race, but I would always come back and do a rewrite. I rewrite anywhere between twelve to twenty drafts of everything. It usually doesn't take me very long to write the first draft, but finalizing it can take years.

What inspires you?

People, situations, and scenes of beauty. Though there are days when I just make myself write, whether or not I feel like it.

My work cuts across time, space, and geographical barriers, as I always like to think we are all global people. I always felt I could belong anywhere no matter what my passports say.

My family is from all over the world. There was a time when I thought that I ought to write a global novel, where everyone in it would speak in different accents, which was what I tried with *Tripmaster Monkey*. It had slang from the 1960s and had a variety of accents and different characters from all over.

Are your inspirations drawn from imagination or observation?

My first couple of books were almost all drawn from Chinese and Chinese American characters, as that was my life then. It is not the world I inhabit now, so I have become more inclusive. Though I do find that, in poetry, I am able to go very far inward of myself to explore the essence of humanity, as that works very well in that medium.

You know, with the *Woman Warrior*, I remembered feeling very fulfilled that my writings created jobs for Asian actors and musicians, as it was made into a play and staged in Berkeley.

I recall, we had a Chinese jazz band and the actors were of Korean, Singaporean, Vietnamese, Filipino, Hong Kong, and Hawaiian descent. It was just beautiful. Of course, there were purists who criticized the play. They made a political argument that the accent was inauthentic. But I think the play succinctly captures how we speak now, as we all have a variety of accents while speaking English. I thought it was just the right thing to do and felt that the diversity was what made the play even more amazing.

You are clearly very forward thinking. But how did you deal with all your naysayers?

I stuck out it because I was one of the first ones around. Back then, there was just Amy Tan and me. We were the only two women and we helped each other.

But yes, we were hit hard, as we were women and all the critics were men. It was really very bad in the early years, as they really did try to squash us. As I wrote these feminist books, the guys saw it as an attack on them personally. Oftentimes, the critics would fight it out amongst themselves, though there have also been critics who are supportive.

I recall Frank Chin brought a charge against me and said I was fake and that I had messed with the Chinese myths, when I never subscribed to any notion of authenticity in the first place.

In fact, on the contrary, I don't think there is such a thing as an authentic Chinese or an authentic Chinese American and we are, in fact, always creating that person all the time, as we are always in the making. By so doing, we are creating American culture, a world culture.

But it was very hard in those early years when I first started out. They used to say such hurtful things, like we were in bed with the white, publishing establishment. They were very harsh on us, as we were of the same race as them, but we were women.

I was never on the offensive, but would clarify my position when I was quizzed in an interview or presentation. It took a long while for their criticism to die down and those guys have since disappeared. It was hard, but I just kept on writing.

On that note of self-identity, who do you identify with?

It is so easy to identify. I am a global citizen. Just take my recent trip to Japan. We have so many things that are different, but there's also so much that we have in common. We are two people who have fought terrible wars, but my son, who married a Japanese, has wonderful in-laws. I feel so connected to their family in Japan and my family here in Hawaiʻi and California. My granddaughter is half Japanese, a quarter Chinese, part Jewish, quarter Portuguese, Irish with some French, and a bit of a Neanderthal from my husband's side.

While we were in Japan, my son noticed that his baby was related to all these diverse people around the room by blood. How amazing is that?

And you know, my works have been taught in British universities, as it's seen as American Literature, but it is also studied in the English departments as it is written in English. So we are all global citizens.

Do you ever suffer from writer's block?

No, no but knock on wood. There was actually a time when I stopped writing after I graduated from Berkeley, as I was doing so much reasoning, logic, and critical thinking that I felt devoid of feeling and imagination.

So I came here to Hawai'i and spent the next year and a half painting. Painting was like writing, as it was primarily working with imagery, metaphors, perspective, and having a point of view.

After that time I spent painting, the writing came back. I see it as akin to cross-training in sports. These seemingly distinct disciplines all have a sense of continuity, even though we are doing it in different mediums.

How did you manage motherhood and your career?

I don't think I was a very good mother. I didn't spend enough time with my son, as I would lock him up so that I could write. I always thought I would run out of time and would focus on my writing. Now, I understand what it means to give somebody attention. It is really giving them your love.

Today, I can afford the now, but back then, I didn't know if I could afford all that time, as I would sacrifice the writing if I spent time with the baby.

If there is one thing I could change, I would change that, and spend more time with my son. I learned now that I would have had time. There probably would have been enough time for me and I probably didn't need to be in such panic. But I'm glad this is only hypothetical, as we can't turn back the clock now.

You know, Virginia Woolf said her sister was a wonderful painter but she was never going to be a great painter, as she had all those kids. She, of course, never had kids and was a great writer. I only have one. That's a choice I made. I did it so that I was able to write and be a mother to one. In hindsight, I think it is possible to have a career and be an excellent mother, but I guess it is easy for me to say now that I'm seventy-nine.

What do you think is one of your biggest failures?

I think I failed in that I could be a better mother and a better daughter. I also think I could be a better teacher. I often think back on the students that I had when I was younger and I don't think that I did right by them. It was only in the later years that I became a very good teacher.

Which is your favorite work to date?

There isn't a favorite, but I am proud that I have been able to solve the difficulties of each of these works.

The easiest one to write is the latest one, as I returned to poetry and wrote whatever came to mind. It seemed to flow easily, perhaps, because I'm older and less harsh on myself. I don't think I try as hard as when I was younger.

Perhaps because I have had some measure of success, this latest came to me in less time, as I could express whatever I wanted fully.

What advice would you give to an aspiring writer?

Just keep working at it every day. Do something every day. That's it.

What advice would you give to your thirty-something self, who was a writer at the crossroads of choosing her career and motherhood?

I would tell her that there really is enough time in the day. I would tell her that she could give her baby five hours and she could still write with one hour. It was only in recent years that I started to take Sundays off.

I have learned over time that if I had limited time, I could still write and I could do it fast. Conversely, if I gave myself more time, then I would also take more time to write.

Lately, I made up my mind that I really shouldn't sacrifice family and friendships. I used to pass up on luncheons or parties, as I noticed that lunch is never over until 2:30 p.m., even if you just grabbed a sandwich. But nowadays, I will go and tell myself that I can still do the writing by being more productive with the less time that I have.

Share with us the misogyny you experienced as an up-and-coming writer.

It was more racism than sexism. There was a time when Amy and I wrote at the same time, but because I was published, she was turned down as the publishing house had "met their quota." It was as if having one Asian writer was enough.

Later, her second book came out about the same time as my book. *Mother Jones*, a liberal magazine, reviewed her but they could not review me, as Amy was already reviewed. Amy was later featured on the cover of a magazine and she was so generous as to pose with my book, as she knew that I would not be featured if she was. So you know, in those days, the discrimination was more racial.

Yet, at the same time, the *Ms. Magazine* and the feminist movement was starting. I had initially resisted being labeled as a feminist writer, but I knew it was going to happen. It was less about the feminist label than I just didn't want to be pigeonholed. I wanted people to be able to read my book as a human being and not in gender specific terms.

Would you be comfortable being labeled a feminist today?

I am because my work has been reviewed as being everything else. But in the early days, I just didn't want to be placed in any box.

I have also learned over the years that I am not pigeonholeable. My work has been taught in African American Studies, Asian American Studies, English, American Literature, Anthropology, Sociology, and all over, so I am very comfortable with any label today.

How do you think publishing has evolved?

It's so hard to see it as we are in the middle of it. But what is evident is that the small publishing houses are gone. There are so few independents, like Mutual Publishing, left. Today, publishing is dominated by conglomerates and huge corporations. Many of the publishing labels all belong to a larger corporation.

The next big change is, of course, the advent of computers. I remember how unhappy I was when I mailed in a manuscript and was told to transfer the data to a floppy disk. I didn't know how to do that! *(laughter)*

People want to know whether it's easier or harder to publish today. I'm thinking about Virginia Woolf again, as she was self-publishing. She had her own press and her husband published all her works. They didn't have to rely on anybody else and that was very honorable.

Today, we can do the same with desktop publishing, but the problem is distribution. How do you get to the bookstores when the bookstores themselves are also vanishing? Many bookstores don't carry self-published books either, so how can one distribute their books with increasing competition?

So my vision of publishing is this—that we are going to have a few big New York publishers dominate and then we will also have the small, independent press. We will see a rise in desktop publishing and there will be bestsellers from all these publishers. But what I think young writers can do is to find a writing partner or group. I started to join one, after my manuscript burned in my home during the big fire of Oakland in 1991.

After that, I started a writing group with some war veterans, as I wanted to write a book of peace. These veterans and I got together to meditate, write, and we have been going on for twenty-five years. The camaraderie really helps to keep the energy going and you can also receive constructive criticism and helpful feedback. From that group, we have seen people publish short stories, novels, and poems. I can attest to how group support can really help people flourish.

> You have been given many awards including two from President Clinton and President Obama. Which was most memorable?

They both are, though I really loved meeting President Obama. He said *Woman Warrior* taught him how to write and that is how he learned to write his autobiography. He is just such a humble man and a good person.

I later read his autobiography and I get it. He said some not too flattering things about his mother and I think he learned that from me—that it is OK to say not so nice things about your mother. I mean, we all have mothers and stories of our mothers who are not always nice. We love them, but they're not perfect, but they did their best as they didn't know better.

> What can we expect from you in the near future?

I am writing my posthumous book. I decided that I would write something that will be published 100 years from now. I have a standing agreement with my agent and am free to write anything in any form I want, so that's what I'm doing now. She asked if I meant it metaphorically, as she wanted to read it now and publish it ahead of the one-hundred years, but I mean it quite literally!

> If you were writing your memoir, what would the title be?

Woman Warrior was in many ways my memoir, so let's call this *Woman Warrior: The Posthumous Novel*.

You were born in Stockton. How did you end up in Hawai'i?

It was during the Vietnam War and we were living in Berkeley. It felt as if the war was being fought right there. Back then, everybody was on drugs and every peace demonstration turned into a riot. We thought we would leave America to go to Japan, where they have a peace constitution, but we stopped at Hawai'i on our way and we just stayed and got engaged here in the sanctuary church. We ended up staying for seventeen years.

We later went back to California, as both our parents were getting old. My husband's parents are fourth-generation Oaklanders. They have all since passed away and, now, we have our granddaughter, so we're planning to move back.

How has Hawai'i changed since you left?

So much has changed. Every time I come back, some buildings have gone and something new has come up. We used to stay in a very poor area on the Windward Side, and even that has changed. The area where we used to live has been made into a state park.

It disturbs me to see the new towns being built all the time, like some science fiction movie. But this is not only happening to Hawai'i but all over the world, even in California where I am. I used to drive for miles on country roads, but now the skyline has changed.

What changes would you like to see in Hawai'i?

What comes to mind right away is solar heating. When it first debuted, everyone said it was great and then later, we were told we could only have a limited number of solar panels. I wish to ask, who controls these conversations in Hawai'i?

There was another similar conversation on electricity, but I don't know what's happened. I would like to see environmentally good developments take shape. I am glad we got rid of the Superferry, but I wonder what is happening with the rail and hope it works out. I hope to see fewer cars and better highways.

I am also very pleased that Hawai'i signed a bill to adopt the goals of the Paris Climate Agreement, despite Trump's pulling out of the global accord.

: What book is a must read for someone visiting Hawai'i for the first time?

Hawai'i's Story by Hawai'i's Queen, which is a book written by Queen Lili'uokalani.

: What advice would you give to a young woman reading this book?

That women have really special powers, distinct points of views, and perspectives. They are able to nourish and make lives and the world wonderful, so they have to really get to know and develop themselves.

: How do you want Hawai'i to be remembered?

For its original inhabitants, who were incredible. They lived the concept of aloha and were one with the environment. You can feel the inclusive love from the people. I have been to American Indian dance festivals, but what we have in Hawai'i is truly special.

Perhaps it has to do with the deep connection the people have for their land, ocean, and nature. This seeps into their bodies and nourishes them and makes them so loving and truly unique.

: Who would you like to have a sit-down dinner with?

I already did with President Clinton, Hillary, President Obama, and Michelle. The Obamas are truly lovely. You know, when I took my sister to the awards ceremony, she saw Michelle and fell to the floor. She was so floored by her beauty and stature. *(laughter)*

The Clintons are also very wonderful and have this golden aura around them.

: Who is your favorite author?

I have so many. OK, so let's just say Grace Paley. She's my role model.

: What book would you recommend is a must-read, either yours or someone else's?

For a writer, that's a really tough question. That's like saying I am stranded on an island and can only take one book and there is no Kindle.

If I was stranded, I would ask for a blank book so that I can write!

That's too greedy! *(laughter)* **What would you say when you meet God?**

That's like meeting my mother. Hmm, I'll say, "I'm glad to see that you exist."

(laughter) **What is your life philosophy on a bumper sticker.**

Oh, we had one on our car. It's *Live Aloha*.

That's real nice. How do you want to be remembered?

I am writing my posthumous novel and it's already like a thousand single-spaced pages, so that won't fit on the tombstone and, besides, I don't want a tombstone.

I'm going to have my ashes scattered in all of my favorite places, which includes Oakland, Hawai'i, and also the Grand Canyon, where we've lived. So no epitaph, but I would like to be remembered as a good human being like, "She did OK."

THE SHARP SHOOTER
Shirley Daniel

It is good to see women supporting each other more openly. That's very important and I hope that stays the case. In the end, it really boils down to money and power. When you look at the sexual harassment and discrimination cases, it is less about sex than power and what people can do with money. Women need more assertiveness training. [They] need tools and techniques to deal with things that they're going to encounter. So I think if women were taught to be more proactive, they could demand higher pay for what they are worth.

Shirley J. Daniel PhD is professor of accountancy and director of the Pacific Asian Management Institute (PAMI) in the Shidler College of Business Administration at the University of Hawai'i (UH). She received her PhD from Oklahoma State University, majoring in accounting with minors in economics and quantitative methods. Since joining UH in 1986, Shirley has served in a number of leadership positions, and currently serves as secretariat for the Pacific Asian Consortium for International Business Education and Research (PACIBER), a consortium of business schools from the Americas, Asia, and Oceania. She has generated over $25 million in sponsored research and training programs at the University of Hawai'i, and serves on the executive committee of the University of Hawai'i Association of Research Investigators (UHARI).

Shirley is a licensed CPA, a past president of the Hawai'i Society of CPAs, and a member of Financial Executives International and the Hawai'i Chapter of Women Corporate Directors. She served on the board and audit committees of Hawaiian Electric Industries (NYSE: HE) from 2002–2011, and currently serves on the board of directors and audit committee of American Savings Bank in Hawai'i.

I first met Shirley at a Women on the Move conference, held at Singapore Management University, and played host by showing her around my hometown, without an inkling that I would soon be seeing a lot more of her in Hawai'i when I moved to Honolulu years later. Shirley became one of my first friends in Hawai'i, generously opening doors for me by introducing me to like-minded folk and giving me good advice each step of the way as I quickly moved to settle into the island beat. My relationship with Shirley underscores for me the importance of genuine hospitality, mutual reciprocity, and the magic of karma, for you never know when your kindness will pay off one day ! But above all, Shirley is that straight-talking, take-no-prisoners mentor whose actions speak volumes. In her own words, "Who do you trust to get things done? Give it to a busy person." And yes, you can certainly count on Shirley to #getitdone.

Share with us who you are. I recall you telling me your father was a pastor.

Yes. My father grew up in Texas. As a kid, he learned music from The Salvation Army. His family was poor, as many were in West Texas during the Great Depression and dust bowl. During those days, The Salvation Army had street corner bands, and he and his brothers learned to play music and received help from The Salvation Army during those tough times. He also met my mother at church then. Patriotism is very strong in my family, and my father and his three brothers all served in various branches of the U.S. military during WWII. My father was such a good musician when he joined the army that he was assigned to the band and also served as a stretcher-bearer. He was in the Battle of the Bulge. After the war, he went to college at Trinity University in Houston on the G.I. Bill to study music, and then went on to seminary with The Salvation Army. He served in The Salvation Army for about ten years, then decided to go into teaching in public school. He also preached at the Methodist Church on the weekends. Actually, my youngest brother is now with The Salvation Army and has been for over twenty years.

I was born and raised in Oklahoma. There were six of us—two older brothers and two older sisters, then there's my younger brother and me. The three oldest siblings were born in Texas, but my father was transferred to Oklahoma with The Salvation Army in about 1950, so my older sister and I were born in Oklahoma, and my youngest brother was born in a little town in Kansas just north of the Oklahoma border.

How did you end up in Hawai'i?

I went to college at Oklahoma State and majored in accounting. After graduation, I was practicing as a CPA in Tulsa, Oklahoma. One of my college friends had moved out here, and I came out to visit her on vacation. I started making friends with some of her friends in Hawai'i and I fell in love with a local Japanese American man that she worked with. After a long-distance relationship for a year or so, he came and lived in Oklahoma to study law. After he graduated law school, he came back to Hawai'i, and I decided to join him.

While my boyfriend was in law school, I was exploring career options in case I relocated to Hawai'i. It just so happened that one of my college professors and mentors from Oklahoma State was hired by the University of Hawai'i to develop a master in accountancy program here. My college friend called me to relay this news, so I contacted my former professor to see if there might be a job available for me at UH if I did move to Hawai'i. He said there was a possibility, but I needed a PhD. So that's when I decided to obtain my PhD. What are the odds that this gentleman who was my undergraduate professor and one of my greatest mentors at Oklahoma State would end up here in Hawai'i?

> Were you one of a handful of females reading your PhD then, and what adjustments did you have to make?

I went back to school in 1982 so I was probably one in four women. It wasn't unheard of, but women were not represented equally in business PhD programs as they are now.

When I first got to Hawaiʻi, there were definitely adjustments I had to make as Hawaiʻi was very expensive. And because my love relationship ended within six months of my arrival here, I had to find a new apartment, new hairdresser, and doctor, as all these connections were through friends and relatives of my then ex-boyfriend. The adjustment was not easy, but you just do what you have to do, and at least I had a good job and the status of being a UH professor.

I was lucky that at the University of Hawaiʻi I had the opportunity to get involved with international business research. There were other scholars in the college that were already on that path who helped me a great deal. The hot topic in the late 1980s was the Japanese economic success, or the Japanese miracle. We did a large-scale research project to examine Japanese manufacturing and accounting systems and compare them to practices in the U.S. We studied worker and management attitudes, productivity systems, and quality management, and that turned out to be a very good career move.

It was also very enriching for me personally, as until then, I was just a small town girl from Oklahoma. The first time I ever flew on an airplane was when I completed my masters and went to work as a CPA at the age of twenty-two. I didn't even see the ocean until I was twenty-three! Coming to Hawaiʻi, living in a multicultural society, doing research on Japan, getting to know other scholars and experts in Europe, and later, Chinese management and culture really changed me. I expanded my horizons and had the chance to travel.

> What would you say was your biggest takeaways working and navigating between the Japanese and Hawaiʻi's residents?

There was a lot of literature out there that talked about the Japanese success being based on their homogeneous society and emphasis on harmony. But my research refuted the idea of harmony as the main element of their success. You could clearly see that successful Japanese firms had very defined management systems, tracked important operating metrics and focused on continuous improvement. It was also clear that the Japanese labor market was not very mobile. The disadvantage to lifetime employment is that moving up the ladder was hard in Japan so one could potentially spend thirty years as a fairly low-level factory foreman. It is not a bad job, but you don't have the labor mobility that you would in the U.S.

If a Japanese man left his mid- to lower-level management job with a large Japanese company, he would not likely get a similar job with another large Japanese company. This labor mobility issue creates a lot of power for the company as long-term service with a major corporation is seen to be prestigious. Losing or quitting your job with a major Japanese company would result in a loss of status, and your family is probably not going to be very happy about that. So life for a Japanese salary-man was stressful and hard work.

One thing I learned from this experience was that Hawai'i has elements of the East and West. When I first came to Hawai'i, there was a feeling that this could be this international business hub or gateway to Asia. But that notion is a bit naive because even though we are an island of immigrants from Asia, the people who had immigrated were mostly from an agricultural background, rather than from the Asian business community. And after Pearl Harbor, there were rational reasons why the local Japanese Americans didn't maintain their Japanese language skills.

During the Japanese bubble, a lot of real estate investment was coming in to Hawai'i from Japan, so there was a lot of enthusiasm, and people in Hawai'i hoped this was going to really benefit the local economy. Articles proposed that Hawai'i could become the Geneva of the Pacific. But Japanese investors did not come to Hawai'i to do business deals with people from the U.S. Mainland, at least that's not my perception. While Hawai'i has some bilingual individuals and the University of Hawai'i Asian Studies programs are strong, there are not enough people with sophisticated business and language skills. Except for some real estate investment, there are not enough business opportunities with Asia to drive a fundamental a change in Hawai'i's economic base. As is common in many U.S. cities, most Hawai'i businesses need translators to negotiate deals with Asia, and the Asian firms will have their English-speaking person available rather than the other way around.

> That is an astute observation. What do you think are some of the biggest obstacles or challenges that you faced as a female academic and business consultant?

I think that being at the university made it easier for me, as sexism was less of an issue than it would have been in a regular business environment. You are evaluated on publishing in blind-peer reviewed journals, and on your student evaluations. UH faculty come from all over the world, and being a professor is relatively well respected in the community. People are supportive of the university.

The business community also did not view you as a threat or competitor, so that made it easier to make connections. As a result, I did not have the challenges that friends of mine from the Mainland, who were working in accounting and health care, had when they were trying to establish themselves here in the business community. Naturally, people are not so welcoming if you're competing against them for clients. To become integrated into the Hawaiʻi business community as a professor, I joined the professional accounting organizations and advised the student clubs. This allowed me to work with the business community in a symbiotic and non-competitive way. That said, I had to work very hard to establish myself and publish my work to keep my job. Within the university, some people were supportive, but the business school is a very male-dominated environment.

If you look solely at the statistics, it is still true that there are fewer women hired at the entry-level business schools, and when you move up the ladder, there are fewer and fewer women. Making that hurdle to get tenure and then promotion to full professor is a big challenge. Hawaiʻi is a very expensive place to live and raise a family. There is a lot of attrition, especially of women, and it is even worse in engineering than business. From a practical standpoint, the higher paying the field, the more sexism you will probably encounter as the competition is tougher for a higher paying job than a mediocre paying job.

How did you survive the sexism and the competition?

It's a combination of things. I would say there were some men in positions of authority that were supportive of me, and of other women. Because I had worked in the private sector and was already in my thirties when I got to the university system, I knew a few things about career management and organizational politics. In the classroom, I used my background in public accounting and was able to succeed in teaching in our MBA and executive training programs. As I mentioned, researching on Asia was also another niche. I got myself into a new research stream which was an advantage when it came to publishing.

I also worked very hard to gather data that nobody else had and could therefore publish some studies that were unique. So I will say it was a combination of flexibility and hard work. That, and having some sponsors and mentors. I read somewhere that you should always know your boss's boss. That has been a very good philosophy for me. As I moved on up in my career,

I developed networks across the university so I knew people in other fields. That not only gave me a network of people that would help professionally, but sometimes when your own department or college is having problems, it can be very refreshing to have a frame of reference of people that aren't in the middle of the fray that you can go to for your own sanity. I have colleagues in engineering, medicine, and science at UH and at business schools across the U.S. and the world. These broader networks help you keep a balanced perspective when the local office politics get rough.

Share with us more about the discrimination action suit you filed.

In 2001, I was awarded a prestigious endowed professorship through a competitive process and an international search. After six years of serving, the dean appointed an all-male review committee to evaluate my performance. The committee decided not to renew my appointment. I disagreed with this decision, as I had secured more extramural funding grants than any other professor in my college. I filed a grievance through the faculty union, then later an EEOC complaint, and then finally the discrimination complaint in court. The legal process took a very long time—over five years—and it was very expensive.

In the end, we reached a settlement. It was a very stressful and unpleasant process, but I felt like I needed to do it it to take a stand against bias in the system. I knew there was a lot of gender discrimination in the university and that it is common across academia. I had hoped that things were changing, and I was proud to be the first woman in the college to be awarded an endowed chair after my success in research, teaching, service to the accounting profession, and obtaining significant extramural funding. I was heading our federally-funded international business center and had obtained over twenty million dollars in grants to improve education in Hawai'i.

In fact, none of the men on my review committee had achieved this level of accomplishment across so many areas of the academic spectrum. I knew that if the UH could treat me this way, then there were many other women who were also being discriminated against in the system who were even more vulnerable and that gender bias remained a bit problem.

In the process of gathering evidence and taking depositions, it was very disappointing to see people, who you worked with for a long time and who you thought were supporters, suddenly "lose their memory." It is interesting when you get into a deposition how people forget conversations and events that happened. But on the other hand, you will find a few people, very few, who step up and back you up, regardless of the potential negative repercussions to them. That means a lot.

It sounds like a very painful and expensive experience. What advice would you give to another woman who was in your shoes?

I'm single and didn't have to justify to a husband or a family why I should spend hundreds of thousands of dollars on legal fees that may never be recovered. Many women would not have a tenured position and without tenure most women filing such a grievance and then a law suit would probably have been terminated. Even tenured professors in fields that pay less probably could not afford the legal fees to fight this type of discrimination. Further, as we have heard many times, the EEO offices and process in the workplace organization are created to protect those further up the hierarchy, not the employee. So to anyone considering filing a discrimination suit, I would say: You have to really think about it hard before you decide to go the legal route. You need to know what you want out of it because when you are dealing with a large organization, reasoning isn't necessarily going to rule. Some organizations may decide they want to fight for the sake of fighting especially when they are spending the state's or the insurance company's money. Generally you as the plaintiff are paying your lawyer out of your own pocket while the administration's legal fees are paid by the employer (in my case the UH/State of Hawai'i and insurers).

In the long run, I did all right when we settled. But in the short run, the costs really add up. So, I will say you have to be realistic that the deck is probably not stacked in your favor. And you'll be surprised how people you thought would be in your corner may not be. The conventional old boys' club sticks together.

Do you see what is happening now with #MeToo and the Women's March as a step in the right direction? Or do you think this is going to be a moment in history, and we will fall back to the usual modus operandi?

I'm not too optimistic. It is good to see women supporting each other more openly. That's very important and I hope that stays the case. In the end, it really boils down to money and power. When you look at the sexual harassment and discrimination cases, it is less about sex than power and what people can do with money.

When you are a lower-level employee, and unfortunately most young women start out in that position, you are not in a position to give up your job because of something that happened at work. Most workplaces have HR policies or departments to protect the executives, not the women. I was very lucky that I was a member of a labor union. Even though they didn't support me through the whole process, they did support me through the first and second grievance levels, where I was able to obtain documentation for things such as review committee reports and emails, and policies and legal documents that were very helpful later. Most women wouldn't have that. When I went to talk to lawyers, a lot of them were not interested because they considered the situation too vague since I had not been fired, but rather demoted and the criteria for performance can be very subjective. The EEOC had limited resources, so they preferred to pursue cases that were blatant discrimination or something over the top where they can fine the organization to recover their costs and justify the involvement of their very limited staff.

My case was not an open-and-shut case, but it was about why my prestigious endowed chair position should be taken away. It was easy to dismiss it as jealousy and not necessarily easy to make a legal case for discrimination. Being realistic about the organization is important because you know you are competing against men in the workforce. The more lucrative and prestigious the position, the greater the competition and motivation for discrimination.

So how would you advise someone stepping into this domain—to go against the tide, play with it, accept it, or get smart about it?

Research shows that it's very difficult to have a good solution. Many women leave organizations and start their own business for that reason. I think staying connected is important. You want to be connected with other women and also other men who have influence in the organization. That is your best strategy in the short run. And if it gets to a stage where you are being discriminated against, then talking to an attorney is not a bad idea. The EEOC is an easy and inexpensive way to begin the process if you do not have a bargaining unit to help. I have seen some women in my organization who are repeatedly discriminated against and exploited. But fighting the system takes lot of resources, both emotionally, financial as well as your time for an uncertain outcome.

One of the reasons I felt compelled to go ahead with the legal route was because I just didn't want to be continually jerked around and I wanted to stand up for all the women that couldn't.

What changes would you like to see implemented in your lifetime?

Women need to have more assertiveness training. This isn't necessarily my problem but I think women need tools and techniques to deal with things that they're going to encounter. It goes back to power and money—economic resources. So I think if women were taught to be more proactive, they could demand higher pay for what they are worth. You need to have a good idea what's going on in the talent market so you can learn strategies to ensure you get paid what you are worth. And in terms of the personal harassment or sexual harassment, the earlier you learn how to deal with people like that, the better you can put a stop to these things in a diplomatic way, especially if it is someone above you in the organization. It is important to let the person know that this is an unwanted situation and you're not comfortable with it. Then keep a contemporaneous record of each incidence including dates, places, witnesses, and as many specific details as you can. If things don't improve after you make it clear advances are unwanted, these documents can be helpful later and at least you don't feel so helpless because you are keeping a written file of your experiences.

Unfortunately, women are taught to be polite and deferential so when someone says something inappropriate, we smile and let it go even if we know it is sexist, demeaning and that the person is basically encroaching on our boundaries in subtle ways.

What sacrifices have you made along the way?

I'm not sure I would call it sacrifices but I would say choices. I like being financially independent and I've always wanted to have my own money and be able to support myself. So I've always focused on what my career opportunities would be even when I had personal reasons why I wanted to relocate.

It was also a conscious choice to leave public accounting for academia. I sacrificed a more lucrative job for more control over my time. I made that decision as I did not want to be assigned clients that I did not enjoy working with. I wanted to have a little more predictability and control over my time and that was a choice I never regretted.

Once I got through the PhD, which was not an easy time to get through given the pay decrease and uncertainty, the early years of being a professor required good classroom teaching as well as research publications. Achieving tenure is hard work and definitely feels risky. But overall, I'm very glad that I made the switch to be an academic instead of staying in public accounting, particularly after the dot-com meltdown.

What are some of your biggest victories or highlights in your career?

I would say there are two things I've accomplished that I really enjoyed and felt proud of. One of them, I really can't take too much credit for, but I spent about thirteen months being the interim chancellor for the community college on the Big Island. It was a lot of fun and one of the most rewarding assignments I ever had. It was unusual that I would have the chance to do that, but it was really wonderful to work with the people there and to see another part of the university that I hadn't seen before. Being on the neighbor island was, in some ways, a little like going home for me as I grew up in a small, rural town. I can understand people in a close community like that. Many people in the upper administration in Honolulu didn't understand, but I understood that culture and I loved it. I felt like I was making a difference. I learned a lot from the people that I worked with and I enjoyed that.

The other thing I might take a little more credit for is founding the Hawai'i State GEAR UP program for which we got a large federal grant to help low-income youth prepare for college. Again, this was unusual as a business school professor. I wasn't the natural person to write the proposal for this grant and start the project but when I found out that no one else at UH was going to do it, I felt I had to. I saw this as an opportunity that Hawai'i should take advantage of. The people in the College of Education were busy with other things and I had worked with the Hawai'i Business Roundtable on an earlier project so I knew that improving education was a high priority for the business community. In the late 90s, many were questioning if Hawai'i's workforce was going to be able to meet the needs of new technologies or society. We had a shortage of doctors, and certain skills needed for the future, and we needed a better education pipeline to meet the needs.

With the help of my staff, we wrote a proposal and got funded. I was very proud when we received $10 million dollars to work on this project for five years, and then five years later, we got another $16 million dollars. That program still exists under the leadership of some of my protégés that worked on it. On the first grant alone, we worked with over seven thousand students in Hawai'i and we saw that we made a real difference to the lives and the prospects of these students who would normally not think about going to college. That was a lot of fun and extremely rewarding.

Would you say a woman can have it all?

I would turn that around and say women get it all because most women don't have a choice!

Most women want a career but will also have a family, whether they end up in a long marriage or not. And we know the divorce rate is what it is. So, I think the question is how can a woman have a happy life when you have all these things to contend with? I have friends who have a career and children and it can be very stressful. So having a support network is very important to have. And it's not all about money, though it certainly helps.

Some women have to go back to work after a very short maternity leave. It is never easy to leave a six-month-old kid with strangers, but that is a choice many women have to make. Having an extended family that can help with the childcare makes it easier, but as women have children later, their mothers are growing older, too, and may not be able to take care of a toddler, or grandma may be working to support herself, too! So I think we're almost past that point to say that women can have it all, because I don't know very many women who are stay-at-home mothers, especially in Hawai'i.

What changes have you seen in Hawai'i since you got here?

There is an increasing feel of urbanization and you see developments popping up everywhere. There is less agriculture and more condos and houses. The entire stretch from Ala Moana to Waikīkī is becoming almost solid retail and luxury condos. There is a lot more commercialism. Even though the Japanese bubble burst in 1992, there is still a lot of cash coming in through real estate from Japan, China, and elsewhere. America, overall is still considered a safe place to invest, and Hawai'i is very comfortable for most real estate investors. But of course, this is exacerbating the homelessness and housing shortage issues.

What sort of changes would you like to see in the next few years?

We need to make sure that the income inequality doesn't continue to accelerate. I'm biased but I believe a part of the answer to that is education. I would like to see a commitment to the K–12 system. I can understand why people send their kids to private schools in Hawai'i, but if that ends up resulting in the abandonment of public education, that's not going to be good for our society in the long run. Sometimes I wonder what Hawai'i's public education system would look like if all our top community leaders had to send their kids to public schools instead of private schools. I am quite sure that our public education system would be one of the top in the nation because the whole community would be invested in it. And there would be a better understanding between different races, cultures, and economic sectors in the long run. The increasing divide between our societal sectors is not a good thing.

We need to have a broad-based educated workforce to support our community. I think attaining a more egalitarian society and maintaining the opportunities for everyone is very important. We also need to manage some of the environmental pressures that we face, and education needs to be a part of that.

What are your hopes and aspirations for Hawaiʻi?

I think maintaining our own cultural identity is important here. We need the diversity and a multicultural environment. We have to try to maintain the idea that everyone should have the chance to get an education, a job that supports them, and we shouldn't have people who were born and raised here living in tents. That's not right.

Where is home for you now?

Although I was not born here, after over thirty years, Hawaiʻi is my home now.

You are an avid traveler. Where is your favorite destination?

The place I haven't been yet. *(laughter)* But I am active so I like to go do things. I know Polynesia has a lot to offer. So perhaps Fiji or French Polynesia because I like watersports. But for culture, I'll say Italy is pretty high on my list.

You are so well exposed to different cultures and work environments. Which do you admire and appreciate the most?

It's hard to say because I am still at heart an American so I'm partial to the American system. If I had to live my life all over again, I would still choose to be an American and live in America as you have a chance to reinvent yourself. You can go back to school in your thirties or change careers in your fifties. Even our bankruptcy laws are geared toward starting over. I appreciate this attitude of enterprise and getting a second or third chance if you are still willing to work hard.

What makes you angry?

My parents used to say, "The world doesn't owe you a living," so you have to get out and figure out what you can do to make a living. There's a certain segment of population that feels like they should be entitled to certain privileges, but that's not the way the world works.

I relocated thousands of miles away from where I grew up and I have a better life because of it. I have relatives and friends who stayed in Oklahoma who could do better if they would even just move a hundred miles away to get a better job. But they won't even try and, instead, idealize on how things used to be fifty years ago. It's unrealistic. So what makes me angry is when people feel like they're entitled for any reason. I just don't see it quite the same way. The world doesn't owe you a living, so you've got to get yourself together, get an education, relocate, or get a job to support yourself and your family. Americans have been doing this for centuries, so get over it.

Who would you like to have a sit-down dinner with?

Barack Obama.

What would you say if you met God?

Thank you for everything you've given me.

What is one piece of accounting advice you live by?

Keep track of where the money is going—cash is king.

What is your best investment?

My education.

Your life philosophy on bumper sticker?

This is not necessarily a bumper sticker, but it is some advice from one of my friends from Malaysia:

"When it comes to knowledge, always compare yourself to people higher than you; When it comes to money, always compare yourself to people lower than you."

Is that your secret to happiness?

Yes, I think so. Because if you really look around, you can always see somebody who has less material than you, and you feel lucky and grateful. But when it comes to knowledge, you should never feel like you're the smartest person on earth because there's always something more to learn. If you compare yourself to people who are more knowledgeable, then you have something to strive for.

Finally, the title of your life memoir would be …

Dumb Luck.

THE COMMUNITY INNOVATOR
Karen Tan

One of the biggest lessons I've learned is to say yes to incredible opportunities. Be open to letting all your life experiences get you to where you are and appreciate that. I've learned to accomplish all the things I've said yes to in my career, in spite of being afraid, thanks to being open to support, guidance, and mentorship, and not being afraid of criticism or making mistakes.

Karen Tan is president and CEO of Child & Family Service (CFS), one of Hawai'i's largest nonprofit organizations with a budget of nearly $30 million and over four-hundred employees island-wide. CFS provides nearly fifty programs across the state that help Hawai'i's families to address serious life challenges, such as poverty, abuse, and neglect, and to create healthy, thriving futures.

Karen is a Licensed Clinical Social Worker (LCSW) and has twenty-four years of management experience in leading nonprofit organizations. She served as an executive level leader for eleven years, during which, she brought national best practices to the work of CFS to meet the needs of Hawai'i's multicultural communities. She holds a master's degree in social work from the University of Hawai'i at Mānoa and a bachelor's degree from Seattle Pacific University, and is certified through the Executive Leadership Institute, University of Michigan, and through The Alliance for Strong Families and Communities.

She is also a nationally recognized speaker and was recently accepted to the Omidyar Fellows, and serves on several boards focused on addressing the wider human services needs of Hawai'i. She welcomes me to her spacious office in 'Ewa Beach and shares with me her newly constructed Innovations Lab, signaling to me that this human services executive is no traditionalist, but a dynamic creative game-changer, keen to fuse enterprise, energy, and experimental innovations into her nonprofit entity.

Do share with us a little about your upbringing and your family.

I learned early on to be adaptable and able to manage changing situations. My father was a minister and had different assignments, so we moved often and I had to get to know new people and make new friends. Since my dad was the leader of the church, our family lived in the spotlight, and we were mindful that it was important how we were perceived by others. So I've always been attuned to people and their perspectives.

How have your formative years influenced you?

Yes. My dad was a true servant leader. He was someone who really cared for people in a genuine way, in a way that we all strive to be. He did everything, and nothing was above him; he would set the church's vision and take out the trash as well. He cared for others and, even though we didn't have much money, he would give those in need money for a meal.

When I was a kid, my dad would take me along with him to do counseling with parishioners every Saturday. I witnessed firsthand how he could help people, how being willing to listen could change their lives. He cared for people the way social workers do.

Life changed for me when I was twelve years old. My father died of cancer, and all of a sudden, my mom was left on her own to raise two children.

Through the tragedy of my father's passing, I could identify when the families and staff we work with go through tough situations or experiences, and understand that life isn't always what we want it to be, but it creates resilience. The help and support of others can change the trajectory of their lives. Even a little shift can change people for the better, in lasting ways.

When my father died, my mom was left to support two children. She was a stay-at-home mom, so she was without work experience and skills at that time. She knew she had to lead the family, and so she went to college to get a bachelor's degree around the time that I started going to college.

We then decided to go into social work together. In fact, we earned our master's degrees together, taking the same courses at the same school. She later worked as a group facilitator for individuals struggling with addiction.

My mom depicted the resilience in the people we help now and showed me what hope is. That's why I believe in the best in people, as I've seen it come out in my mom.

How did you end up to Hawaiʻi?

I came to Hawaiʻi for my master's degree at the University of Hawaiʻi. The plan was to return home afterwards, but I met my husband, Felix. We have since been married twenty-one years. I was literally packed and ready to go, but ended up staying and this has been my life ever since. Our meeting changed everything. Felix is a local boy of Filipino ancestry. He loves people and is my best champion in my life, as a parent, and in my career.

Coming from the Mainland, was it hard for you to adapt to Hawaiʻi?

When I first came to Hawaiʻi, I had to adapt to a different culture, but my approach has always been one of curiosity and openness. I'm not one to judge or react very easily. Having lived in different environments, it was second nature to me to listen and to ask questions; to bring people to the table with different ideas, and to make connections.

I had a lot of people around me to support me, including my friends from the school of social work and colleagues. They would joke about what I didn't know, but they helped me to better understand Hawai'i and the local culture. The support of others was valuable and helped to shape my thinking and understanding of what makes Hawai'i special.

What got you interested in diverse, minority cultures and social work in the first place?

In my field, people who receive services tend to be from minority cultures and are over-represented. In fact, when I was interning as an undergraduate at the King County Detention Center in Seattle, about ninety-five percent of the kids in the youth correctional facility were of minority ethnic backgrounds.

I asked myself, "Why can't people thrive equally? How can we create the opportunities to change the trajectory of people's lives?" That's what prevention programs do. We can prevent children from struggling to learn and from dropping out of high school, and, instead, enable them to strive to go to college and go on to have successful careers. We can help families prevent tragedies and abuse, rather than having to help them heal from the trauma afterwards.

You ended up having a twenty-four yearlong career in nonprofit work, and counting. How did this come to be?

The social services professional is all about systems, about how things work together. In Hawai'i, the system includes things, like family, home life, work, school, education—these are all intertwined and this is how social workers view the world. It's a systems approach I value. I am a licensed clinical social worker (LCSW), which required training and experience working in clinical settings for counseling and therapy. But a CEO has to look at all the systems at play — how they work together and how to advance all the pieces for the better good while leading an organization of five hundred people.

We work with families very tough situations and our staff members bring a great depth of experience and knowledge about the best practices that work. Having this background myself helps me better understand and support our team in our systems approach to bringing all the parts together to help families to thrive.

What have been some of the biggest lessons learned over all this time?

One of the biggest lessons I've learned is to say yes to incredible opportunities. Be open to letting all your life experiences get you to where you are and appreciate that. I've learned to accomplish all the things I've said yes to in my career, in spite of being afraid, thanks to being open to support, guidance, and mentorship, and not being afraid of criticism or making mistakes.

I've also learned to really listen to all sides when dealing with issues. Laser-focused plans don't always work. Don't move so quickly that you miss the opportunity to make the best decision.

With the benefit of hindsight, how do you think you ended up as the president of the CFS?

My journey gave me opportunities to see that I could do it, and there were always people along the way who inspired my growth. I had many mentors along the journey. I attribute my career to the leaders around me, who saw potential and put me into coordination, supervisory, and later, leadership roles that I had no idea I was even capable of. I think I was always lucky to have that one senior staff that would see my potential and would challenge me out of my comfort zone.

I hope to do that for others from where I am today, to help inspire our next generation of leaders.

What have you learned in your years of being a leader?

I learned to not shy away from leadership, because it offers the power to influence change. People are resilient, and I believe that on an individual, as well as systems, levels that there can be positive change, and, as a result, amazing things can happen in people's lives and in our larger community.

You've had a lot of mentors along the way. In my personal experience and in talking to other women, I realized that women can sometimes be harsher on other women. What are your thoughts about this?

I think we women tend to be critical of other women, as we have a critical eye. But I have had the fortune of being surrounded by people who gave me opportunities and are optimistic about my contributions.

You're also only a leader if people follow you. If you genuinely care for others and the work you do, then you'll be a good leader. I couldn't do the job I do without caring for all walks of life and our community. It drives what I do every day and is a passion I take seriously.

Has motherhood changed your style of leadership?

What I appreciate from having three daughters is how uniquely different they are, just like the team I lead. Each child approaches life in a unique way. My oldest is a driver and gets things done. My middle daughter is led by feelings and emotions, while my youngest is a wonderful cheerleader—all different ways of being, despite having the same parenting.

Having this perspective makes me a better leader as you appreciate the differences, and use the differences in a positive way.

Have you made any sacrifices along the way?

I don't like to call it sacrifices. You can have a high-level career and a family life that's very healthy, but you have to give a little on each side. You can't value one more than the other, or one will suffer. There can be a balance, but you have to be deliberate. I give my full attention to work in the morning, and when I leave at the end of the day, I give my full attention to my family. If I've had crazy busy days at work, I find those crazy busy times for my family as well.

I also give full credit to stay-at-home moms, because it's really a tough job. I tried it for a few months and it wasn't for me, and I'm so impressed with those who do it.

What advice would you give to a young person who is keen on a career in social work?

I tell young professionals to practice self-care because it is the hardest work you'll ever do. And when you finally make headway with families, celebrate those victories, and keep that hope alive. Don't give up and believe in the good intentions of those you serve. You'll wake up every day happy, knowing that you're making a difference in the community.

What are some community trends, patterns, demographics, and observations you've made since being here in CFS?

In the largest-ever national study of its kind called The National Imperative, the Alliance for Strong Families and Children surveyed forty-thousand community-based organizations (CBOs) through their Form 990 filings, an Internal Revenue Service form that provides the public with financial information about a tax-exempt organization.

The study found that America's CBOs impact the lives of an estimated one in five Americans, contributing nearly $200 billion in economic activity through the cost of delivering services. In Hawai'i, more than three-hundred human services organizations in Hawai'i contribute more than $650 million annually to our economy.

Despite that impact, the study said our communities face significant risks if CBOs are not financially strong. The report identified a number of challenges that CBOs face, such as persistent operating deficits, few or no financial reserves, and lack of access to capital to invest in technology and systems.

Hawai'i is not immune from these impacts. We commissioned a supplemental, Hawai'i-focused report funded by the Hawai'i Community Foundation. While we compared slightly better than the national average in categories like insolvencies and cash liquidity, these findings give us pause as to the ability of our sector to deliver on helping people to reach their full potential.

Given this scenario, what can be done to make a difference?

The good news is that the Alliance report also identified what they call five "North Star" initiatives to improve the financial health of CBOs: a commitment to measure longterm outcomes; investing in the capacity for innovation; forming strategic partnerships; developing new financial policies and practices; and driving regulatory modernization.

We convened a group of sixty-five local CBOs to identify specific initiatives in each of these categories that can make a difference in our collective ability to ensure the financial health of our CBO community, and in turn, achieve more and greater measurable impact by supporting thriving individuals and a healthier community.

We are already moving forward on action steps that include working in cooperation with legislators to help streamline the contract process to make it as effective as possible, and most importantly, for the families we serve. Hawai'i's community-based organizations are also forming partnerships to more efficiently bid on contracts and leverage the strengths of each of our organizations to maximize impact.

So you are hopeful for the families in Hawai'i?

Yes, there's always hope. We collectively have the power to help families to achieve lasting change, and we are working collaboratively to get resources out to families so that they can be purposeful and successful. There's so much support for those in need in our community, and by working together strategically, we can make significant change.

How do you leverage partnerships to tackle tough social problems?

When you're a leader, you have to stay relevant to the issues in your community. Take, for example, the whole issue of sexual harassment in the workplace. It is unacceptable. If we don't take the initiative to lead, then who will?

As a systems person, I'm also very clear that we're not going to do this alone, that we all need each other. So, I connected a group of twelve women CEOs to initially discuss the issue, and we quickly found common purpose. We have already created a safe spaces, or work places, partnership and are finding ways to help companies to create a safe environment for all of their workers.

How do you reach out to communities who feel ashamed to seek help? Speaking as an Asian, I know the idea of saving face is integral to one's identity, so how do you get to this population?

Meeting families where they are and working with them in a nonjudgmental way is critical to how we help families. We need to build relationships with family members. We make our services available, show the opportunity and create a safe place to share stories, without judgment. If you are genuine and make it OK to share and don't force it, families will open up and reach out for help.

What about the growing issue of child abuse in our communities?

I don't believe anyone intends to hurt their children. It happens due to a variety of factors. It may be due to lack of resources and stresses that cause parents to react. We, as leaders, need to make sure there are necessary supports to prevent it, whether through the companies we work for, or the families we serve directly.

The neat thing is child abuse is preventable. In fact, any form of abuse is preventable, as no one intends to do it. The question is how do we get more resources and support for the focus on prevention?

> Based on what you just shared, how does CFS work to help in the prevention aspect?

We have a program that is near and dear to my heart called Healthy Families. This is a home-visiting program that is purely voluntary. We identity at-risk families, such as single-parent homes, a parent who has been abused, or other possible factors, and we invite them to be part of the program. Many say yes, and we work with them by going to their homes and supporting them in their child-rearing experiences.

Ninety-nine percent of the families, who stay with us for a year or more, report no abuse or neglect to these high-risk families. This is a program we started in Hawaiʻi and we have many partner-providers in the state that support the program.

> Any other pressing issues facing children in Hawaiʻi?

There are so many issues—poverty, early education, reading, nutrition, and health, to name a few. It really is the need to look at what it is we want to prioritize. Human trafficking is certainly more prevalent, with our local kids being trafficked. My job is to make sure we pay attention, stay relevant, and ensure we are meeting needs with a forward-thinking perspective.

I also make sure I'm listening to our staff. They have their boots on the ground and are a fantastic source of knowing what is happening in the community and why. They also know when we should be looking at this or that issue. My job is to listen and set the vision.

> You speak a lot on innovation and showed me your Innovations Lab. How do you foster fresh thinking at CFS and can you share with us your ideas on the lab?

It starts the minute new staff walk through the doors at employee orientation. I tell our staff to be innovative, to try new things, and that it's OK to make mistakes. We set up the value system and a culture that it's okay to be uncomfortable. We challenge everyone, from the frontline staff to the executive leadership team, to stretch, be bold, and take risks.

From there, we create an environment that follows through, literally and figuratively. When I assumed the job as president and CEO, I gave up the old CEO office and turned it into an Innovations Lab. We tore down walls and put up high-tech whiteboards, so that the best and brightest ideas can keep growing. And we use it, not only internally, but also, we bring together community leaders to come up with new solutions to our most pressing social issues.

Through our leadership academy, we are also creating adaptive leaders, who are willing to take an issue and really step back from it to hear different sides and get to the root cause and solutions. It embraces a willingness and permission to not stick to the status quo.

Rather than technical solutions, we're looking at adaptive solutions that will be more effective, and save money in the long term. I have a great staff, so smart and wise, so that already makes my job easier. I love seeing their creativity.

What else can we expect from you in the years ahead?

We have a lot of work to do. Homelessness, a livable wage, moving people out of poverty—these are huge adaptive challenges. Our goal is always that our community would thrive and be healthy so that our work would be eliminated.

But these challenges are staring at us vividly, and our job is to manage it. What we're doing is reaching out nationwide to find programs and initiatives that work, including evidence-based models. We test and adjust the models to Hawai'i's multicultural environment, and when they work, we expand services statewide to help more families.

We make sure to capture the data that prove our services are helping people and that they are really better off after receiving our services. I see great opportunity for Hawai'i to lead the nation in developing new standards of this data model as well.

What about the future of the social services sector in Hawai'i?

We'll see a lot more organizations coming together because partnerships are essential; it's what we all need to do. Over the next three to five years, there will likely be strategic mergers and partnerships to create a stronger continuum of care and streamline services. We also need to work together on some of the regulations that govern organizations, so that we can collectively address which regulations are needed and which can be lifted.

> **You've been here for twenty-seven years. What has changed for you and what have you noticed has changed about Hawaiʻi?**

Hawaiʻi is not immune from the national trends that we see such as crime, violence, addictions, and stresses of life. But we also come together as a community to help those in need, and that sense of family is still important to all of us.

All of my children's friends grew up together. We have an extended ʻohana that is unique to Hawaiʻi. Even though I have my biological family on the Mainland, I have such an amazing family here with aunties, uncles, and cousins galore, even though no one is blood related! This is very special and unique to Hawaiʻi that you don't get on the Mainland.

> **What are your fondest memories being here?**

My children were born and raised here in such a diverse and beautiful place. I have fond memories of taking my kids to the beach, and I ask myself, "Who wouldn't want to live here and call this place home?" Despite Hawaiʻi's high cost of living, there's no price tag on that sense of beauty and ʻohana.

> **What are some misconceptions of Hawaiʻi that you would like to see debunked?**

Many people think of Hawaiʻi as a vacation paradise or wonderland, which makes it hard for people to understand that there are needs here. This can make it difficult for us to compete for funds from the federal government or other national foundations.

> **How do you want Hawaiʻi to be remembered?**

As a place where we care for our ʻohana and where we are compassionate toward each other.

> **Who would you like to sit-down to dinner with?**

Since taking on the role as president and CEO, I have had opportunities to sit with so many amazing leaders in Hawaiʻi who have been generous in sharing their values, ideas, strategies, and their encouragement. I would like to keep doing more of that.

Who are or were your role models?

My mother. She met challenges head on, did the hard work to make her life better, and we were buddies going down on the same education path together. I measure my success against her many successes.

What would you say if you meet God?

I would be speechless and wouldn't know what to say. I hope he would say to me that I have been a good and faithful servant so, "Welcome!" (*laughter*)

Where is your favorite spot in Hawaiʻi?

Waimea on the Big Island, for its beauty and small-town feel.

What makes you happy?

Family and doing what I love to do every day.

Describe yourself in three words.

Hopeful, compassionate, and innovative.

What is your life philosophy on a bumper sticker?

Don't be afraid to say yes to possibilities.

Finally, how do you want to be remembered?

I hope people remember me as someone who cared compassionately and made strategic decisions to help our community thrive.

THE CULINARY CONNOISSEUR
Lynette Lo Tom

You have to know and be true to yourself and figure out your passion, as that fuels your work. The second thing is to not stress out too much if something is not working out as it may not have been a good fit. Everything happens for a reason.

Lynette Lo Tom is a woman of many accomplishments: former news reporter and anchor, Hawaiian Telecom spokeswoman, marketing diva, mother, and cookbook author. The self-proclaimed news junkie started out at All News Radio KHVH, KGMB and PBS before single parenthood spurred her to start her own company.

For the next twenty years, Lynette's Bright Light Marketing was a force in local public relations and marketing. While growing her one-person public relations consultancy into the thriving, full-service marketing agency that it was, Lynette learned that focusing on the success of her clients was the secret of success in her own company. When Bright Light was in business, more than 90 percent of its clients came from business referrals. In 2011, Lynette was a finalist in Pacific Business News' *Women Who Mean Business Award.*

It is this same bubbly personality, unbridled enthusiasm and compulsion to succeed that Lynette held onto when she decided to whittle down her client list over six years ago, to focus on her passion for food. An unquenchable thirst to learn about new things and the same inquisitive drive now propels Lynette to hunt for long lost recipes from her Chinese heritage.

Lynette holds a master's of business administration degree from the University of California at Berkeley and graduated with honors in journalism from the University of Colorado at Boulder. She was selected to serve as vice chair on the five-member volunteer Citizens Advisory Commission on Civil Defense for the City & County of Honolulu. She was the marketing chair for the Honolulu Japanese Chamber of Commerce, was on the board of the YMCA Honolulu and also assists numerous nonprofit organizations.

Today, she invites me for a meal at TOWN in Kaimukī and it is clear she is well-loved by the community, judging by how many people walk by to say hello.

It's great talking to you. My first question is, why Lo Tom?

I am born Lynette Lo to Chinese parents and my first husband was Tom from San Francisco. I am re-married now but I kept my ex's last name as my professional name, as people know me as such from the news and television.

You have an eclectic background. Share with us some of your interesting incarnations including your cookbook writing!

Yes, things happen! I was born and raised here but left after high school for the Mainland and lived in Colorado, Michigan, Berkeley, California, and worked in D.C. I moved back here armed with an MBA from Berkeley and a journalism degree. I also studied Chinese politics while in Michigan, so I wanted to be the best business journalist on the island, but there was a recession, so I just did whatever I could. I became a radio producer for News Radio and was later hired by the CBS affiliate to work in television. I also worked with the public PBS affiliate. So I've worked all over.

Later, I started my own PR and marketing firm and had that for many years. About six years ago, I wanted to do something different and knew I wanted to write a cookbook, as my mom was starting to forget some of her recipes and she was a very good cook. So I decided to let all my staff at Bright Light marketing go their own ways and went solo. I kept a few clients just to earn enough money for the ingredients because I want to cook. Later, I started writing the cookbook. So that's my first cookbook. The *Honolulu-Star Advertiser* then asked me to be part of their ethnic cookbook series, so I wrote the Chinese one, which was the fourth in the series. The series features different ethnicities, including Portuguese, Korean, Hawaiian, Japanese, and Filipino.

I featured my mom, both maternal and paternal grandmothers' recipes, as they were all very good cooks. I also started asking around for good family recipes and many people would laugh, as about a third would say they can't tell me because it's a family secret. I'll then ask, "Who makes the dish now?" and they will say "Nobody" as it is a family secret, but I was worried that if nobody cooks, then the recipe will be lost forever! Eventually, people did share their family recipes.

Did you learn anything interesting in the process of your writing?

My fifth grandfather on my mother's side came to the U.S. in 1850, so I'm a fifth-generation American. By writing the cookbook, I learned so much about my Chinese culture, as I did not care much for it when I was growing up. My uncle would tell me to be proud of my Chinese ethnicity, as we invented fireworks and this and that, but I was just not interested back then, as you think your parents and your grandparents will be around forever. I wouldn't even know how many siblings my grandfather had if not for the book!

I learned so much from writing the book and, at the start, it was so embarrassing. I spent time in Singapore, Taiwan, and China to research, and the people were so amused that I could not speak Mandarin and Cantonese, except for some of the food names! (*laughter*)

Why did you decide to find out about your Chinese heritage? Was it the food or the familial ancestry?

It was the food, as that has always been my hobby. Since I was eleven, my mom always made me cook dinner, as I'm the oldest of five children. It is unlike in Singapore, where cooked food is readily available or most household have domestic helpers. We had to do everything, so you're lucky if you get to learn from the cook, but if you are not paying attention, then you end up not being able to make anything.

I came to love cooking dinner with mom. I also realized that life is short, so I wanted to do something else and focus on my mom and her recipes. As I was researching, I had to ask, "Why is our food like this? and "Why is it different from L.A., San Francisco, or Singapore? And the answer is because 80 percent of the Chinese who came to Hawai'i came from Zhongshan, which is just above Macau.

When I went to visit the Sun Yat Sen museum in Zhongshan, I started laughing as they had plastic figurines of taro and kau yuk! It reminded me so much of Hawai'i and what my grandfather used to make. They came two-hundred years ago and we are still making that kind of food!

How was it like getting back in touch with your roots?

I had to start questioning everything and asked my mom many questions. I learned that my grandfather actually had fourteen children, but one died within the first year. I also learned that his brother had leprosy and had to live on the leper colony in Moloka'i. I would also ask people how they made their versions of the same dish and all the stories will come out like, "Your grandfather used to add too much sugar"—it was like an Italian family, where everyone makes things differently. I had so much fun!

I also learned that both my father's mother and father were Hakka and about 20 percent of the Chinese who came to Hawai'i were from there. They were originally northern people, but they kept getting kicked out and were like gypsies and, eventually, settled in the rocky areas that were barely farmable areas.

There must have been so much corruption and poor standards of living for people to want to move to all over the world—Singapore, Taiwan, Hawaiʻi, the Philippines—I mean the Chinese went all over the world!

One of my calabash aunties asked me to speak to her my mom, who was then 101 years old, but still had all her marbles. She passed away five years ago, but I remember when we had lunch, auntie would ask me what my grandmother's Chinese name was and I realized I don't know! Auntie tells us that her name was Ah Kim and that she knew her very well! She would tell me that one of my grandmother's favorite soups was Lotus Root Pork Bone Soup! All this was so interesting to me! I had thought my grandmother's name was Louise Kim with Kim being Korean, but it was actually Kim (also spelled Gim) in Chinese, which means gold! All this was so fascinating for me.

I was raised very American because my grandparents would tell us to have a good English education in order to succeed. Today, we are getting our children to speak Mandarin, but in those days, an education in English was what was needed to get ahead. So the learning has been enormous and I am writing the second one now on local food.

So now that you have gotten more in touch with your roots, what is being Chinese American to you?

I think it is how I am. I can't pretend that I am not Chinese and am raised with the usual Chinese family values, expectations, and told not to bring shame upon the family. We are also taught to always work hard so a B+ was never good enough. And the love of food! Every family gathering would have been filled with food and the most embarrassing thing that can happen in a Chinese party is to run out of food, so we always have to have plenty.

But it is interesting because being Chinese American in Hawaiʻi is very different from being Chinese American in New York or San Francisco. The major difference is that we are so established here in Hawaiʻi because of the plantation culture. In fact, the local plate lunch arose from all the races eating together in the plantation, except by the time the Filipinos came to eat in the fields with the Japanese, the Chinese had largely fulfilled their terms and went back to Chinatown, which is why the Chinese cuisine remained largely intact and unchanged from its origins.

So your Asian values shaped you and drove you to succeed?

Yes, I think so, as I always feel these expectations. But I'm not too traditional, as I got divorced and that is seen as a taboo in Asian culture. It's like, if you don't want to get married, the Chinese will go, "What's wrong with you?" So there are norms that I follow, but there are also those that I disregard as I think we have to be ourselves.

I also loved having my own business and did very well. Now, I write for food column *Easy Kine* in the *Honolulu Star-Advertiser* and published my second cookbook, *Back in the Day*, in October 2018. So, I have re-invented myself many times, though I have stayed true to who I am.

You radiate positivity. What do you do to stay positive?

When I have a bad day, I try to distract myself. Some will clean the yard or the porch or do art, while I cook to de-stress. And even better now that I get to talk about food all the time!

I also feel it has to do with creativity and how I was raised. We just power through and did our best no matter what. But in hindsight, it was also why I couldn't keep a job until I started my own company and could create. I didn't like to be told what to do, as I had such a strong personality and had to be my own boss.

So if I was giving advice to somebody, I would say, you really need to know yourself. Can you have a boss? Are you a better follower or a leader? Are you willing to take the risks? For me, I had to do it my way which also meant that I had to hustle, especially when I had fifteen people in my agency! But to me, the pressure was worth it as I got to do good work on my terms. So the key is, know yourself.

Were you one of the first females in media and how was that like?

I was not one of the first few females in the media but I was certainly the first to be shown pregnant on television in the 1980s, and everybody was shocked. I remember the production crew trying to shoot me from belly up and viewers were concerned that there was a pregnant news anchor. We don't think about it today but back then, there weren't many women on television and certainly none were shown pregnant so it was a big deal.

What are some of the changes you have seen since your time as a news anchor in the 1980s?

News is news so what is newsworthy is newsworthy, but computing and social media are game changers as the news cycle is so much faster. But I think it's great as things are always going to change just like food. It morphs with the times and you can't have it stay the same unless you specifically will it to be so, such as the traditional Chinese New Year dinner with the jai and gau, which are symbolic of the families sticking together.

You are a blend of the East and the West, so where do you draw the line between sticking with tradition and embracing change?

They are not mutually exclusive. Let's stick with the news as a metaphor. The news is just news but it can be interesting or scandalous depending on how it is portrayed. So today, instead of doing an editorial piece of a newsworthy event, you take a picture and load it on Instagram, right? It is the same piece of news but a different format. So tradition and change are really the same, just different perspective and formatting.

Following on your news metaphor, do you think the media and objectivity is in crisis given all the "fake news" that abound?

The one thing that is constant is that you should never listen to hearsay or blindly follow what you read. Always research, even in food. I was listening to *The Splendid Table* on public radio and the founder, Lynne Rossetto Kasper, was saying her first book was on Tuscany and she had to address many myths and rumors about cheese! She had to research on the stories to find out about its true origins. So always research and not take everything out there as fact.

What are some of your fondest memories growing up in Hawaiʻi?

I just loved growing up at the beach by Kualoa Ranch. My late uncle had a beach house, so all five kids would be there all weekend camping out, picking seaweed and shells, fishing, and playing games. There were many cousins, so we just played all day. I remember my dad carrying us out of the car, sleeping. Looking back, it is probably why I have so many freckles! *(laughter)*

> What are some of the changes you have seen in the past years?

I'm sixty-three and I feel that things have gotten very expensive. It's not an easy place for people to raise their families. People are working long hours and holding two jobs. When I grew up, we were not rich at all, but my parents still managed to raise us and take off on the weekends.

Today, there is little leisure time as people are stressed, which is why I started *Easy Kine* to encourage families to make their own meals, even if it is easy from a can or pre-made mixes, as the act of preparing a simple meal and eating together is a de-stresser. I recall growing up how we would all have family time together—the adults would sit, eat, and bond, while the children are nearby playing. The key is having free time and playing. Being able to create allows one to be more relaxed.

But it is increasingly tough financially, especially the younger ones starting out. Many of my friends have moved to North Carolina and Tennessee, and they are less stressed about finances now as things are much cheaper there, so they can enjoy a better quality of life.

> I think you have answered my next question, which is what are some of the changes you would like to see?

Yes! I would love for my daughter and family to move back to Hawai'i. They are in Santa Clara, Silicon Valley, as there are so many opportunities there.

> Put on your journalistic hat and share with us what you think we need to do to make that change happen?

I love it when people are entrepreneurial and creative—starting new books and businesses, as I think that is the answer to creating jobs.

> Would you say you define yourself as, first and foremost, a creative?

Yeah. I get bored easily which is a downside, too.

> What have been your biggest boons and banes in your career?

My husband said that I am the worst employee, as I can't be told what to do as I don't like procedures and I like to create.

Professionally, I have been lucky, as most of my clients have become my good friends so it creates win-win situations. But I am not a natural manager, so people-management is one of my biggest regrets. I was not very nurturing of the people who worked for me and can be harsh, as I felt the business pressure very strongly. I shouldered the responsibility of their paychecks and families they were raising so that was all too real for me.

In hindsight, I wish I was more nurturing, kind and more of a mentor, but otherwise, I have been so lucky, as PR, like journalism, allows you to meet different people and not work by rote as that's the death of me.

What advice would you give to a young entrepreneur?

As shared, you have to know and be true to yourself and figure out your passion, as that fuels your work. The second thing is to not stress out too much if something is not working out as it may not have been a good fit. Everything happens for a reason.

When I was younger, I would be very disappointed if we lost a pitch, but years later, I find out that the prospect would have been a bad client, as they were crooks or bad paymasters. Learn to let things go because they are not meant to be, it won't happen and, later on, something better may be in store.

How was it like for you being a single mom in those early years because, as you said, it was atypical of an Asian to get a divorce then?

I got into business because my ex-husband went back to San Francisco, and I had a young daughter to support and raise by myself. Having my own business allowed me the flexibility—I could work all night if I had to and work from home if she was sick.

Later, when she was in elementary school, she went to an after care not back home. Once she told me that she would like to be a "go home girl," so when she grew up, she wanted to be housewife! *(laughter)* Today, she is a stay-at-home mom, as she just had a baby.

In Singapore, there is a great push towards mom-entrepreneurship. Do you think it is possible to encourage moms in Hawai'i to work from home?

It is for some people but not for others. I always said, I had to give it to my mom as she raised me! It is probably easier to work than to raise a child, as you have to pay full attention and are responsible for every second. Whereas at work, you can at least daydream for a few minutes! So I will say that for some, go ahead and multitask if you can but for others, focus on being a mom.

It goes back to being yourself. I think all of us should take stock of our lives almost every ten years and plan what we want to do for the next decade.

Which takes me to, what is in store for you in the next ten years?

I want to keep on writing about food, as I am still so fascinated and passionate. But cooking is a physical act, so who knows what I want to do when I'm seventy? But if I were in my twenties, I would want to open a restaurant, as physically, I'd be stronger to cope with the long hours and heavy lifting and it seems like so much fun!

Now for trivia. What would be your favorite dish?

I love so many foods. Right now, I keep trying to better my Spanish paella.

What dish or food best represents you?

Currently, when I do cooking demos, I favor crispy skin roast pork. I show people that it is easy to do. But if I had to pick a traditional dish, it would be my grandfather's kau yuk with taro in red sauce.

What food best symbolizes Hawai'i?

That would be a combination plate lunch with foods from different ethnicities.

What is your life philosophy on a bumper sticker?

My car license plate reads "char siu" but it is spelled "CHARSU." When I am driving around town, people just start laughing. I lease a car, so usually I lease it in red but they didn't have red this time, so I leased brown and said it was a well-done char siu *(laughter)*

If you could meet God, what would you say?

Hi! Can I cook you something? *(more laughter)*

THE CHIEF STAFFER
Jennifer Sabas

Change is hard. Risk taking is, well, risky. But, you got to keep doing it, one step at a time. And, I am all about focusing on the next generation of leaders and giving them the opportunity and encouragement to develop into the bigger, well-informed thinkers they are destined to be to move Hawai'i forward.

Jennifer Sabas

With many years working on Capitol Hill, Jennifer Sabas has seen a lot and learned important lessons. She continues to follow some basic rules, such as your word is your bond, compromise is not a bad word, and you can disagree without being disagreeable. After all, she learned from the best—working for U.S. Senator Daniel K. Inouye for more than twenty-five years in both D.C. and Honolulu, serving as his chief of staff, until his passing in 2012.

Jennifer had the opportunity to work on all major federal infrastructure projects, as well as federal education, health and human services, and science-related programming investments in Hawai'i. This, of course, included the military. Senator Inouye was a steadfast proponent of a strong military presence in Hawai'i because of its strategic location, as well as its economic importance to the state. As Inouye's chief of staff, Jennifer came to understand, value, and advocate for the commands and their missions in Hawai'i. A memorable test came in 2005 when Pearl Harbor Naval Shipyard found itself on the BRAC list. Hawai'i's civilian leaders came together to both support and then to insist on a higher level of performance at the shipyard. Whether it was the shipyard, Schofield Barracks, Pacific Missile Range Facility, or the F22's for the Hawai'i Air National Guard, Jennifer ably served as the senator's trusted representative and voice, ensuring that D.C. never forgot about Hawai'i's important priorities.

Following the loss of Hawai'i's senior senator, Jennifer worked with Irene Inouye to establish the Daniel K. Inouye Institute, a program fund of the Hawai'i Community Foundation to carry on his legacy. Today, the Institute enjoys partnerships with the Library of Congress, Smithsonian Institution, University of Hawai'i, and Zocalo Public Square. The last significant naming opportunity was for the destroyer USS Daniel Inouye, with the laying of the keel done in spring 2018.

Jennifer established a consulting practice, Kaimana Hila, and continues to carry forward initiatives from her senate days. She serves on a variety of boards, including the Hawai'i Community Foundation, Hawai'i Leadership Forum, Public Schools Foundation, Pacific International Center for High Technology Research, Transportation for America Advisory Board, Partnership for Pacific Resilience, and Zocalo Public Square.

A graduate of Castle High School, University of Hawai'i, and Georgetown University Law Center, Jennifer is married to John Sabas, and they have three handsome sons, Ioane, Naki, and Kauanui.

Share with us a little bit more about your background, family, and how it was for you growing up.

I am your typical local girl who grew up in Kāneʻohe, attended public schools and went to the University of Hawaiʻi. I am the oldest and only daughter who decided I wanted to see the world. Even though my parents were politically active, when I moved to Washington, D.C. for law school, I was not planning on entering the world of politics.

I interned for Senator Inouye after my first year of law school. It was exciting to be in law school in our nation's capital. After graduation, I didn't want to come home just yet. I taught legal research, writing, and moot court at The Catholic University law school. As I submitted the final grades for my students and began packing my bags to come home, Senator Inouye was tapped to be the Iran-Contra Senate Chair. Senator was looking for a few lawyers from Hawaiʻi who would backfill on his personal staff as the more senior staff were moving to the committee. It was a fast turnaround, about two weeks to a month. That was how I ended up on the senator's staff.

This is where I pause and say that, sometimes, it's better to be lucky than to be smart. I was right there at the right place and time. I thought I was going to be a casual hire until the work of the Iran-Contra hearing was done. Famous last words.

So that was your big break?

Yes, I was lucky lady. As I learned my way around Capitol Hill, the legislative process, the appropriations process, working with colleagues on and off the Hill, and then, my favorite, working with our constituents at home. I was given the opportunity to learn about the campaign side of the business. The senator's longtime political confidant and chief of staff, Henry Giugni, became my political "dark side" mentor.

I learned about campaign finance, fundraisers, polling, advertising, basically all the elements of running a campaign. I traveled ahead to many cities, supporting the senator and Henry, at fundraising events in New York, Philly, Chicago, Denver, Los Angeles, and Seattle. I also worked the National Democratic Conventions in New York, when Bill Clinton accepted the nomination for his first term as president, and in Denver, when Barack Obama accepted the nomination for his term as president. It has been an incredible journey.

What do you think Senator Inouye saw in you?

I would like to think he saw me as a representative of Hawai'i's community. A hard-worker, with a sense of humor, and adventure. A quick study. We got along early on, because I also wasn't afraid to disagree with him, or to ask him to consider another option or solution. With that said, once he made his decision, the team lined and executed.

The senator wouldn't always just give you the answer; he wanted you to figure it out for yourself. He was macro in his thinking and direction, and deferred to the staff to fill in the blanks, the details, and to bring the policy direction to life. I loved the challenge, and because I was quite good at it frankly! *(laughter)*

What are some highlights of your career?

There were so many leadership lessons from my time in D.C. and upon my return home to Hawai'i. I returned in 1993 after being in D.C. for ten years to lead the senator's Hawai'i operation. After a bruising election in 1992, I felt we needed to have a more open-door approach to our constituents. At that time, the senator was perceived as a respected national figure, revered and feared, but I also wanted him to be beloved.

The first step we had to take was a more active, accessible operation in Hawai'i—everything from immigration and veterans to social security casework, to congratulatory or memorial messages—I knew we needed to have a full-service operation. We needed to be more visible in the community to include additional field representatives on the islands, and we certainly had a need for more ears on the ground. We already had staff on Kaua'i, Maui, and Hilo; and we added Kona and Moloka'i.

The big, additional personal bonus was that I met my hubby on Moloka'i as I recruited him to be our Moloka'i representative! *(laughter)* We also needed to have more of a local, political presence, not just a national one, and foster closer relationships with Hawai'i legislators, councilmembers and mayors. With a more active and connected Hawai'i operation, we could provide our D.C. office with better insights and intel to be able to make more informed decisions. And, the Hawai'i input needed to matter.

Senator Inouye gave me the opportunity and wide latitude. I took and ran with it. The office became active and connected. Staff from D.C. and Hawai'i traveled and spent time in each other's offices. That said, our D.C. legislative team—personal and committee staff—were the best on Capitol Hill. With the changes implemented, the Hawai'i staff more directly supported legislative and appropriations requests with their D.C. counterparts, and Hawai'i was better served.

What were some of your most memorable projects with the senator?

There were many projects, no matter how big or small, and we came at it with the same commitment and vigor. Japanese American redress, return of Kaho'olawe to the state of Hawai'i and funding for its cleanup, to bringing the USS *Missouri* to Hawai'i. We worked on the H-3 and placed thousands of acres into conservation as national parks and reserves. With each project, I learned valuable lessons—tactical and strategic, empathy and heart.

Let me share a story to illustrate: We got a call from the office of the U.S. Transportation Secretary Ray LaHood,[1] letting us know that the secretary would be in Hawai'i, and inquiring whether the senator had a few priority transportation projects he'd like the secretary to see while in the Aloha State. This is normal protocol, so we picked a big project and a "little big" problem: Honolulu rail and Kalaupapa.[2] With everything going on, we should have asked for more help from Secretary LaHood on the Honolulu rail. (*laughter*) In all seriousness, Secretary LaHood would have signed the Honolulu Full Funding Grant Agreement in the Senate Appropriations hearing room in the capitol, as planned, but, the day after, Senator Inouye passed away on December 17, 2012.

Anyhow, Kalaupapa is one of the most serene, sad places I will ever visit. It was the senator's pu'uhonua, or "place of refuge." He would spend the eve of each of his re-elections at Kalaupapa with, as he would say, the most beautiful people on earth. Disfigured from leprosy, and with every reason to be bitter, the people of Kalaupapa accepted their lot with pragmatism and aloha. We would always have a party with good food and music and the senator would

---

1 Ray H. LaHood (born December 6, 1945) is an American politician who served as United States Secretary of Transportation from 2009 until 2013. A Republican from Illinois, LaHood represented Illinois' eighteenth congressional district in the U.S. House of Representatives from 1995 to 2009, and served on the House Transportation and Infrastructure Committee from 1995 to 2000. In 2008, President-elect Barack Obama announced he would nominate LaHood to be the next transportation secretary. After serving to the end of Obama's first term in 2013, he announced his plans to step down as transportation secretary. He did not seek any public office after that, and instead entered the private sector.

2 Kalaupapa is a small, unincorporated community on the island of Moloka'i, within Kalawao County. In 1866, during the reign of Kamehameha V, the Hawai'i legislature passed a law that resulted in the designation of Moloka'i as the site for a leper colony, where patients who were seriously affected by Hansen's disease could be quarantined, to prevent them from infecting others. At the time, the disease was little understood and was believed to be highly contagious and incurable. Its sea cliffs are one of the highest in the world, rising to two-thousand feet (610 m) above the Pacific Ocean. The area has been preserved as the Kalaupapa Leprosy Settlement and National Historical Park, and remains one of the most remote locations in Hawai'i.

thank them for the honor of representing them in congress and for continuing to restore his faith in humanity.

As a result, we were dedicated to the community and, if there was anything we could do to make their life better, we had standing orders to just do it, as the Nike tagline goes. And we did. We preserved some of the old buildings, which separated the patients from their families, to ensure that their stories would live on, and even got them cable television hook-ups!

Getting back to the link with Secretary LaHood, what had transpired was that a very mean-spirited commuter air carrier had the essential air service contract to serve Kalaupapa. They were gouging the residents who could no longer afford to travel as often. The air carrier also removed ramps and lifts, making it near impossible for some of the commuters to get into the small planes. We asked for the opportunity for the residents to plead their case directly to the secretary, who had the discretion to cancel the contract for cause. Upon making the request, and we expected it, the office of the secretary went, "Wait, what? Where? How do you spell that!?"

But, long story short, we chartered a plane from Kalaupapa to Honolulu and brought some of the patients for a meeting with Secretary LaHood and Senator Inouye. The room was packed with lawyers, bureaucrats, and congressional staff. The residents shared their sorrow through song, and when they were done, there wasn't a dry eye in the airport conference room. Needless to say, that carrier was removed from the route and actually from Hawai'i altogether! The new Hawai'i carrier today does a good job of providing compassionate and reasonable service.

Clearly, your career is so intertwined with the late senator's. What do you think were some of his biggest legacies and what would you personally continue to champion?

I have listed out memorable projects and there are many of them on every island and in every sector. They were all impactful to the economy, environment, culture, and soul of our community. But his greatest legacy is his investment in the people who worked for and with him. With all the glass ceilings he broke throughout his life, he encouraged all of us to step it forward and aspire large. He pushed us to believe in ourselves, and to know that we were good enough, smart and tough enough to compete straight on and succeed in whatever we choose to do. And he also let us know that he had our backs, win or lose.

I am honored to serve now as the director of the Daniel K. Inouye Institute. Our initial priority was to archive all of his papers from thousands of boxes, and videos/tapes, and to make gifts of the many items that were given to him over his fifty-year career. We also focused on events, which brought people together on a variety of topics in Washington D.C. and Honolulu. This is the last year of a five-year lecture series with the Library of Congress, with the underlying theme of bi-partisanship which is, ironically, a very novel concept in Washington, D.C., these days! *(laughter)*.

Our first lecture, Bipartisanship Beyond our Shores featured former Secretary of States Madeline Albright and Colin Powell, and our last will feature Karl Rove and David Axelrod in Civility in Presidential Politics. At home, we have partnered with the Smithsonian, Zocalo Public Square, and Hawaiʻi Public Radio to put on quarterly Talk Story gatherings now in Kakaʻako on a variety of topics. They range from the serious, like climate change and limits on tourism, to lighter fare, like the poke craze sweeping through the continental U.S., the power of being from Hawaiʻi, and why we don't vote!

The senator had the ability to inspire conversations that are bigger than ourselves, so our events honor this part of his legacy which encourages people to come together to talk story, learn a few new things, and even make a few new acquaintances.

Our last major initiative involves the University of Hawaiʻi and working to establish a School of Public Policy. Denise Konan, dean of the School of Social Sciences is my academic lead. She is an incredible wahine leader and we are working together to provide students with policy-focused educational pathways that are more applied and less theoretical. One of my goals is to better prepare students for a career in government, whether in budget and finance, health policy, sustainability, or climate change policy, just to name a few.

On that note, how do you maintain that balance between "keeping the local, local" and charting for future development?

It is expensive to live in Hawaiʻi and local families are really struggling to make ends meet. You got to get the economics right and, of course, it is all about balance. Tourism will always be our life blood, but that should not keep us from leaning forward and continuing to invest in technology, even encouraging some of the tech giants to invest in a presence in Hawaiʻi. There is much we can do in expanding educational pathways in IT and cybersecurity as careers of the future. The military is the second largest economic sector which will remain steady, if not grow. We need to be supportive of their presence for our economy, as well as the good of our nation.

How can you try to foster that sense of urgency, competitive edge, and productivity?

Change is hard. Risk taking is, well, risky. But, you got to keep doing it, one step at a time. And, I am all about focusing on the next generation of leaders and giving them the opportunity and encouragement to develop into the bigger, well-informed thinkers they are destined to be to move Hawai'i forward.

You are also the executive director of Move O'ahu Forward. What are you doing to gain more buy-in from the people?

Our mission has always been to provide support for the Honolulu rail project. There have clearly been ups and downs, and bumps in the road, like funding constraints, leadership constraints, and bickering. Unfortunately, there are more hurdles ahead.

I still believe that a rail system is the right thing and right project for Honolulu. Our bus system is maxed out and, once we are connected to rail, the traffic congestion from the west side of O'ahu will improve. It is like the construction of the H-3—that was a similarly brutal project and took decades to complete. But once it was done, it has been well-used with no protest or guff. For me, I will keep the faith and support for the rail project until it is up and running. I know I just have to keep working it.

You were also involved in the NextEra deal that fell through. What are your sentiments about it now that time has passed?

If the merger had gone through, we would have seen transformation a lot quicker because of the financial clout and technology investments. NextEra was welcomed by the Abercrombie[3] administration, but the tides turned with a new administration. It is hard to know whether the outcome would have been different had NextEra bought on our team earlier, but it may not be as

---

3 Abercrombie was sworn in as Governor of Hawai'i on December 6, 2010, and succeeded Republican Governor Linda Lingle. Governor Abercrombie was a longtime advocate of the undersea cable. In January 2014, during the State of the State address, Abercrombie mentioned only one company, NextEra. But in early August 2014, Governor Abercrombie suffered a landslide defeat in the Democratic Gubernatorial Primary Election. According to polls, in October 2011, Abercrombie was the most unpopular governor in the country, with a 30 percent approval rating. By August 9, 2014, Abercrombie was defeated by State Senator David Ige, taking just 31 percent of the vote to Ige's 67 percent, making him the first incumbent governor to lose a primary in Hawai'i's history with the largest margin of defeat in the primary by any incumbent governor in United States history.

well because the new administration made their position very clear by sending clear smoke signals to the Public Utilities Commission.

But because the merger fell through, the signal sent was that, while we are headed to 100 percent renewable energy by 2045, it is on us as a community and our local utility to get there without a bigger partner to have our back. We will need to rise our own tide from a leadership standpoint and this is happening, which, to me, is the silver lining.

Which is the perfect segue to our segment on leadership. What do you do when you see a crisis in leadership?

Hit the pause button, and get some intel. One of my skill sets is as a fixer, and I am always tasked to find out what happened. Was it a slow burn or a rapid-fire crisis? Are we able to quickly fill in the leadership void, or is there a work-around and is adjustment possible? These were some the first lessons I learned from Senator Inouye—that is, to stay focused on the objectives to be achieved and then figure it out. There are other times when you just have to step back and let the blood splatter, and be there to help put the pieces back together. If you can, put up some bumper guards to minimize the mess.

How do you deal with negative criticism and with naysayers?

Take a deep breath. Go home and pout for a bit if you need to, then get over it and get strategic. Be a good listener, be respectful, and try to maintain some level of communication as long as you can. As a public servant, sometimes you just need to toughen up your skin and take it, whether deserved or not. It does suck, though.

That said, the importance of being of able to work together cannot be understated, and then to learn how to disagree without being disagreeable. This was the basis of Senator Inouye's long-standing working relationship and friendship with Republican Senator Ted Stevens of Alaska. They voted together only 10 percent of the time and did so with passion and vigor, and found compromise in a variety of others.

How do you feel as a woman leader ahead of your times?

I really do not think of myself as ahead of my time. When I think back on the early days in the late 1980s, senators could smoke anywhere including in hearings. Cocktails over lunch were common. And up until very recently, no baby or child was allowed on the senate floor. The U.S. Senate had to pass a resolution in 2018 so Senator Tammy Duckworth of Illinois could bring her infant to the senate floor. How times have changed for the better. But late night sessions remain universal.

Has gender been a boon or bane?

There were very, very few women chiefs of staff in the U.S. Senate when I started on Capitol Hill so there were no role models or playbook. Whether male or female, the basic rule for succeeding on Capitol Hill is that your word is your bond. And if, due to changing circumstances, you needed to change your position or your ask, then you needed to explain it personally. If your word was not good, you could not be effective. And, if you worked for Senator Inouye, he taught us that compromise was not a bad word. It was OK to take half a loaf, even if we could power play for the full loaf because you make friends with others when they have something to take back to their home states.

That all said, it was not easy at the outset. I had just graduated from Georgetown Law School and had just finished teaching first-year law students at The Catholic University law school. I thought I was brilliant, unstoppable, and a tad spoiled! Of course, I ran head-first into a couple of brick walls.

One of my favorite anecdotes to tell was my assignment of the agriculture portfolio, which for a Hawai'i, meant sugar and pineapple in the late 1980s. This meant working with the national sugar growers, who came primarily from the South. I walked into my first meeting and was immediately asked to get all the "good ol' boys" some coffee with sugar! Whaaat!?!!! Dumbfounded, I got them coffee. This went on for awhile and it compounded their refusal to consider any of my suggestions as I was the "lil missy from Hawai'i." Whaat?!!!

I stormed into the senator's office to complain about my mistreatment, even though I wasn't even sure what I wanted him to do! He just looked at me and said, "You're a smart woman, you will figure it out. And, since when do you do something, just because they tell you to? I don't think that of the person I hired. I will give you a hint. One day, when they need something from me, they will need my vote." Best advice ever. I went home, kicked the pillows, cried, and sulked. Then, I really did figure it out.

First, stop acting like the victim. Second, I didn't need their approval. At the next meeting, I was a new person. I gave them nicknames and asked the "sweetie from Florida" to get me a refill of coffee—Ha! It worked. And, just as the senator predicted, they did come asking for his vote. They tried to get around me to speak directly to him, but all phone messages and meeting requests were placed on my desk. In the end, we became friends and I earned the respect of those old Southern dogs.

Do you think you worked harder because you are a woman?

Maybe, but not necessarily. Staff, especially the senior staff, work long hours when congress is in session. Both women and men. As women, we had to learn not to take things personally, especially as negotiations were heating up. I learned it was more satisfying to get even, or better, than crying about it. And, I will say, women are way, way better multitaskers, so very likely we got more done!

How has the tide changed for you? What have you observed since you first came on the scene?

As I shared above, there were very few women chiefs on Capitol Hill when I started. No role models, really. And definitely no mentoring, as there was no time for such coddling. I admired Congresswoman Patsy Mink from afar. She was bold, passionate, fearless, impatient, and, at times, angry. She could both lecture and sweet talk the other members of the Hawaiʻi delegation: Inouye, Akaka, and Abercrombie, and usually got her way! It was wonderful to watch. I would have loved to have been mentored by Patsy Mink but I also understood that she really had no time (I say it with much affection). She had many wrongs to right, many inequities to make more just. And, that she did.

But I did promise myself, if I ever got to a position of leadership, that I would be a mentor. I would spend time and listen, make suggestions, and encourage young professionals to overtake me in the path ahead. This is most satisfying and meaningful.

Today on Capitol Hill, women chiefs in the senate equal men. At the time of Senator Inouye's passing in 2012, there were more women in senior posts than men on our personal staff as well as the committee staff. There are twenty-five women U.S. senators today compared to two in my early days, and a record number of women running for president in 2020. This speaks volumes about expanding pathways for women in politics. Opportunities are bright.

But my pet peeve is women are oftentimes harsher critiques of fellow women and on the most shallow of matters: hair, wardrobe, or shoes, rather than on an important policy matter. For example, the fixation with Colleen Hanabusa and her clogs, or Hilary Clinton and her pant suits. Really?! These are among the smartest, toughest women I will ever know, and that's what we want to poke about? So, my one ask—when you find yourself on the verge, or are with a friend getting ready to make some chatty comment, which demeans the ability of women in this tough, political arena, hit the pause button and refocus those comments on a hard-hitting policy question worthy of discussion.

What do you think has been your biggest obstacle?

It was me. I had to learn to play the game with the boys! Once I figured it out, it was fun. It became about the art of negotiation and winning—all in the name of delivering for Hawai'i, of course. We perfected the "macadamia nut diplomacy," bringing and sharing omiyage with colleagues on both sides of the aisle.

What are your thoughts on the #MeToo movement?

This is an important movement, as it has provided a voice for many women who were victimized. By shining a spotlight, it puts all on notice that there is no place for such behavior now and in the future. As professional women, we need to be watchful for ourselves and those women who come after us.

How did you balance your career and family?

I came home from D.C. to have my family. I am blessed with a wonderful husband and amazing parents, who helped raise our three sons when I traveled to D.C. When I was home, weekend sports were paramount. During campaign season, we made campaign activities our family activities— sign waving, canvassing, rallies, hanging out in HQs. My kids were the best campaigners. Our activities were not typical, but as I learned, it is all about being together. As they got older, there wasn't a fundraiser event they wouldn't join us for, provided we could assure them there would be noodles, mac salad, teriyaki chicken, or chili! I would like to think that being around elected officials as much as my sons have, has taught them respect; about being confident in conversing with adults, and the power of networking.

I tell young women that you don't need to always have play dates for your kids. If your job requires you to be in the office on the weekend or attend an evening event, take your kids with you and make some family fun out of it. Bring them into our work and let your colleagues and boss know them. Don't place a huge divide between family and your work.

Given how they were raised, do you think your children are going into politics?

I don't know. I would like to think that they are confident and aware enough should they want to dabble in it. Hopefully, it is not diving head first into the pool. Our oldest son works as the IT Manager for a government/public relations firm in Seattle. Some of their clients are political in nature. Our second son spent a summer with Congresswoman Colleen Hanabusa. He loved it. And, our youngest is a sophomore in college and still in an exploring phase so maybe a congressional internship at some point?

What are your fondest memories growing up in Hawaiʻi?

I love Hawaiʻi. I grew up in Kāneʻohe, and after many years in D.C., I returned home to Kāneʻohe where we raised our sons. My childhood friends are still my best friends. It is the simplicity and comfort for which I am still making memories.

What are some of the biggest changes you've seen in Hawaiʻi, or what are some of the changes you would like to see?

The biggest change is probably the fact that more people who were not born in Hawaiʻi now call Hawaiʻi home, as compared to those of us who are born and raised here. Add to that, the high cost of living, which pushes Hawaiian families to the Mainland and keeps our collective kids from coming home, believing there is no longer a place for them.

There is no silver bullet, instead, there needs to be a commitment to build more affordable housing, for sale or rent, and then to invest in additional sectors to diversify our economic base. We need to set a goal, for example, in IT, data analytics, cyber security, and innovation, and drive to it from economic development/investment and education/workforce paths. We should be marketing to some of the tech giants to have a lab or hub here.

For now, I hang on to Hawaiʻi's aloha spirit where people still really care about each other, sharing what we have with friends and family. There is a fundamental goodness in these islands for which we all cherish and come home to.

What do you do to relax?

Being with my family. Even when there were hectic times, when the family is together, I am in my happy place. Our house was the gathering place as our boys were growing up, and still is. Their friends are always welcome for barbecues, beer parties, and sleepovers for a dozen or more, just to be safe.

I enjoy my Sunday morning walks around Ala Moana Beach Park and Magic Island with my dad. It's relaxing and enjoyable, and, halfway through, we make our big decision, "Where to eat lunch?!" And, I am always up for a pedicure and facial.

Where is your favorite travel spot?

I travel a lot and I love to spoil my sons in between my travels. Now that they're adults, we can enjoy wonderful meals and a cocktail or two. So, my favorite travel spot is anywhere my sons are, either Portland, Seattle, and, now, Orlando.

What would you say if you met God?

Wow! Aloha plenty—which way to the party?

What pisses you off?

Those who do not keep their word. This is not to say that there are times when circumstances change, but when they do, have the courtesy to let me know. I can take it. Going back on your word or bullshitting is totally unacceptable.

Who would you like to have a sit-down dinner with?

My mom, for one last Christmas dinner. She passed away on Christmas Eve after making my sons' favorite dessert, and having prepared our Christmas dinner. I miss her a lot.

What are your thoughts on Hillary Clinton?

Hillary Clinton is a brilliant and accomplished leader. Her loss taught us that we cannot take anything for granted. You have to connect with everyday people and play to win all the time. Don't take your eye off the target.

And, oftentimes, to my personal irritation, women are the hardest and most critical of other women. We can be catty and focus on attire or hair, rather than on a woman's qualifications and leadership skills. We are not going to move forward when we are our own worst critics on the superficial and shallow stuff.

What advice would you give to someone who is starting his or her career?

Find a mentor, work hard, and be a risk taker. As a young professional, you honestly never ever know where your career path will take you. Also, pick a nonprofit that speaks to you, and make giving back to our community a part of your DNA early.

What is your life philosophy on a bumper sticker?

Bring It On, Baby!

What would be the title of your memoir if you wrote one?

No Challenge Too Big, No Opportunity Too Small. Somewhere along those lines. Many focus on achieving the one big project or goal. As for me, I have learned that it is the little steps that can get you further and make you smarter because you learn something from each new step.

How do you want to be remembered?

As someone who cared and made a positive difference in my family, community, state, and nation.

What can we expect from you in the near future?

I love my life now. I have one employee who has been my assistant for thirty years. We work together so well, and we do what we like, and we don't when we don't. Although, I can be talked into taking on a tough project or two … Oh, my soft, bleeding heart! (*laughter*)

Today, I am able to balance by own time with my hubby and our three grown sons—the loves of my life. All that said, I am always up for a challenge, especially if it supports our beloved Hawai'i.

The Women of Waiʻanae (WOW) Scholarship

Part of the proceeds of the book will go towards a Women of Waiʻanae scholar who enrolls in Leeward Community College–Waiʻanae Moku campus. The scholarship aims to help the recipient overcome the obstacles of tuition costs, books and supplies, and transportation fees.

The Waiʻanae Coast, or the Leeward Coast of Oʻahu, stretches north to south from Kaʻena Point through the communities of Mākaha, Waiʻanae, Māʻili, and Nānākuli. This part of the island is noted for its arid, rugged and remote coastline, deep, awe-inspiring ampitheater valleys and majestic mountains.

The Waiʻanae Coast is home to the largest concentration of Native Hawaiians on Oʻahu. They take pride in keeping the Hawaiian traditions of hula, surfing, cultural practices, values, and the spirit of aloha alive.

In 1989, a small group of women in Waiʻanae held yard and chili sales to build funds to help residents return to school. The group named itself the Women of Waiʻanae (WOW). The first award of $356 in 1990 went to a mother of two children who was in nursing school. That awardee is now a resident nurse at a Mākaha nursing home. In 2017, WOW awarded $21,000 in scholarships to eleven non-traditional Waiʻanae students. With the rising cost of education, WOW aims to increase its capacity and size of scholarships.

Today, WOW continues to offer annual partial financial scholarships to the non-traditional student residents of the Waiʻanae Coast.

Leeward Community College–Waiʻanae Moku Campus

Leeward Community College–Waiʻanae Moku is a full-service education center that aims to provide residents of the Waiʻanae Coast access to a high quality college experience in a supportive and respectful environment within their own community.

The campus offers more than sixty-five Leeward CC credit classes in the fall and spring semesters. Classes offered in language arts, mathematics and science, fine arts and humanities, social sciences and education, business and vocational education meet the requirements for a liberal arts degree so a student can complete the entire associate in arts degree program at Waiʻanae Moku.

The campus offers the advantages of being close to home for Waiʻanae Coast residents, small class sizes, friendly and helpful staff, as well as caring, competent, and knowledgeable instructors and counselors.

About the Author

Firebrand Dr. Loretta Chen is an award-winning director, professor, and best-selling author of *Woman on Top: The Art of Smashing Stereotypes and Breaking All the Rules*; *The Elim Chew Story: Driven by Purpose, Destined for Change,* and *Madonnas and Mavericks: Power Women in Singapore* when she interviewed seventeen of Singapore's most illustrious women, including the incumbent President.

Hailing from city-state Singapore, Dr. Chen was the Creative Director of The Activation Group, a creative agency with offices around Asia. During her twenty-year career, she helmed campaigns for clients such as Samsung, BNP Paribas' inaugural all-star Women's Tennis tournament featuring Serena Williams and Maria Sharapova; Louis Vuitton, Adidas, and World Wide Fund among others. She also directed numerous theatrical productions including *Victor Victoria* that was staged during President Obama's historic APEC visit to Singapore and *The F Word* (2011), which premiered at the Edinburgh Fringe Festival, garnering Dr. Chen an Amnesty Freedom of Expression Award for bringing the plight of sex trafficked women to light.

Other career highlights include being nominated as Nominated Member of Parliament, having her eponymous radio show on Lush 99.5FM, instituting a Young Designer's Scholarship at Raffles Design Institute, and being voted one of Asia's Most Inspiring Women. She was also the International Consultant to Druk Holdings and Investments (DHI), the government investment arm of Bhutan, and is working to create a pilot leadership program for the Kingdom.

She holds a Doctorate in Philosophy and a Certificate in Leadership from Harvard University and is a Visiting Professor at numerous institutions including Stanford, University of Southern Maine; Trinity University of Asia, the 400-year old Colegio de San Juan de Letran in The Philippines, and APU Ritsumeikan University in Japan. She is currently pursuing an Advanced Certificate in Service Leadership & Innovation with Singapore Management University.

However, what she takes most pride in is her work with women, LGBTQIA, and youth advocacy. She is the co-founder of two social enterprises, A Common Purpose (ACP) in Bhutan and Beyond Individual Good (BIG) in The Philippines.

Now happily married and living her dream in Hawaiʻi, she teaches at University of Hawaiʻi-Leeward Community College and started a theater program on the Waiʻanae Coast as well as Caravan Theater, a community theater outfit for leadership and social change. Dr. Chen believes in compassion, karma, and is cat mom to seven fur babies.

Inspiring Women of Hawaiʻi marks Loretta's first collaboration with Mutual Publishing and is now working on *M/others*, a celebration of stories from teenage, single, gay, incarcerated, surrogate, foster moms, and other alternative modalities of motherhood.

For inquiries and collaborations, log on to www.drlorettachen.com.